### SEVENTH EDITION
# GRAMMAR IN CONTEXT 2B

**SANDRA N. ELBAUM**

Australia · Brazil · Mexico · Singapore · United Kingdom · United States

National Geographic Learning,
a Cengage Company

*Grammar in Context 2B*, Seventh Edition
Sandra N. Elbaum

Publisher: Sherrise Roehr

Executive Editor: Laura Le Dréan

Managing Editor: Jennifer Monaghan

Director of Global Marketing: Ian Martin

Heads of Regional Marketing:

  Joy MacFarland (United States and Canada)

  Charlotte Ellis (Europe, Middle East, and Africa)

  Kiel Hamm (Asia)

  Irina Pereyra (Latin America)

Product Marketing Manager: Tracy Bailie

Content Project Manager: Beth F. Houston

Media Researcher: Leila Hishmeh

Art Director: Brenda Carmichael

Senior Designer: Lisa Trager

Operations Support: Rebecca G. Barbush, Hayley Chwazik-Gee

Manufacturing Planner: Mary Beth Hennebury

Composition: MPS North America LLC

© 2021 Sandra N. Elbaum

ALL RIGHTS RESERVED. No part of this work covered by the copyright herein may be reproduced or distributed in any form or by any means, except as permitted by U.S. copyright law, without the prior written permission of the copyright owner.

"National Geographic," "National Geographic Society" and the Yellow Border Design are registered trademarks of the National Geographic Society ® Marcas Registradas

---

For permission to use material from this text or product, submit all requests online at **cengage.com/permissions**
Further permissions questions can be emailed to
**permissionrequest@cengage.com**

---

Grammar in Context 2B ISBN: 978-0-357-14029-1
Grammar in Context 2B + OLP ISBN: 978-0-357-14055-0

**National Geographic Learning**
200 Pier 4 Boulevard
Boston, MA 02210
USA

Locate your local office at **international.cengage.com/region**

Visit National Geographic Learning online at **ELTNGL.com**
Visit our corporate website at www.cengage.com

Printed in China
Print Number: 01  Print Year: 2019

# CONTENTS

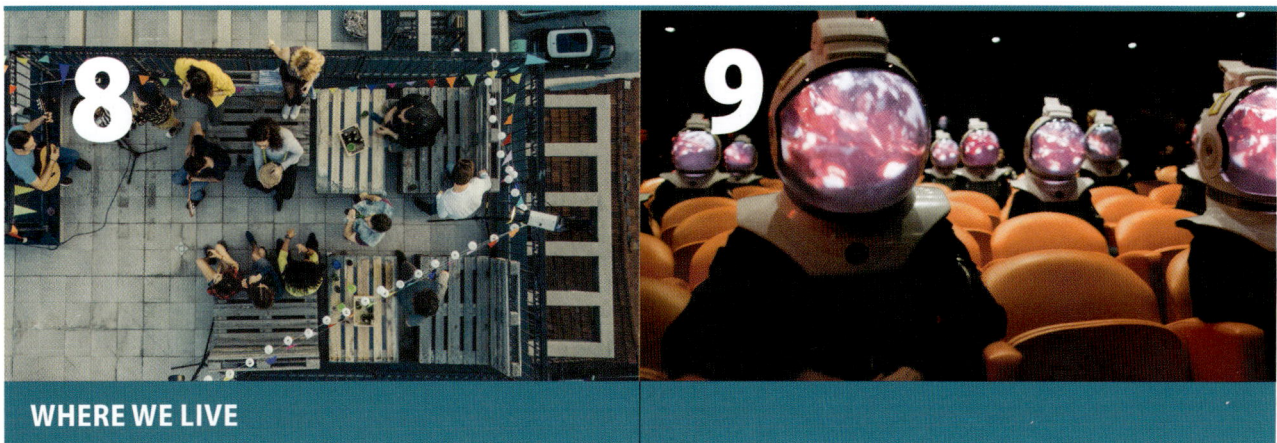

## 8 WHERE WE LIVE

| | | |
|---|---|---|
| **GRAMMAR** | **Modals** | |
| **READING 1** | **An Apartment Lease** | **196** |
| 8.1 | Overview of Modals | 197 |
| 8.2 | Phrasal Modals | 197 |
| 8.3 | Obligation/Necessity—*Must* and Phrasal Modals | 199 |
| 8.4 | Permission/Prohibition—*May* and Phrasal Modals | 200 |
| 8.5 | Expectation—*Be Supposed To* | 201 |
| 8.6 | Ability/Permission—*Can, Could*, and Phrasal Modals | 202 |
| **READING 2** | **Frequently Asked Questions: Recycling Plastic in Your Home** | **204** |
| 8.7 | Advice—*Should, Ought To, Had Better* | 205 |
| 8.8 | Negatives of Modals | 207 |
| **READING 3** | **Starting Life in a New Country** | **211** |
| 8.9 | Conclusions or Deductions—*Must* | 212 |
| 8.10 | Possibility—*May/Might* | 214 |
| **READING 4** | **How to Furnish Your New Apartment Cheaply** | **216** |
| 8.11 | Using Modals for Politeness | 217 |
| **UNIT SUMMARY** | | **220** |
| **REVIEW** | | **221** |
| **FROM GRAMMAR TO WRITING** | | **222** |

## 9

| | | |
|---|---|---|
| **GRAMMAR** | **The Present Perfect** **The Present Perfect Continuous** | |
| **READING 1** | **Google** | **226** |
| 9.1 | The Present Perfect—Forms | 227 |
| 9.2 | The Past Participle | 229 |
| 9.3 | The Present Perfect with an Adverb | 233 |
| **READING 2** | **Crowdfunding** | **234** |
| 9.4 | The Present Perfect—Overview of Uses | 235 |
| 9.5 | The Present Perfect with Continuation from Past to Present | 236 |
| 9.6 | The Simple Past, the Present Perfect, the Simple Present | 238 |
| **READING 3** | **Khan Academy** | **240** |
| 9.7 | The Present Perfect with Repetition from Past to Present | 241 |
| 9.8 | The Present Perfect with an Indefinite Time in the Past | 243 |
| 9.9 | The Present Perfect vs. the Simple Past | 246 |
| **READING 4** | **Genealogy and the Genographic Project** | **248** |
| 9.10 | The Present Perfect Continuous—Forms | 249 |
| 9.11 | The Present Perfect Continuous—Use | 251 |
| **UNIT SUMMARY** | | **254** |
| **REVIEW** | | **255** |
| **FROM GRAMMAR TO WRITING** | | **256** |

Contents  iii

# 10 JOBS

**GRAMMAR** Gerunds
Infinitives

**READING 1** Finding a Job — 260
- 10.1 Gerunds—An Overview — 261
- 10.2 Gerunds as Subjects — 263
- 10.3 Gerunds as Objects — 265
- 10.4 Preposition + Gerund — 267

**READING 2** Employee Engagement — 270
- 10.5 Infinitives—An Overview — 271
- 10.6 Infinitives after Expressions with *It* — 272
- 10.7 Infinitives after Adjectives — 273
- 10.8 Infinitives after Verbs — 274
- 10.9 Objects before Infinitives — 276
- 10.10 Infinitives to Show Purpose — 277
- 10.11 Infinitives or Gerunds after Verbs — 278

**UNIT SUMMARY** — 280
**REVIEW** — 281
**FROM GRAMMAR TO WRITING** — 282

# 11 MAKING CONNECTIONS

**GRAMMAR** Adjective Clauses

**READING 1** Reconnecting with Old Friends — 286
- 11.1 Adjective Clauses—Overview — 287
- 11.2 Relative Pronouns as Subjects — 288
- 11.3 Relative Pronouns as Objects — 291

**READING 2** Making Connections Using Meetup — 295
- 11.4 Relative Pronouns as Objects of Prepositions — 296
- 11.5 *Whose* + Noun — 298

**READING 3** The Science of Friendship — 300
- 11.6 Adjective Clauses with *Where* and *When* — 301

**UNIT SUMMARY** — 304
**REVIEW** — 305
**FROM GRAMMAR TO WRITING** — 306

## 12 SPORTS AND ATHLETES

**GRAMMAR** Superlatives
Comparatives

**READING 1** Gregg Treinish: Extreme Athlete and Conservationist  310
**12.1** The Superlative Forms of Adjectives and Adverbs  311
**12.2** Superlatives—Use  313

**READING 2** Americans' Attitude toward Soccer  316
**12.3** The Comparative Forms of Adjectives and Adverbs  317
**12.4** Comparatives—Use  319

**READING 3** An Amazing Athlete  323
**12.5** As . . . As  324
**12.6** As Many/Much . . . As  326
**12.7** The Same . . . As  327

**READING 4** Football and Soccer  330
**12.8** Showing Similarity with *Like* and *Alike*  331

**UNIT SUMMARY**  334
**REVIEW**  335
**FROM GRAMMAR TO WRITING**  336

## 13 THE LAW

**GRAMMAR** Active and Passive Voice

**READING 1** The Supreme Court  340
**13.1** Active and Passive Voice—Overview  341
**13.2** The Passive Voice—Form  342

**READING 2** Jury Duty  344
**13.3** The Passive Voice—Use  345
**13.4** Negatives and Questions with the Passive Voice  347

**READING 3** Who Owns the Photo?  349
**13.5** Transitive and Intransitive Verbs  350

**UNIT SUMMARY**  354
**REVIEW**  355
**FROM GRAMMAR TO WRITING**  356

Contents **v**

## 14 MONEY

**GRAMMAR**   Articles
*Other/Another*
Indefinite Pronouns

**READING 1**   **Millennials and Money**   360
**14.1**  Articles—An Overview   361
**14.2**  Making Generalizations   362
**14.3**  Classifying or Defining the Subject   363

**READING 2**   **Kids and Money**   365
**14.4**  Non-Specific Nouns   366
**14.5**  Specific Nouns   367
**14.6**  Specific or Non-Specific Nouns with Quantity Words   370

**READING 3**   **Billionaires**   372
**14.7**  *Other* and *Another*   373
**14.8**  More about *Other* and *Another*   374
**14.9**  Definite and Indefinite Pronouns   376

**UNIT SUMMARY**   378
**REVIEW**   379
**FROM GRAMMAR TO WRITING**   380

## APPENDICES

| | | |
|---|---|---|
| A | Summary of Verb Tenses | 382 |
| B | Nonaction Verbs | 383 |
| C | Irregular Verb Forms | 384 |
| D | Gerunds and Infinitives | 386 |
| E | Verbs and Adjectives Followed by a Preposition | 387 |
| F | Noncount Nouns | 388 |
| G | Uses of Articles | 390 |
| H | Connectors | 394 |
| I | Capitalization and Punctuation | 396 |

## GLOSSARY 398

## INDEX 402

## CREDITS 407

# ACKNOWLEDGMENTS

The Author and Publisher would like to acknowledge and thank the teachers who participated in the development of the seventh edition of *Grammar in Context*.

A special thanks to our Advisory Board for their valuable input during the development of this series.

## ADVISORY BOARD

**Andrea Gonzalez,** BYU English Language Center, Provo, UT, USA
**Ellen Rosen,** Fullerton College, Fullerton, CA, USA
**Erin Pak,** Schoolcraft College, Livonia, MI, USA
**Holly Gray,** Prince George's Community College, Largo, MD, USA
**John Halliwell,** Moraine Valley Community College, Palos Hills, IL, USA
**Katherine Sieradzki,** FLS Boston, Boston, MA, USA
**Maria Schirta,** Hudson County Community College, Jersey City, NJ, USA
**Oranit Limmaneeprasert,** American River College, Sacramento, CA, USA
**Susan Niemeyer,** Los Angeles City College, Los Angeles, CA, USA

## REVIEWERS

**Adriana García,** Institut Nord-America, Barcelona, Spain
**Alena Widows,** Institut Nord-America, Barcelona, Spain
**Augustine Triantafyllides,** So Easy, Athens, Greece
**Bilal Aslam,** GTCC, High Point, North Carolina, USA
**Carmen Díez,** CFA Les Corts, Barcelona, Spain
**David Finfrock,** QU, Doha, Qatar
**Deanna Henderson,** LCI, Denver, CO, USA
**Ellen Barrett,** Wayne State University, Detroit, MI, USA
**Francis Bandin,** UAB, Barcelona, Spain
**Jonathan Lathers,** Macomb Community College, Warren, MI, USA
**Karen Vallejo,** University of California, Irvine, CA, USA
**Kathy Najafi,** Houston Community College, Houston, TX, USA
**Katie Windahl,** Cuyahoga Community College, Cleveland, OH, USA
**Laura Jacob,** Mt. San Antonio College, Walnut, CA, USA
**Leah Carmona,** Bergen Community College, Paramus, NJ, USA
**Luba Nesterova,** Bilingual Education Institute, Houston, TX, USA
**Marcos Valle,** Edmonds Community College, Lynnwood, WA, USA
**Marla Goldfine,** San Diego Community College, San Diego, CA, USA
**Milena Eneva,** Chattahoochee Technical College, Marietta, GA, USA
**Monica Farling,** University of Delaware, Newark, DE, USA
**Naima Sarfraz,** Qatar University, Doha, Qatar
**Natalia Schroeder,** Long Beach City College, Long Beach, CA, USA
**Paul Schmitt,** Institut d'Estudis Nord-Americans, Barcelona, Spain
**Paula Sanchez,** Miami Dade College, Miami, FL, USA
**Paulette Koubek-Yao,** Pasadena City College, Arcadia, CA, USA
**Robert Yáñez,** Hillsborough Community College, Tampa, FL, USA
**Samuel Lumbsden,** Essex County College, Newark, NJ, USA
**Sarah Mikulski,** Harper College, Palatine, IL, USA
**Steven Lund,** Arizona Western College, Yuma, AZ, USA
**Teresa Cheung,** North Shore Community College, Lynn, MA, USA
**Tim McDaniel,** Green River College, Auburn, WA, USA
**Tristinn Williams,** Cascadia College, Seattle, WA, USA
**Victoria Mullens,** LCI, Denver, CO, USA

# A WORD FROM THE AUTHOR

My parents immigrated to the United States from Poland and learned English as a second language as adults. My sisters and I were born in the United States. My parents spoke Yiddish to us; we answered in English. In that process, my parents' English improved immeasurably. Such is the case with many immigrant parents whose children are fluent in English. They usually learn English much faster than others; they hear the language in natural ways, in the context of daily life.

Learning a language in context, whether it be from the home, from work, or from a textbook, cannot be overestimated. The challenge for me has been to find a variety of high-interest topics to engage the adult language learner. I was thrilled to work on this new edition of *Grammar in Context* for National Geographic Learning. In so doing, I have been able to combine exciting new readings with captivating photos to exemplify the grammar.

I have given more than 100 workshops at ESL programs and professional conferences around the United States, where I have gotten feedback from users of previous editions of *Grammar in Context*. Some teachers have expressed concern about trying to cover long grammar lessons within a limited time. While ESL is not taught in a uniform number of hours per week, I have heeded my audiences and streamlined the series so that the grammar and practice covered is more manageable. And in response to the needs of most ESL programs, I have expanded and enriched the writing component.

Whether you are a new user of *Grammar in Context* or have used this series before, I welcome you to this new edition.

*Sandra N. Elbaum*

**For my loves**
Gentille, Chimene, Joseph, and Joy

# WELCOME TO *GRAMMAR IN CONTEXT*, SEVENTH EDITION

*Grammar in Context*, the original contextualized grammar series, brings grammar to life through engaging topics that provide a framework for meaningful practice. Students learn more, remember more, and use language more effectively when they study grammar in context.

## ENHANCED IN THE SEVENTH EDITION

**National Geographic photographs** introduce unit themes and pull students into the context.

**Unit openers** include an inspirational quote to help students connect to the theme.

**New and updated readings** introduce the target grammar in context and provide the springboard for explanations and practice.

**New Think About It questions** give students the opportunity to personalize and think critically about what they are reading.

# CROWDFUNDING

Read the following article. Pay special attention to the words in bold.

■ **Have** you ever **had** an idea for a business but no way to fund it? **Have** you **asked** relatives and friends for money to help you? If you **have done** these things, you know it isn't easy to get people interested in investing in your dream. After getting money from relatives and friends, it's hard to find more people willing to invest. Lately, people **have found** a different way to raise cash: through crowdfunding. Crowdfunding is a method of "collecting small amounts of money from a lot of different people, usually by using the Internet." While the idea **has been** around for possibly hundreds of years, the word *crowdfunding* **has** only **existed** since 2006.

Crowdfunding websites, which started to appear on the Internet in 2010, **have helped** individuals raise billions of dollars worldwide. So how does it work? A person demonstrates his idea in a short video and states his financial goal and the time frame for raising money. Usually the first investors are family and friends. Little by little, strangers become interested and donate money.

Not all crowdfunding plans are for profit. Some people **have used** crowdfunding websites that are specifically for philanthropic[1] projects. These sites **have attracted** people who want to make the world a better place. The 97 Supermarket in Changchun, China, is one example of this. Jiang Naijun used crowdfunding to get the money to open a supermarket. She named her market 97 because that was her age when she did this. Since she became profitable, she **has given** at least half the money she earns to charity[2], to help children in need. "I wanted to do more for society," she said.

If you want more information, just google "crowdfunding" and you will find a number of different sites specializing in different types of projects.

Crowdfunding has become one of the most popular ways for people to raise money for a cause, project, or event. In 2017, $34 billion was raised globally. This number is expected to grow to more than $300 billion by 2025.

[1] philanthropic: intended to help others
[2] charity: an organization that helps people in need

98-year-old Jiang Naijun used crowdfunding to start her supermarket and donates the profits to charity.

**COMPREHENSION** Based on the reading, write T for *true* or F for *false*.

1. _____ Sometimes strangers help fund a crowdfunding project.
2. _____ The idea of crowdfunding is old, but it has become easier to do with the Internet.
3. _____ The "97 Supermarket" project didn't reach its financial goal.

**THINK ABOUT IT** Discuss the questions with a partner or in a small group.

1. What would you like to crowdfund for? Why?
2. What might be some challenges with crowdfunding? Explain.

## 9.4 The Present Perfect—Overview of Uses

| EXAMPLES | EXPLANATION |
|---|---|
| People **have used** crowdfunding since 2010. Google **has been** in existence for over 20 years. | We use the present perfect to show that an action or state started in the past and continues to the present. |
| I **have used** my laptop in coffee shops many times. How many articles about crowdfunding **have** you **read**? | We use the present perfect to show that an action repeated during a period of time that started in the past and includes the present. |
| **Have** you ever **asked** relatives for money? | We use the present perfect to show that an action occurred at an indefinite time in the past. |

**EXERCISE 7** Tell if the sentences show continuation from past to present (C), repetition from past to present (R), or an indefinite time in the past (I).

1. Larry Page has been interested in computers since he was a child. __C__
2. How many emails have you received today? _____
3. I've had my laptop for one year. _____
4. The word *crowdfunding* has been in existence since 2006. _____
5. Internet security has become a big problem. _____
6. Has your computer ever had a virus? _____
7. My cousin has used crowdfunding two times. _____
8. Have you ever used your laptop in a coffee shop? _____

**GRAMMAR IN USE**
When an event happened in the recent past, and the effect is still felt, we often use the present perfect. This is especially common for speakers of British English. In American English, we use either the present perfect or the simple past.

Someone **has just donated** $10,000!     Someone just donated $10,000.
I **have forgotten** my password again.     I forgot my password again.
**Have** you **heard** the news?     Did you hear the news?

**New Grammar in Use** notes highlight practical usage points to help students communicate more effectively.

**New listening comprehension activities** encourage students to listen for meaning through natural spoken English.

**EXERCISE 17** Listen to the information about the U.S. Census. Write T for *true*, F for *false*, or NS for *not stated*.

1. _____ At first, children were not counted in the census.
2. _____ All census information is available to everyone.
3. _____ Most Americans complete the census questionnaire.

**New Fun with Grammar** allows the class to practice grammar in a lively game-like way.

**Summary and Review** sections help students revisit key points and assess their progress.

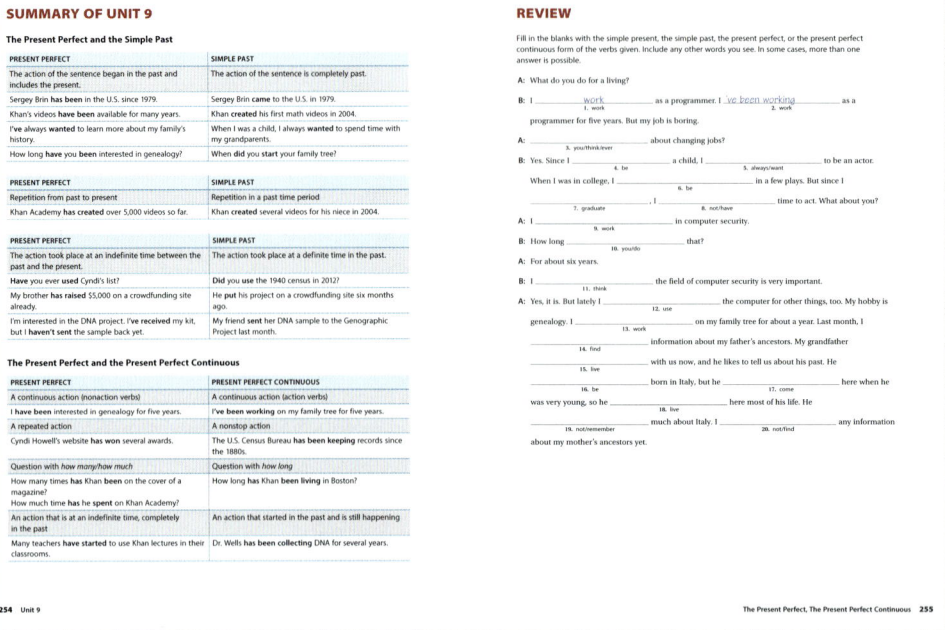

**From Grammar to Writing** gives editing advice and practice to set students up to successfully apply the grammar to writing.

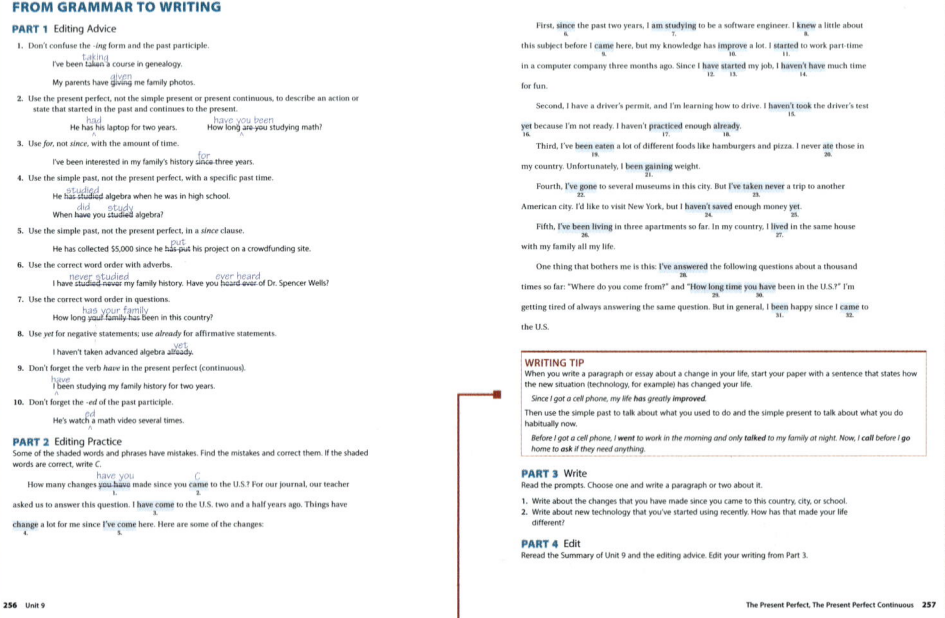

**New Writing Tips** further connect the grammar to the unit writing task.

## ADDITIONAL RESOURCES

**FOR STUDENTS** The **Online Practice** provides a variety of interactive grammar activities for homework or flexible independent study.

**GO TO ELTNGL.COM/MYELT**

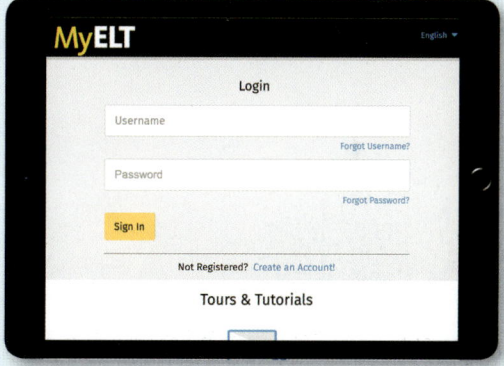

**FOR TEACHERS** The **Classroom Presentation Tool** allows the teacher to project the student book pages, open interactive activities with answers, and play the audio program.

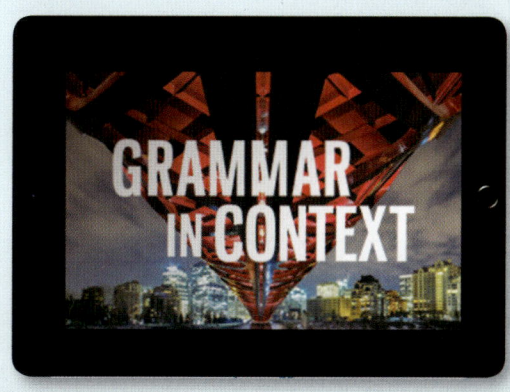

**The Teacher's Website** hosts the teacher's guide, audio, and ExamView® Test Center, so teachers have all the materials they need in one place.

**ELTNGL.COM/GRAMMARINCONTEXTSERIES**

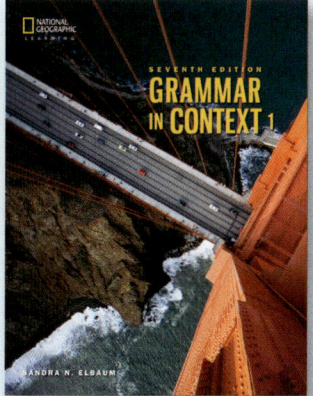
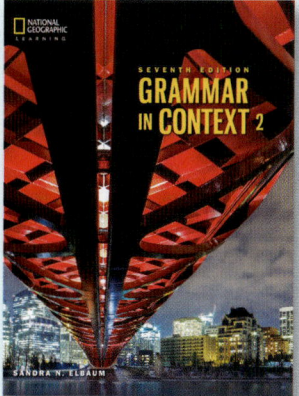
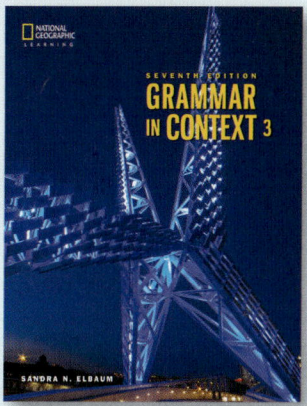

UNIT

# 8
Modals

# Where We Live

Quality of life actually begins at home - it's in your street, around your community.

CHARLES KENNEDY

Friends gather on a rooftop in Bulgaria.

# An Apartment Lease

Read the following article. Pay special attention to the words in bold. 8.1

Do you live in an apartment? **Did** you **have to sign** a lease? **Could** you **understand** what you signed? A lease, or rental agreement, **can be** hard to read, but you **should try** to understand what you are signing.

Your lease is a legal agreement between the owner (landlord[1]) and you, the renter (tenant). A lease states the period of time for the rental, the amount of the rent, when the tenant **must pay** it, who pays for utilities[2], and any rules the renter and the landlord **must follow**. Some leases contain the following rules:

- Pets **are not permitted**.
- Renters **may not change** the locks without the owner's permission.
- Renters **must pay** a late fee if they don't pay their rent on time.

The lease **might** even **state** how many overnight guests you **may have** and where you **can** or **cannot park**.

Many of the rules in the lease are for the benefit of the owner. The owner protects his or her property by requiring a security deposit. Usually a renter **has to pay** one to two months' rent as a deposit. The owner **can use** part or all of the money to repair any damage the renter causes. However, the landlord **may not keep** the renter's money for normal wear and tear[3].

There are also rules that protect the renter. For example, owners **must provide** heat during the winter months. In most cities, they **must put** a smoke detector in each apartment and in the halls. The owner **may not raise** the rent during the period of the lease.

When the landlord gives the renter the lease, it looks like an unchangeable document, but it isn't. Renters **don't have to accept** and sign the lease as is. If they don't agree to all the terms, they **can ask** for changes before they sign. For example, if you **would like to have** a pet, you **can ask** for permission by offering to pay a higher security deposit.

There **has to be** trust between the landlord and the renter. When looking for a new apartment, if you have a bad feeling about the landlord, you probably **ought to look** elsewhere.

---

[1] landlord: the owner of a rental property. If the owner is a woman, she is called "landlady."
[2] utilities: basic services such as water, electricity, or gas
[3] normal wear and tear: the normal use of something

A young woman takes a break from unpacking to video chat with family.

**COMPREHENSION** Based on the reading, write T for *true* or F for *false*.

1. _____ A renter cannot ask for changes to a lease.
2. _____ The owner can use the security deposit to pay for a renter's damages.
3. _____ The owner can raise the rent during the term of the lease.

**THINK ABOUT IT** Discuss the questions with a partner or in a small group.

1. Imagine the following situation. You are a tenant with a one-year lease. After two months, you receive a letter from the landlord that rent is increasing by $100. What would you say or do?
2. What are some issues that a tenant and landlord might need to negotiate? You can use ideas from the article or your own experience.

## 8.1 Overview of Modals

Modals add meaning to the verbs that follow them. The modal verbs are *can, could, should, would, may, might,* and *must*.

| EXAMPLES | EXPLANATION |
|---|---|
| A renter **must sign** a lease.<br>A tenant **can ask** for changes before signing the lease. | The base form of the verb follows a modal.<br>A modal never has an *-s* ending. |
| You **should not pay** your rent late.<br>I **cannot understand** my lease. | To form the negative, we put *not* after the modal. The negative of *can* is written as one word: *cannot*. The contraction for *cannot* is *can't*. |
| If you don't trust the landlord, you **should probably look** for another apartment. | We can put an adverb between the modal and the main verb. |

Notice these seven patterns with a modal:

| | |
|---|---|
| AFFIRMATIVE STATEMENT: | We **can have** a cat in the apartment. |
| NEGATIVE STATEMENT: | We **can't have** a dog. |
| YES/NO QUESTION: | **Can** we **have** a bird? |
| SHORT ANSWER: | Yes, you **can**. |
| WH- QUESTION: | Why **can** we **have** a cat? |
| NEGATIVE WH- QUESTION: | Why **can't** we **have** a dog? |
| SUBJECT QUESTION: | Who **can have** a dog? |

## 8.2 Phrasal Modals

Phrasal modals are expressions that are like modals in meaning.

| EXPRESSIONS | EXAMPLES |
|---|---|
| have to | He **has to sign** the lease. |
| have got to | He **has got to return** the security deposit. |
| be able to | He **is able to pay** the rent. |
| be supposed to | I'm **supposed to pay** my rent by the first of the month. |
| be permitted to | You **are not permitted to park** on the side of the building. |
| be allowed to | You **are not allowed to change** the locks in your apartment. |
| ought to | You **ought to respect** your neighbors. |
| had better | You **had better read** your lease carefully before signing it. |

**EXERCISE 1** Listen to the statements. Then write T for *true* or F for *false*. 8.2

1. _____ It is possible that a landlord will let you out of your lease early.
2. _____ If there is damage to the apartment, the landlord probably won't return the security deposit.
3. _____ A landlord cannot refuse to rent to a person based on sex, race, or religion.

**EXERCISE 2** Listen again to these sentences about renting an apartment. Fill in the blanks with the words you hear. 8.2

1. When a lease is up for renewal, the owner _____can_____ offer the renter a new lease, or he _____ ask the renter to leave.
2. The owner _____ notify the renter if he or she wants the renter to leave.
3. If you pay your rent late, you _____ have to pay a late fee.
4. If you want to make changes to the lease, you and the landlord _____ initial the changes.
5. What if you _____ move before the lease is up? What _____ you do?
   You _____ inform the landlord as soon as possible.
6. _____ the landlord make you pay until the end of your lease? Yes, he _____.
7. Some landlords _____ let you out of your lease by keeping your security deposit.
   Or a landlord _____ make you pay until the end of your lease.
8. The landlord _____ return your security deposit if there is no damage to the apartment.
9. The landlord _____ obey the law. He _____ refuse to rent to a person because of sex, race, religion, nationality, or disability.
10. If the landlord doesn't keep his end of the agreement, you _____ need a lawyer.

**EXERCISE 3** Read each statement. Fill in the blanks to complete the question.

1. You should read the lease before you sign it. Why ____should I____ read the lease before I sign it?
2. You can't have a dog. Why _____ a dog?
3. We must pay a security deposit. How much _____?
4. Someone must install a smoke detector. Who _____ a smoke detector?
5. The landlord must return the security deposit. When _____ it?
6. The landlord said I can pick up the key tomorrow. What time _____ the key?

## 8.3 Obligation/Necessity—*Must* and Phrasal Modals

| MUST | PHRASAL MODAL | EXPLANATION |
|---|---|---|
| The landlord **must provide** smoke detectors. | The landlord **has to provide** smoke detectors. | We use *must* and *have to* for rules and obligations. *Must* is more formal than *have to*. |
| | I**'ve got to call** my landlord today. I **have to tell** him about a problem in my bathroom. | We use *have to* or *have got to* for personal obligations or necessities. |
| | At the end of my lease last June, I **had to move**. I **had to find** a bigger apartment. | *Must* has no past form. The past of both *must* and *have to* is *had to*. |

**Notes:**

1. *Have got to* is usually contracted with a subject pronoun.

    I have got to = I've got to    He has got to = He's got to

2. We don't use *have got to* for questions or negatives.
3. Many legal documents use *shall* for obligation.

    *If the security deposit does not cover the cost to repair any damages, the tenant shall pay the additional costs to the owner.*

**Pronunciation Note:**

In informal speech, *have to* is often pronounced "hafta." *Has to* is often pronounced "hasta." *Got to* is often pronounced "gotta." In informal speech and writing, people often say or write "gotta." (I gotta go now.)

---

**EXERCISE 4** Fill in the blanks with one of the items from the box. Use the correct form of *have*.

| have to notify | have to move | must put | must give ✓ |
|---|---|---|---|
| have got to obey | have to sign | have to return | have got to clean |

1. The landlord ____must give____ you heat in cold weather.

2. You _____ the lease with a pen. A pencil is not acceptable.

3. The landlord _____ your security deposit if you leave your apartment in good condition.

4. The landlord _____ you if he wants you to leave at the end of your lease.

5. The landlord _____ a smoke detector in each apartment and in the hallways.

6. I _____ the rules of the lease.

7. My new apartment is dirty. I _____ it before I move in.

8. My old apartment was too expensive, so I _____ last month.

**ABOUT YOU** Make a list of personal obligations you, your roommate, or your family members have in your apartment or house. Practice *have to* and *have got to*. Share your answers with a partner.

1. I've got to throw out the garbage twice a week.
2. My roommate has to clean the kitchen on the weekend.
3. _____
4. _____
5. _____

**ABOUT YOU** Make a list of things you had to do last weekend. Share your answers with a partner.

1. I had to do my laundry.
2. _____
3. _____
4. _____
5. _____

## 8.4 Permission/Prohibition—*May* and Phrasal Modals

| MAY | PHRASAL MODALS | EXPLANATION |
| --- | --- | --- |
| The landlord **may enter** the apartment in case of emergency. | The landlord **is permitted to enter** the apartment in case of emergency. | We can use *may*, *be permitted to*, and *be allowed to* for permission or prohibition. We often see *may* in legal documents. |
| The tenant **may not leave** items in the hallway. | The tenant **is not allowed to leave** items in the hallway. | |

Notes:
1. *May not* and *must not* have the same meaning—prohibition.

    Tenants **may not park** behind the building.

    Tenants **must not park** behind the building.

2. Many legal documents use *shall* (*not*) for permission or prohibition.

    The tenant **shall have** one parking space behind the building.

    The tenant **shall not change** the locks without the owner's permission.

**EXERCISE 5** The rules for driving in the United States are similar in most states. Fill in the blanks with one of the phrases from the box to complete each sentence.

| aren't allowed to ride | must reduce | may not go | have to go |
| aren't permitted to hold | may drive | must have | must wear ✓ |
| may not pass | have to get | may not park | may use |

1. You _____must wear_____ a seatbelt.

2. If you are from another state or another country, you _____ with a valid license. However, you _____ a license in the state where you're living (usually within 90 days).

3. You _____ in a disabled parking space unless your vehicle has a disabled license plate or a removable windshield card.

4. Bicycle riders _____ against traffic. They _____ in the same direction as traffic.

5. A driver _____ insurance.

6. You _____ on a hill or curve if you are not able to see the oncoming vehicles.

7. In many places, you _____ a cell phone in your hand while driving. However, you _____ a hands-free device.

8. Drivers _____ their speed in a school zone during school hours.

9. When a school bus stops for children to get on or off, you _____ around it.

## 8.5 Expectation—Be Supposed To

| EXAMPLES | EXPLANATION |
| --- | --- |
| The landlord **is supposed to give** you a copy of the lease.<br>When **am I supposed to pay** the rent?<br>My friend **is supposed to help** me move. | *Be supposed to* expresses an expectation. We expect something because of:<br>   a law or a requirement.<br>   a personal obligation. |
| We**'re not supposed to have** cats in my building, but my neighbor has one.<br>I **was supposed to pay** my rent yesterday, but I forgot. | We use *be supposed to* when someone broke a rule or did not meet an expectation. |

**Pronunciation Note:**
We don't pronounce the *d* in *supposed to*.

**EXERCISE 6** Finish these statements. Use *be supposed to* (present or past, affirmative or negative) and one of the verbs from the box. Use contractions wherever possible.

| use | paint | provide | pay ✓ | clean | take out |
|---|---|---|---|---|---|
| return | fix | replace | wash | have | |

1. I **'m supposed to pay** my rent on the first of the month.
2. Pets are not permitted in my apartment. I _____ a pet.
3. In which months _____ the landlord _____ heat?
4. The tenants _____ the apartment before they move out.
5. My stove isn't working. My landlord _____ it tomorrow.
6. We're going to move out next week. Our apartment is clean and in good condition. The landlord _____ our security deposit.
7. The janitor _____ the garbage every day.
8. When we moved in, we _____ the back stairs, not the front stairs.
9. My smoke detector doesn't work. The landlord _____ it.
10. My landlord _____ the walls of my apartment last month, but he didn't do it. I'm still waiting.
11. My roommate _____ the dishes last night, but she forgot.

## 8.6 Ability/Permission—*Can, Could*, and Phrasal Modals

| CAN/COULD | PHRASAL MODALS | EXPLANATION |
|---|---|---|
| I **can clean** the apartment by Friday. <br> I **can't understand** the lease. | I **am able to clean** the apartment by Friday. <br> I **am not able to understand** the lease. | Ability/ Inability |
| I **could understand** the first page of the lease. <br> I **couldn't understand** the rest of the lease. | I **was able to understand** the first page of the lease. <br> I **wasn't able to understand** the rest of the lease. | Past Ability/ Inability |
| I **can have** a cat in my apartment. <br> I **can't have** a dog. | I **am permitted to have** a cat in my apartment. <br> I **am not allowed to have** a dog. | Permission/ Prohibition |
| I **could have** a cat in my last apartment, but I **couldn't have** a dog. | I **was permitted to have** a cat in my last apartment, but I **wasn't allowed to have** a dog. | Past Permission/ Prohibition |

Notes:
1. We also use *may* for permission. *May* is more formal than *can*.
2. A common expression with *can* is *can(not) afford*.
   I **can afford** a one-bedroom apartment. I **can't afford** a two-bedroom apartment.

**Pronunciation Note:**

*Can* is not usually stressed in affirmative statements. In negative statements, *can't* is stressed, but it can be hard to hear the final *t*. So we must pay attention to the vowel sound and stress to hear the difference between *can* and *can't*.
      I "can" go. (kIn)      I "can't" go. (kænt)

In a short answer, we pronounce *can* as /kæn/.
      "Can" you help me later?   Yes, I "can." (kæn)

---

**EXERCISE 7** Fill in the blanks with one of the words from the box to complete this conversation.

| can't carry | can give | can't do | couldn't reach |
|---|---|---|---|
| wasn't able to find | 're not allowed to use ✓ | can you put | can cook |
| 'm not allowed to leave | 're not permitted to use | are you able to wash | can't afford |

**A:** How do you like your new apartment?

**B:** The apartment is great. But I don't like some of the rules. For example, we <u>'re not allowed to use</u> (1.) the laundry room after 11 p.m. I work late, and I _____ (2.) my laundry in the daytime.

**A:** _____ (3.) your clothes on Sundays?

**B:** Yes, but that's when most people do their laundry. Also, I like to barbecue on the porch. But we _____ (4.) a fire grill. We _____ (5.) on a gas grill, but I prefer a fire grill. Here's another problem: I use my bike every day, but I _____ (6.) it in the hallway. I'm on the third floor, and there's no elevator. I _____ (7.) my bike upstairs every day.

**A:** _____ (8.) your bike in the basement?

**B:** I don't know. I don't have a key to the basement. I called the landlord yesterday to ask him about it, but I _____ (9.) him.

**A:** Try again. Is your roommate happy with the apartment?

**B:** I don't have a roommate. I _____ (10.) one. But the rent is high, and I _____ (11.) it on my own.

**A:** I have a friend who's looking for a roommate. I _____ (12.) you his phone number.

**B:** Thanks.

In the U.S., people buy over a billion plastic bottles every year. We recycle only 25% of them.

# FREQUENTLY ASKED QUESTIONS:
## Recycling Plastic in Your Home

Read the following FAQs. Pay special attention to the words in bold. 8.3

Q: Why **should** I **recycle** plastic?

A: In the United States, we produce tons of plastic waste every year, but we recycle only about nine percent of it. A lot of this plastic goes into the ocean, and it is killing sea animals. Plastic is appearing in our food and drinking water now, too. As one expert said recently: We**'d better do** something about this problem. . . before it's too late. Everyone **ought to recycle** *and* **use** less plastic.

Q: Where **should** I **recycle** plastic items?

A: If your city has a recycling program, your dorm or home will have a bin. (It's usually blue or gray.) You **should put** your plastic items here.

Note: In many U.S. cities, all recyclable items (plastic, glass, paper, metal) go in the same bin. However, in some cities (e.g., New York City), plastic, glass, and metal items go in one bin and paper in another. If you aren't sure what to do, you**'d better check** online. Residents can be fined[1] for not putting items in the correct bin.

Q: **Should** I **put** plastic bags in the recycling bin?

A: **No,** you **shouldn't**. Many recycling centers do not take them. If possible, you **ought to keep** the plastic bags and take them to a supermarket. Many stores recycle them.

Q: **Should** I **clean** plastic containers first?

A: **Yes,** you **should**. Dirty bottles and other containers cannot be recycled, so you **shouldn't leave** food or liquid in them. Also, you **ought to remove** the caps[2] from bottles and jars. (The cap and container are usually different kinds of plastic.)

Q: I want to use less plastic, but it's hard. What **should** I **do**?

A: Over 40 percent of all plastic waste comes from single-use plastics (shopping bags, cups, bottles). You **ought to stop** using these items. Instead, you **should buy** and **use** your own bag or bottle. Many coffeeshops and stores give a discount[3] when you bring your own bottle or bag. By doing this, you can make a big difference—and you'll save money, too!

---
[1] fined: charged money as a punishment for breaking a rule
[2] cap: the cover on top of a bottle, jar, or other container
[3] discount: a little bit of money subtracted from the regular price

**COMPREHENSION** Based on the reading, write T for *true* or F for *false*.

1. _____ In many U.S. cities, you should put plastic in one bin and glass, metal, and paper in another.
2. _____ In many U.S. cities, plastic bags go in the recycling bin.
3. _____ It is OK to put a dirty container in the recycling bin with the cap on.

**THINK ABOUT IT** Discuss the questions with a partner or in a small group.

1. According to the reading, why should we reduce and recycle? Explain in your own words.
2. The reading gives tips for using less plastic. What are they? Do you do these things? What else should you do? Think of at least one more idea.

## 8.7 Advice—*Should, Ought To, Had Better*

| EXAMPLES | EXPLANATION |
|---|---|
| You **should bring** your own shopping bag to the store.<br>You **shouldn't put** plastic bags in the recycling bin. | For advice, we use *should*.<br>  *Should* = It's a good idea.<br>  *Shouldn't* = It's a bad idea. |
| Everyone **ought to recycle** plastic. | *Ought to* means the same as *should*. We don't usually use *ought to* in questions or negatives. |
| Plastic is in our food and drinking water. We **had better do** something about this problem before it's too late.<br>We**'d better not wait** much longer. | When it is probable that something bad or unpleasant will happen, we use *had better (not)*.<br>The contraction for *had* (in *had better*) is *'d*.<br>  I'd  you'd  he'd  she'd  we'd  they'd |

**Note:**
*Should* is for advice. *Must* is for obligation or necessity.
Compare:
  You **should bring** your own shopping bags to the store. (advice)
  You **must pay** 10 cents for each new bag at the store. (obligation)

**Pronunciation Note:**
Native speakers often don't pronounce *had* or the *'d* in *had better*. You will hear people say:
  *If you are unsure about the recycling rules,* **you better ask**.

**EXERCISE 8** Complete each sentence with *should/ought to, shouldn't,* or *'d better*.

1. The blue bin is for recycling. You ___shouldn't___ put garbage in there.
2. All glass and plastic bottles _____ go in the recycling bin.
3. You _____ not pour cooking oil down the sink. It can block the drain.
4. Everyone _____ use less plastic. It's good for the environment.
5. You _____ put broken glass in recycling. It goes in the garbage bin.
6. You _____ bring your own cup to a coffeeshop. You'll get a discount.

**EXERCISE 9** It is the end of the school year, and two college students are cleaning their dorm room. Unscramble the words to complete the dialogue.

**A:** OK, we packed our clothes. ____What should we do____ next?
   1. should/we/what/do

**B:** I think _____ the trash.
   2. should/we/throw out

**A:** OK. _____ all these plastic bottles in the garbage?
   3. put/I/should

**B:** No. _____ in recycling.
   4. go/those/ought to

**A:** Oh, right. And these old batteries? _____ them?
   5. I/where/put/should

**B:** I'm not sure. _____ online.
   6. better/check/you'd

**A:** Good idea. It says _____ batteries in the garbage.
   7. shouldn't/we/put

_____ to the campus recycling center.
   8. them/we/take/should

**B:** OK. What about this microwave oven? It doesn't work anymore. _____ here?
   9. we/it/leave/should

**A:** _____. The school charges money if we leave things in the room. I'll take
   10. better/not/we'd

it with me.

**EXERCISE 10** Read about the recycling rules in one community. For each item, write a sentence that explains the rule. Use *should/ought to* and *shouldn't*.

| SHOULD THESE ITEMS GO IN THE RECYCLING BIN? | | | |
|---|---|---|---|
| ITEM | RECYCLING | GARBAGE | OTHER |
| 1. plastic bags | | ✓ | ✓(recycle at a supermarket) |
| 2. milk cartons | ✓ | | |
| 3. paper napkins | | | ✓(put in the compost bin; use cloth) |
| 4. laundry soap bottles | ✓ | | |
| 5. light bulbs | | ✓(regular bulbs) | ✓(CFLs: take to a recycling center) |
| 6. magazines | ✓ | | |
| 7. old pens | | ✓ | |
| 8. an old phone | | | ✓(take to a recycling center or donate) |
| 9. takeout containers | ✓ | | |
| 10. batteries | | | ✓(put in a bag on top of the garbage bin) |

1. Plastic bags shouldn't go in the recycling bin. You should put them in the garbage bin or recycle them at a supermarket.

2. _____

3. _____
4. _____
5. _____
6. _____
7. _____
8. _____
9. _____
10. _____

## 8.8 Negatives of Modals

| EXAMPLES | EXPLANATION |
| --- | --- |
| Tenants **are not supposed to leave** bikes near the door, but someone always does. | *Be not supposed to* shows that something is not acceptable by rule or custom. |
| Renters **must not change** the locks.<br>Renters **may not change** the locks.<br>Renters **cannot change** the locks.<br>Renters **are not allowed to change** the locks.<br>Renters **are not permitted to change** the locks. | *Must not, may not, cannot, be not allowed to,* and *be not permitted to* show prohibition. |
| I **cannot** open this water bottle.<br>I **am not able to** open this water bottle. | *Cannot* and *be not able to* show inability. |
| You **shouldn't put** plastic bottles in the garbage bin. They go in recycling. | *Shouldn't* shows that something is not advisable. |
| Renters **don't have to accept** the lease as is. They can ask for changes. | *Don't have to* shows that something is not necessary. It often means that there is an option. |
| You **had better not make** noise at night. You will disturb your neighbors. | *Had better not* shows that a negative consequence can result. |

**Note:**
Even though *have to* and *must* have basically the same meaning in the affirmative, in the negative they are completely different.

    You **must sign** the lease. = You **have to sign** the lease.

    The landlord **doesn't have to renew** the lease. (He has a choice.)

    He **must not enter** your apartment without your permission. (This is prohibited.)

**EXERCISE 11** Circle the correct words to complete this list of advice on living in the United States. In some cases, both answers are possible, so circle both options.

1. Americans are generally on time for appointments. You (*can't/shouldn't*) keep people waiting.

2. You (*shouldn't/must not*) visit friends without an invitation. If someone says, "Let's get together sometime," wait for a specific invitation.

3. Americans don't like to wait in line, but if they have to, they're usually courteous. You (*shouldn't/don't have to*) push to try to get ahead of someone.

4. Bribing[1] an official is against the law. You (*must not/don't have to*) offer a bribe if a police officer gives you a ticket or a government official turns down your application.

5. When you buy new items in a store, you (*had better not/shouldn't*) try to negotiate the price. Prices in stores are fixed. However, a major exception is when buying a new car. You (*don't have to/must not*) pay the asking price. The price is negotiable.

6. You (*may not/must not*) drive without insurance in the U.S. You (*must/have to*) have insurance to protect the other car and driver. You (*don't have to/must not*) have insurance to protect your own car.

7. In most places, you (*may not/can't*) use a hand-held cell phone while driving.

---
[1] bribing: the illegal act of offering money in exchange for something

Americans generally don't dress up for casual house parties.

8. A driver's license is often used for identification, but you (*must not/don't have to*) have a driver's license. You can get a state ID. A state ID looks like a driver's license, but you (*can't/aren't allowed to*) drive a car with it.

9. If you have a Social Security number, you (*shouldn't/can't*) give it to strangers over the phone. Someone can steal your identity and cause you a lot of problems.

10. Americans are generally very casual. If you're invited to an informal party at someone's house, you (*don't have to/may not*) dress up.

11. If you are invited to a party, you (*aren't supposed to/don't have to*) bring anything, but many guests will come with something to eat, such as a dessert or something to drink. When you leave, you (*shouldn't/may not*) take that food or drink home. It's the custom to leave it there.

12. If you are invited to a formal wedding, you (*aren't supposed to/must not*) take children unless the invitation specifically invites them.

**EXERCISE 12** Fill in the blanks with the negative of *have to, should, be supposed to, must, had better, can,* or *may* to complete the conversation between students (A) and their teacher (B). In some cases, more than one answer is possible.

**A:** Do I have to sit in a specific seat for the test?

**B:** No, you ____don't have to____. You can choose any seat you want.
                    **1.**

**A:** Is it OK if I talk to another student during a test?

**B:** No. Absolutely not. You _____ talk to another student during a test.
                              **2.**

**A:** Is it OK if I use my book?

**B:** Sorry. You _____ use your book.
                  **3.**

**A:** What if I don't understand something on the test?

**B:** Please ask me if you have a question.

**A:** What happens if I'm late for the test? Will you let me in?

**B:** Of course I'll let you in. But you _____ come late. You'll need a lot of
                                          **4.**
time for the test.

**A:** Do I have to bring my computer for the final test?

**B:** If you want to, you can. But you _____ bring it.
                                        **5.**
There will be school computers you can use.

*continued*

A: Do I have to write my final essay on the computer? Or can I use a pen and paper?

B: You can use whatever you want. You _____ use a computer.
6.

A: Do you have any advice on test-taking?

B: Yes. On the grammar section, if you see an item that is difficult for you, go on to the next item. You _____ spend too much time on a difficult item, or you won't finish the test.
7.

A: Can I bring coffee into the classroom?

B: The school has a rule about eating or drinking in the classroom. You _____ bring food or drinks into the classroom.
8.

A: How long will we have for the test?

B: You'll have two hours. That's usually enough time. If you finish early, you _____ stay. You can leave.
9.

A: If we need more time, can we keep working?

B: You _____ need more time. But I will give you 10 extra minutes if you do.
10.

A: Will we get our test results tomorrow?

B: You _____ expect me to grade 25 tests overnight! You'll get the results by the end of the week.
11.

**FUN WITH GRAMMAR**

Imagine a new student is joining your class. Work with a partner to write a list of class regulations and advice. They can be serious or silly and may include both things you should do and things you shouldn't or can't do.

*Students are not permitted to have pizza delivered during class.*

*You should have two notebooks—one for general notes and one for vocabulary.*

A neighborhood party

# Starting Life in a NEW COUNTRY

Read the following article. Pay special attention to the words in bold. 🎧 8.4

You're about to go to college in the United States. Or your family just moved to the United States. Your friends back home tell you, "It **must be** so exciting to live in a new country." But there are so many new rules and customs to learn. After the excitement wears off[1], there are many questions you'll have and decisions you have to make.

Now you're here, and you find yourself in situations that are completely new to you. You might ask yourself: "Should I buy a car or use public transportation? Should I get a roommate? If so, how and where? How do I find a doctor? Where do I get insurance? How do I find a job? When and where do I tip?" There **must be** hundreds of things you never thought about before.

In addition to those practical things, you **might** also **wonder** about social differences. You **might ask** yourself: "What topics are appropriate for making small talk here? What topics **might not be** so good? Why did the person I am talking to step back from me? Did I say something wrong?" It **might be** that you are standing too close. People in the U.S. like their personal space. This is one of many unspoken rules that **might be** new to you.

Besides questions you have about life in the United States, you're probably discovering that many Americans are curious about you. Of course, they'll ask you where you're from. Keep in mind that they **might not know** much about your country or culture. If you say Sri Lanka, for example, they **may have** no idea where this is. They **might not understand** the differences between different Asian countries. If you're from Brazil, people **might think** you speak Spanish. People who think that **must not know** that Portuguese is the language of Brazil. Just explain where you're from and what language you speak.

With time, you'll learn more about American behaviors, and others will learn more about you and your native culture.

---

[1] to wear off: to go away, little by little

Modals   211

**COMPREHENSION** Based on the reading, write T for *true* or F for *false*.

1. _____ Americans are often curious about foreigners.
2. _____ Some Americans might not know a lot about different Asian countries.
3. _____ Everyone knows that Portuguese is the language of Brazil.

**THINK ABOUT IT** Discuss the questions with a partner or in a small group.

1. Describe a situation in the U.S. that was new or confusing for you. Explain how you handled it.
2. Talk about the questions you wanted answers to when you first moved to the United States. How did you find the answers?

## 8.9 Conclusions or Deductions—*Must*

| EXAMPLES | EXPLANATION |
| --- | --- |
| It **must be** exciting to live in another country.<br>You're from Mexico? You **must speak** Spanish, then. | We often make a deduction or come to a conclusion using *must*. We think our assumption is probably true. (We may be wrong.) |
| I told a classmate that I'm from Brazil. He thinks I speak Spanish. He **must not know** much about Brazil. | For a negative deduction/conclusion, we use *must not*. We don't use a contraction. |

**Note:**
Remember, we also use *must* to express necessity.
    *Students must register for classes.*

**EXERCISE 13** Fill in the blanks with an appropriate verb phrase from the box to complete the conversation between two neighbors. You may use an answer more than once.

| must spend | must have | must get | must not like |
| --- | --- | --- | --- |
| must know | must not be | must be | |

A: Hi. My name's Alma. I live on the third floor. You ____must be____ new in this building.
                                                                                  1.

B: I am. We just moved in last week. My name's Eva.

A: I noticed your last name on the mailbox. It's Gonzalez. Are you from Mexico?

B: No. Actually I'm from the Philippines.

A: I'm so sorry. You _____ that mistake all the time. Are you going to school now?
                                                 2.

B: Yes, I'm taking English classes at Washington College. I'm in Level 5.

A: You _____ my husband, Hasan. He's also in the Level 5 class there.
                  3.

B: Oh, yes, I know him. I didn't know he lived in the same building. I never see him here. He

_____ home very much.
          4.

**A:** He isn't. He has two jobs. By the way, I saw the movers carrying in a crib.

You _____ a baby.
            5.

**B:** We do. We have a 10-month-old son. He's sleeping now. Do you have any kids?

**A:** Yes. I have a 16-year-old daughter and an 18-year-old son. I _____ half my time
                                                                        6.

worrying about them. My daughter texts her friends all day.

**B:** Kids today _____ to talk much. They rely more on texting.
                      7.

**A:** You're right. Listen, I don't want to take up any more of your time. You _____ a
                                                                                    8.

lot to do. I just wanted to bring you these cookies.

**B:** That's very nice of you. They're still warm. They _____ right out of the oven.
                                                              9.

**A:** They are. Maybe we can talk some other time when you're all unpacked.

**EXERCISE 14** Use *must* + base form to show Eva's conclusions about Alma's life when she is visiting Alma in her apartment. Answers may vary.

1. There is a bowl of food on the kitchen floor.

   <u>Alma's family must have a pet.</u>

2. There is a nursing certificate on the wall with Alma's name on it.

   _____

3. There are many different kinds of coffee on a kitchen shelf.

   _____

4. There are a lot of classical music CDs.

   _____

5. In Alma's bedroom, there's a sewing machine.

   _____

6. There's a piano in the living room.

   _____

7. On the kitchen calendar, there's an activity filled in for almost every day of the week.

   _____

# 8.10 Possibility—*May/Might*

| EXAMPLES | EXPLANATION |
|---|---|
| Americans **might ask** you some strange questions.<br>They **may have** little or no knowledge of your country. | *May* and *might* both have about the same meaning: possibility or uncertainty about the present. |
| They **may not know** much about your country.<br>They **might not know** the difference between a Spanish person and a Spanish-speaking person. | For the negative, we use *may not* or *might not*. We don't use a contraction for these negatives. |
| I **may get** a roommate next semester.<br>I **might get** a roommate next semester. | *May* and *might* can give a future meaning. |

Notes:

1. *Maybe* is an adverb. It is one word. It usually comes at the beginning of the sentence and means *possibly* or *perhaps*. *May* and *might* are modals. They follow the subject and precede the verb.

    **Maybe** *he is Mexican.* = *He* **may be** *Mexican.* = *He* **might be** *Mexican.*

    **Maybe** *I will get a roommate next semester.* = *I* **may get** *a roommate next semester.* =

    *I* **might get** *a roommate next semester.*

2. Remember, *must* shows a conclusion, an assumption, or a deduction.
    Compare:

    *You're from Mexico. You* **must speak** *Spanish. (assumption)*

    *He speaks Spanish. He* **might be** *from Guatemala or Peru. (possibility)*

---

**EXERCISE 15** Remove *maybe* from each of the following sentences and rewrite the sentences using the modal given.

1. Maybe some questions seem silly to you. (*may*)

    <u>Some questions may seem silly to you.</u>

2. Maybe Americans don't know much about your country. (*may*)

    _____

3. Maybe you will become impatient with some questions. (*might*)

    _____

4. If you say you speak Spanish, maybe an American will say, "Oh, you're Spanish." (*may*)

    _____

5. Maybe you will be confused at times. (*may*)

    _____

6. Maybe Americans ask you some strange questions. (*might*)

_____

7. Maybe you will learn about Americans from their questions. (*might*)

_____

**EXERCISE 16** Fill in the blanks with a verb to show possibility. Answers may vary.

1. **A:** I'm going to move on Saturday. I'm going to need help. Can you help me?

   **B:** I'm not sure. I may _____*go*_____ away this weekend.

2. **A:** My next-door neighbor's name is Terry Karson. I see her name on the doorbell, but I never see her.

   **B:** Your neighbor may _____ a man. *Terry* is sometimes a man's name.

3. **A:** I need coins for the laundry room. Do you have any?

   **B:** Let me look. I might _____ some. No, I don't have any. Look in the laundry room.

   There might _____ a dollar-bill changer there.

4. **A:** Do you know the landlord's address?

   **B:** No, I don't. Ask the manager. She might _____.

5. **A:** Do they allow cats in this building?

   **B:** I know they don't allow dogs, but they might _____ cats.

6. **A:** Are you going to stay in this apartment for another year?

   **B:** I'm not sure. I may _____. The landlord might _____ the rent. If the rent goes

   up more than 25 percent, I'll move.

7. **A:** I have so much stuff in my closet. There's not enough room for my clothes.

   **B:** There might _____ lockers in the basement where you can store your things.

   **A:** Really? I didn't know that.

   **B:** Let's look. I may _____ a key to the basement with me.

   **A:** That would be great.

8. **A:** When I tell people I'm from Korea, they ask me if I speak Chinese. I get so mad.

   **B:** Don't get mad. Be patient and teach them something about your culture. They may _____

   something new from you.

There are ways to furnish a new apartment without spending a lot of money.

# How to Furnish YOUR NEW APARTMENT Cheaply

Read the following conversation. Pay special attention to the words in bold. 🎧 8.5

Many people need to furnish their home, apartment, or room, but they don't want to spend a lot of money. In this conversation, Student B gives his friend Student A (who moved to the U.S. recently) some tips for furnishing a new place cheaply.

A: The first thing I need for my new place is a bed.

B: OK, **would you rather get** a twin- **or** full-sized bed?

A: I know it's more expensive, but I**'d rather get** a full. A twin is too small.

B: OK. Look, this discount website has a full bed set for $250. They deliver for free, too.

A: Great. **Could you text** that information to me? And **can I use** your pen? I want to do some quick math.

B: Sure, here you go. What else do you need?

A: Some things for the kitchen—plates, glasses, pots.

B: **Why don't you buy** them at a second-hand store? There's one nearby. It sells lots of gently used, inexpensive household items.

A: Good idea. But I'll need help bringing things home. **Will you come** with me?

B: Sure. **Would you like** to go this afternoon?

A: Yeah, that'd be great.

B: Is there anything else?

A: **I'd like to get** a desk and chair, but I don't have enough money.

B: Try Craigslist.org or Freecycle.org. You can find free stuff[1] on those sites. And people often put unwanted items on the sidewalk, too—especially furniture.

A: I can take stuff on the street?

B: Yeah. Many people **would rather give** away unwanted items **than** put them in the garbage. Actually, I have a small desk that I don't use anymore. **Why don't I bring** it to your place later?

A: Really? Thank you!

---
[1] stuff: an informal word for *things*

**COMPREHENSION** Based on the reading, write T for *true* or F for *false*.

1. _____ Student A wants to get a twin-sized bed.
2. _____ Student B suggests buying the bed at a second-hand store.
3. _____ In the U.S., people often put unwanted items on the sidewalk for others to take.

**THINK ABOUT IT** Discuss the questions with a partner or in a small group.

1. Imagine you are renting a new apartment. What furniture do you buy first? Where do you buy it?
2. Do you like to shop at second-hand stores? Why or why not?

## 8.11 Using Modals for Politeness

| EXAMPLES | EXPLANATION |
|---|---|
| **May** / **Can** / **Could** **I use** your pen? | We use *may*, *can*, or *could* + *I* to ask for permission. |
| **Can** / **Could** / **Will** / **Would** **you text** that information to me? | We use *can*, *could*, *will*, or *would* + *you* to make a request. |
| **Would** you **like to go** shopping today? <br> Yes. I**'d like to.** | *Would like* has the same meaning as *want*. *Would like* is more polite than *want*. The contraction for *would* after a pronoun is *'d*. |
| **Would** you **rather get** a twin- **or** full-sized bed? <br> I **would rather get** a full-sized bed (**than** a twin bed). <br><br> I**'d rather get** a full-sized bed. <br> I**'d rather not spend** a lot of money. | *Would rather* shows a preference of choices. We use *or* in questions. We use *than* in statements. The second choice can be omitted if it's obvious. <br><br> The contraction for *would* after a pronoun is *'d*. The negative is *would rather not*. |
| **Why don't you buy** your bed online? <br> **Why don't I bring** the desk to your place? | We can use a negative question to offer a polite suggestion. |
| **May** I **help** you? <br> **Can** I **help** you? | In a shopping situation, the salesperson often uses these questions. |

Notes:
1. When asking for permission, it is more polite to use *may* or *could* rather than *can*.
2. When making a request, it is more polite to use *could* or *would* rather than *can* or *will*.

### GRAMMAR IN USE

Choosing the correct level of politeness for a situation will make your English sound more natural. In formal situations, use these modal phrases:

*May I please speak to …?*

*Could you please tell me where …?*

*I would like to make an appointment.*

In less formal contexts, you can use other phrases:

*Can I speak to …?*

*Can you tell me where …?*

*I want to make an appointment.*

If you are uncertain of the situation, it's better to be too polite than not polite enough.

---

**EXERCISE 17** The conversation takes place in a second-hand store. Person A is a shopper; Person B is a salesperson. Make the language more polite by using modals and other expressions in place of the underlined words. Answers may vary.

**A:** Excuse me.

**B:** Yes? <u>Do you need help?</u> *May I help you?*
    1.

**A:** Yes. <u>I want to see</u> that lamp—the one on the shelf. <u>Show it to me</u>, please.
    2.                                                    3.

**B:** Sure. <u>Wait a minute.</u> I have to get a ladder. *(A moment later)* OK, here's the lamp.
    4.

**A:** Thanks. It's nice, but does it work?

**B:** I think so, but <u>let's check</u>. I'll plug it in. Yes, it works.
    5.

**A:** Great. <u>Tell me how much it is.</u>
    6.

**B:** Let's see. It's 15 dollars.

**A:** OK, I'll take it.

**B:** <u>Do you want to see</u> any other lamps?
    7.

**A:** Yes, <u>show me</u> that blue one, please.
    8.

**B:** Sure, here you go.

**A:** It's nice, but it's 30 dollars, and <u>I don't want to spend</u> that much money.
    9.

**B:** Sure, I understand. <u>Do you want to see</u> anything else?
    10.

**A:** No, thanks. I'm done shopping. I'll just pay for this lamp.

**B:** <u>Do you want to pay</u> by debit or credit card?
    11.

**A:** <u>Is it OK to pay</u> in cash?
   12.

**B:** Yes, of course. Your total with tax is $15.75.

**ABOUT YOU** Work with a partner. Use *would rather* to ask and answer questions. Take notes on your partner's answers.

1. own a house/a condominium

    *A: Would you rather own a house or a condominium?*

    *B: I'd rather own a condominium (than a house).*

2. live in the United States/in another country
3. own a condominium/rent an apartment
4. have young neighbors/old neighbors
5. have wood floors/carpeted floors
6. live in the center of the city/in a suburb
7. drive to work/take public transportation
8. buy new/used items for your home

**EXERCISE 18** Tell a new classmate about your partner's answers in the exercise above.

   *A: Yusef was my partner. He'd rather own a condo than a house because he's single. But I'd rather own a house. A house has more space.*

   *B: My partner was Sofia. Our answer to number one was the same. We'd both rather own a condo.*

Some people prefer an apartment to a house.

# SUMMARY OF UNIT 8

**Modals**

| MODAL | EXAMPLES | EXPLANATION |
| --- | --- | --- |
| can | I **can** stay in this apartment until March.<br>I **can** carry my bicycle up to my apartment.<br>**Can** I write you a check?<br>**Can** you plug in the microwave, please?<br>You **can't** paint the walls without the landlord's permission. | Permission<br>Ability/Possibility<br>Asking permission<br>Request<br>Prohibition |
| should | You **should** change the batteries in the smoke detector.<br>You **shouldn't** leave matches in the reach of small children. | A good idea<br>A bad idea |
| may | **May** I borrow your pen?<br>You **may** leave the room.<br>The tenant **may not** leave things in the hallway.<br>I **may** move next month.<br>The landlord **may** have an extra key. | Asking permission<br>Giving permission<br>Prohibition<br>Future possibility<br>Present possibility |
| might | I **might** move next month.<br>The landlord **might** have an extra key. | Future possibility<br>Present possibility |
| must | The landlord **must** install smoke detectors.<br>The tenant **must not** change the locks.<br>The new neighbors have a crib. They **must** have a baby. | Necessity—Formal<br>Prohibition—Formal<br>Conclusion/Deduction |
| would | **Would** you help me move? | Request |
| would like | I **would like** to buy your used TV. | Want |
| would rather | I **would rather** have a roommate than live alone. | Preference |
| could | In my last apartment, I **couldn't** have a pet.<br>In my country, I **could** attend college for free.<br>**Could** you help me move?<br>**Could** I borrow your car? | Past permission<br>Past ability<br>Request<br>Asking permission |

**Phrasal Modals**

| PHRASAL MODAL | EXAMPLES | EXPLANATION |
| --- | --- | --- |
| have to | She **has to** find a roommate.<br>I **had to** move last month. | Necessity<br>Past necessity |
| have got to | She **has got to** sign the lease.<br>I**'ve got to** pay my rent tomorrow. | Necessity |
| not have to | You **don't have to** pay with cash. You can pay by check. | Lack of necessity |
| had better | You **had better** get permission before changing the locks. | Warning |
| be supposed to | We **are not supposed to** have a dog here.<br>I **was supposed to** pay my rent by the fifth of the month, but I forgot. | Expectation by rule or custom<br>Past: reporting an unmet expectation |
| be able to | I **am able to** carry my bike to my apartment.<br>Everyone **was able to** get out of the apartment during the fire. | Ability<br>Past ability |
| be permitted to<br>be allowed to | We **are not permitted/allowed to** park here overnight.<br>In my last apartment, I **was not permitted/allowed to** leave my bike in the hallway. | Permission<br>Past permission |
| ought to | You **ought to** change the batteries in your smoke detector. | A good idea |

# REVIEW

Circle the correct expression to complete the conversation.

**A:** I'm moving on Saturday. ((Could)/May) you help me?
                                    1.

**B:** I (should/would) like to help you, but I have a bad back. I went to my doctor last week, and she told me
          2.

that I (shouldn't/don't have to) lift anything heavy for a while. (Can/Would) I help you any other way
            3.                                                              4.

besides lifting things?

**A:** Yes. I don't have enough boxes. (Should/Would) you help me find some?
                                            5.

**B:** Sure. I (have to/must) go shopping this afternoon. I'll pick up some boxes while I'm at the supermarket.
              6.

**A:** Boxes can be heavy. You (would/had) better not lift them yourself.
                                   7.

**B:** Don't worry. I'll have someone put them in my car for me.

**A:** Thanks. I don't have a free minute. I (couldn't go/can't go) to class all last week. There's so much to do.
                                              8.

**B:** I know what you mean. You (might/must) be tired.
                                    9.

**A:** I am. I have another favor to ask. (Can/Would) I borrow your van on Saturday?
                                           10.

**B:** I (should/have to) work on Saturday. How about Sunday? I (must not/don't have to) work on Sunday.
         11.                                                      12.

**A:** Sunday's too late. I ('ve got to/should) move out on Saturday. The new tenants are moving
                              13.

in on Sunday morning.

**B:** Oh, I see. My brother has a van, too. He (has to/should) work Saturday, but only for half a day.
                                                  14.

He (must/might) be able to let you use his van.
      15.

**A:** Thanks. (Could/May) you ask him for me? I'd appreciate it.
                 16.

**B:** Sure. I (should/can) ask him later this evening. Why are you moving? You have a great apartment.
                17.

**A:** We ('d rather/'d better) live in the suburbs. And I want to have a dog.
             18.

I (shouldn't/'m not supposed to) have a dog in my present apartment. But my new landlord says
        19.

I (might/can) have one.
      20.

# FROM GRAMMAR TO WRITING

## PART 1  Editing Advice

1. After a modal, use the base form.

   You must ~~to~~ pay your rent on time.

2. A modal has no -s form.

   He can~~s~~ carry his bike upstairs.

3. Don't forget *to* after *be permitted, be allowed, be supposed, be able,* and *ought*.

   We're not permitted ^to^ leave a bicycle in the hallway.

   I don't like my apartment. I ought ^to^ look for a new one.

4. Don't forget *be* before *permitted to, allowed to, supposed to,* and *able to*.

   I ^am^ not supposed to have a pet in my apartment.

5. Use the correct word order in a question.

   What ~~I should~~ ^should I^ do in case of fire?

6. Don't use *can* for past. Use *could* + a base form.

   I ~~can't found~~ ^couldn't find^ a roommate, so I live alone.

7. Don't forget *would* before *rather*.

   I ^would^ rather live with my parents than live alone.

8. Don't forget *had* before *better*.

   You ^had^ better not park here. You can get a ticket.

9. Don't forget *have* before *got to*.

   I^'ve^ got to change the batteries in the smoke detectors.

10. Don't use *maybe* before a verb.

    I ~~maybe will~~ ^may^ move next month.

11. Use *not* for negative modals.

    I don't like garage sales. I'd rather ~~don't~~ ^not^ buy used things.

## PART 2  Editing Practice

Some of the shaded words and phrases have mistakes. Find the mistakes and correct them. If the shaded words are correct, write *C*.

I am renting an apartment, and I **would like to give** [C, 1.] you some advice. First, before you move in, you **should to take** [2.] pictures of the empty apartment, keep a copy of the pictures for yourself, and email a copy to the landlord. The pictures will show the condition of the apartment before you moved in, so the landlord **can't to blame** [3.] you for damage you didn't do. Test everything, like

light switches, toilets, and faucets. You maybe will find that something isn't working properly.
                                              4.
Make a list of these things. You better show this list to the landlord immediately. He should fix
                              5.                                                        6.
these things before you move in. If not, he ought give you a credit on your rent so that you can fix
                                          7.
them yourself, if you rather do it that way. You can finding checklists online. You can search for
               8.                              9.                                  10.
"rental condition checklist." This list may help you identify many common problems.
                                      11.

   Second, you got to take your lease seriously. If the lease says "no pets," that means no pets. If
          12.
you not allowed to have a pet, it's for a good reason. A pet cans cause damage. Dogs make noise,
    13.                                                  14.
too, so this rule protects other tenants. If you are not supposed use the laundry room during
                                              15.
certain hours, this might be because of the noise.
               16.

   Third, before you sign a lease, you should try to find out something about the landlord, the
                                    17.
neighbors, and the neighborhood. How you can do that? You can waiting outside the building
                                         18.            19.
during a busy afternoon or on a weekend and talk to the tenants walking in and out. Interview
them. Are they happy? Are there any problems? What should you know before signing the lease?
                                                      20.
In my last apartment, I didn't do this. I was surprised to find that I couldn't park my car on the
                                                                         21.
street overnight, so I must to park far away. This is not the fault of the landlord or the lease, but
                      22.
this was inconvenient for me. I'd rather don't have this situation again. Find out what you can
                                 23.
before signing a lease for a place where you may don't be happy.
                                              24.

> **WRITING TIP**
>
> When comparing things, there are different ways to organize your ideas. One option is to write about the first topic, for example, apartment life in the United States. You cover that topic completely and then write about the next topic you are comparing, for example, apartment life in Brazil.
>
> Another option is to write about one point of similarity or difference between the two topics, for example, *In the United States, neighbors aren't typically friendly with each other. In Brazil, however, neighbors usually know one another well.* Then you would write about another point of similarity or difference between the two topics.

## PART 3 Write
Read the prompts. Choose one and write a paragraph or two about it.

1. Compare apartment life in the United States with apartment life in another country.
2. Compare driving rules in the United States with driving rules in another country.

## PART 4 Edit
Reread the Summary of Unit 8 and the editing advice. Edit your writing from Part 3.

UNIT
# 9
The Present Perfect
The Present Perfect Continuous

# VIRTUAL COMMUNITIES

National Geographic's Space Projection Helmets allow participants to look at Earth from an astronaut's perspective.

> Technology is nothing. What's important is that you have a faith in people, that they're basically good and smart, and if you give them tools, they'll do wonderful things with them.
>
> STEVE JOBS

# Google

Larry Page and Sergey Brin

Read the following article. Pay special attention to the words in bold. 9.1

How many times **have** you **wanted** a quick answer to something and **gone** to your computer to google it? The word *google* **has become** synonymous[1] with "search". Since its start in 1998, Google **has been** one of the most popular search engines. It **has grown** from a research project of two college students to a business that now employs approximately 85 thousand people.

Google's founders, Larry Page and Sergey Brin, **have known** each other since 1995, when they were graduate students[2] in computer science at Stanford University in California. They realized that Internet search was an important field and began working to make searching easier. Both Page and Brin left their studies at Stanford to work on their project and **have** never **returned** to finish their degrees. In 2014, when they were 41 years old, *Forbes* magazine listed Page's and Brin's net worth at about $30 billion each. Today, they are each worth more than $50 billion.

Brin was born in Russia, but he **has lived** in the United States since he was five. His father was a mathematician in Russia. Page, whose parents were computer experts, **has been** interested in computers since he was six years old.

When Google started in 1998, it did ten thousand searches a day. Today it does more than five billion a day in 40 languages. It indexes[3] 130 trillion Web pages.

How is Google different from other search engines? **Have** you ever **noticed** how many ads there are on other search engines? News, sports scores, links for shopping, and more fill other search engines. Brin and Page wanted a clean home page. They believed that people come to the Internet to search for information, not to see unwanted data. The success of Google over its competitors **has proven** that this is true.

Over the years, Google **has added** other features to its Web site: Google Images, Google Drive, Google Calendar, Google Earth, and more. But one thing **hasn't changed**: the clean opening page that Google offers its users.

---

[1] synonymous: having the same meaning as
[2] graduate student: a student who studies for a higher degree such as a Master's or Doctorate
[3] to index: to sort, categorize, and organize information

**COMPREHENSION** Based on the reading, write T for *true* or F for *false*.

1. _____ Larry Page and Sergey Brin have known each other since they were children.
2. _____ Larry Page has been interested in computers since he was a child.
3. _____ Brin and Page have finished their graduate degrees.

**THINK ABOUT IT** Discuss the questions with a partner or in a small group.

1. What do you know about Google's features such as Google Search, Google Earth, or Google Drive? What have you used them for?
2. If a friend or family member had an idea for a project, would you support their decision to leave school to pursue their project? Why or why not?

## 9.1 The Present Perfect—Forms

| SUBJECT | HAVE/HAS (+ NOT) | PAST PARTICIPLE | | EXPLANATION |
| --- | --- | --- | --- | --- |
| I | have | used | Google. | We use *have* with the subjects *I, you, we, they*, a plural subject, or *there* + a plural subject. |
| You | have not | heard of | Larry Page. | |
| We | have | read | about Sergey Brin. | |
| Brin and Page | have | become | billionaires. | |
| There | have | been | many changes in computers. | |
| Brin | has | lived | in the U.S. most of his life. | We use *has* with the subjects *he, she, it*, a singular subject, or *there* + a singular subject. |
| Google | has not | used | ads on its opening page. | |
| There | has | been | a lot of interest in search. | |

**Notes:**

1. Contractions: have not → haven't, has not → hasn't, he has → he's, we have → we've, there has → there's
2. The apostrophe + *s* can mean *has* or *is*. The verb form following the contraction tells you what the contraction means.

   *He's worked* with computers. (He's = He has)
   *He's working* with computers. (He's = He is)

> **GRAMMAR IN USE**
>
> Contractions are common in speaking, both formally and informally. They make your speech sound more fluent and natural. We also use them in informal writing, such as in emails to friends or personal letters. However, many teachers do not want students to use contractions in formal academic writing (essays, research papers).

**EXERCISE 1** Fill in the blanks with the words you hear. 🎧 9.2

The Internet <u>has made</u> it easy to get information. But it _____
                     1.                                                      2.

also _____ easy for cybercriminals, people who commit crimes through the
       3.

Internet, to steal your personal data. About 32 percent of Internet users in the United States

_____ victims of online crime.
    4.

    Cybercriminals steal important information such as Social Security or credit card numbers.

According to a Consumer Report survey, 62 percent of responders _____ nothing
                                                                                 5.

to protect their online privacy.

    _____ you ever _____ to a coffee shop and _____
          6.                           7.                                                    8.

the Wi-Fi there? If so, other customers can easily gain access to your private information. Also, the

cloud seems like a good place to store data, but it _____ it easy for criminals to steal
                                                                           9.

information.

    Without knowing it, it is possible that you _____ ordinary thieves too much
                                                                          10.

information. _____ you ever _____ news about an upcoming
                 11.                              12.

trip on a social media site? _____ you ever _____ where you're
                                 13.                         14.

going on your next vacation, when you're leaving, and how long you'll be gone? Then you

_____ also _____ thieves know when your house will be empty.
    15.                        16.

    In addition to stealing private information from your computer, hackers—people

who illegally get into computer systems— _____ into bank websites and
                                                      17.

_____ large amounts of money. In 2018, hackers stole nearly $1 billion.
    18.

Hackers _____ information from government sites, too. Since the beginning
           19.

of the Internet, security _____ a problem. _____ you ever
                       20.                    21.

_____ a victim?
    22.

## 9.2 The Past Participle

| BASE FORM | SIMPLE PAST FORM | PAST PARTICIPLE | EXPLANATION |
|---|---|---|---|
| work<br>wonder<br>change | worked<br>wondered<br>changed | worked<br>wondered<br>changed | The past participle is the same as the simple past form for all regular verbs. |
| hear<br>make<br>let | heard<br>made<br>let | heard<br>made<br>let | For some irregular verbs, the past participle is the same as the simple past form. |
| break<br>grow<br>go | broke<br>grew<br>went | broken<br>grown<br>gone | For other irregular verbs, the simple past and the past participle are different. |

For the following verbs, the past form and past participle are different.

| BASE FORM | PAST FORM | PAST PARTICIPLE | BASE FORM | PAST FORM | PAST PARTICIPLE |
|---|---|---|---|---|---|
| become | became | become | bite | bit | bitten |
| come | came | come | drive | drove | driven |
| run | ran | run | ride | rode | ridden |
| blow | blew | blown | rise | rose | risen |
| draw | drew | drawn | write | wrote | written |
| fly | flew | flown | be | was/were | been |
| grow | grew | grown | eat | ate | eaten |
| know | knew | known | fall | fell | fallen |
| throw | threw | thrown | forgive | forgave | forgiven |
| tear | tore | torn | give | gave | given |
| wear | wore | worn | mistake | mistook | mistaken |
| break | broke | broken | see | saw | seen |
| choose | chose | chosen | shake | shook | shaken |
| freeze | froze | frozen | take | took | taken |
| speak | spoke | spoken | do | did | done |
| steal | stole | stolen | forget | forgot | forgotten |
| begin | began | begun | get | got | gotten |
| drink | drank | drunk | go | went | gone |
| ring | rang | rung | lie | lay | lain |
| sing | sang | sung | prove | proved | proven (or proved) |
| sink | sank | sunk | show | showed | shown (or showed) |
| swim | swam | swum | | | |

*For a complete list of irregular past participles, see Appendix C.

**EXERCISE 2** Write the base form and the simple past form for each past participle in the chart. If the simple past and the past participle are the same, write S. If they are different, write D.

| BASE FORM | SIMPLE PAST FORM | PAST PARTICIPLE | SAME (S) OR DIFFERENT (D) |
|---|---|---|---|
| want | wanted | wanted | S |
| be | was/were | been | D |
| | | grown | |
| | | known | |
| | | stolen | |
| | | returned | |
| | | become | |
| | | noticed | |
| | | added | |
| | | changed | |
| | | made | |
| | | had | |
| | | gone | |
| | | done | |
| | | thought | |
| | | told | |
| | | chosen | |
| | | broken | |
| | | gotten | |
| | | lived | |

**EXERCISE 3** Write the past participle of these verbs.

1. eat _____eaten_____
2. go _____
3. see _____
4. look _____
5. study _____
6. bring _____
7. take _____
8. say _____
9. be _____
10. find _____
11. give _____
12. leave _____
13. live _____
14. know _____
15. like _____
16. fall _____
17. feel _____
18. come _____
19. break _____
20. wear _____
21. let _____
22. grow _____
23. drive _____
24. write _____
25. put _____
26. begin _____
27. want _____
28. get _____
29. fly _____
30. drink _____

**EXERCISE 4** Fill in the blanks with the present perfect form of a verb from the box. You can use one verb more than once. Make a contraction with *have* or *has* where possible.

| do     | read | know | use   | be    |
|--------|------|------|-------|-------|
| finish | go   | have | steal |       |

1. I ′ve read _____ several articles about Internet security.
2. You _____ Wi-Fi in coffee shops.
3. _____ you _____ anything to protect your personal information?
4. _____ your friend _____ careful with Wi-Fi at coffee shops?
5. Larry Page _____ Sergey Brin since they were students at Stanford University.
6. _____ they _____ graduate school? No. They left their graduate program to start Google.
7. It _____ easy for hackers to steal information.
8. Some hackers _____ a lot of money.
9. Some hackers _____ to jail for stealing money online.
10. _____ your computer ever _____ a virus?

"Hacker hostels," like this one in Silicon Valley, California, U.S., offer affordable housing to technology entrepreneurs (**not** hackers!).

**EXERCISE 5** Use the words in parentheses to write a question about each statement.

1. Google has changed the way people search. (*how*)

   How has Google changed the way people search?

2. I have used several search engines. (*which ones*)

3. Brin and Page haven't finished their graduate degree. (*why*)

4. They have made a lot of money. (*how much*)

5. Brin has been in the United States for many years. (*how long*)

6. You haven't been careful about Internet security in coffee shops. (*why*)

7. Internet security has become a big problem. (*why*)

8. Hackers have stolen money from banks. (*how much*)

**ABOUT YOU** Use the words to write present perfect questions. Then take turns asking and answering your questions with a partner. Use contractions. Share what you learned with your class.

1. (Internet security/be/problem/for you) Has Internet security been a problem for you?

2. (which/music apps/use)

3. (try/VR)

4. (what/change/in the last 20 years)

232  Unit 9

## 9.3 The Present Perfect with an Adverb

| SUBJECT | HAS/HAVE (+ NOT) | ADVERB | PAST PARTICIPLE | | EXPLANATION |
|---|---|---|---|---|---|
| Page and Brin | have | never | finished | their graduate degree. | We can put an adverb between the auxiliary verb (have/has) and the past participle. |
| Internet security | has | often | been | a problem. | |
| I | haven't | always | been | careful in a coffee shop. | |
| You | have | probably | used | Wi-Fi in a coffee shop. | |

**Note:**
The adverb *already* can come between the auxiliary verb and the main verb or after the verb phrase.
　They have **already** become billionaires.
　They have become billionaires **already**.

**EXERCISE 6** Add the word in parentheses to each sentence.

1. You have used your laptop in a coffee shop. (*probably*)

   You have probably used your laptop in a coffee shop.

2. I have installed an anti-virus program. (*already*)

3. We have heard of Larry Page. (*never*)

4. Page and Brin have been interested in search technology. (*always*)

5. You have used Google. (*probably*)

6. He hasn't finished his college degree. (*even*)

7. I have read the article about Internet security. (*already*)

### FUN WITH GRAMMAR

Race to write. Form three teams. One person from each team goes to the board. Your teacher will say an irregular verb, and you will write the past participle of that verb on the board. Every student has a turn. The first to finish writing the word correctly wins a point.

For an extra challenge, the first to write a sentence using the verb in the present perfect wins another point.

# CROWDFUNDING

Read the following article. Pay special attention to the words in bold. 9.3

**Have** you ever **had** an idea for a business but no way to fund it? **Have** you **asked** relatives and friends for money to help you? If you **have done** these things, you know it isn't easy to get people interested in investing in your dream. After getting money from relatives and friends, it's hard to find more people willing to invest. Lately, people **have found** a different way to raise cash: through crowdfunding. Crowdfunding is a method of "collecting small amounts of money from a lot of different people, usually by using the Internet." While the idea **has been** around for possibly hundreds of years, the word *crowdfunding* **has** only **existed** since 2006.

Crowdfunding websites, which started to appear on the Internet in 2010, **have helped** individuals raise billions of dollars worldwide. So how does it work? A person demonstrates his idea in a short video and states his financial goal and the time frame for raising money. Usually the first investors are family and friends. Little by little, strangers become interested and donate money.

Not all crowdfunding plans are for profit. Some people **have used** crowdfunding websites that are specifically for philanthropic[1] projects. These sites **have attracted** people who want to make the world a better place. The 97 Supermarket in Changchun, China, is one example of this. Jiang Naijun used crowdfunding to get the money to open a supermarket. She named her market 97 because that was her age when she did this. Since she became profitable, she **has given** at least half the money she earns to charity[2], to help children in need. "I wanted to do more for society," she said.

If you want more information, just google "crowdfunding" and you will find a number of different sites specializing in different types of projects.

---

[1] philanthropic: intended to help others
[2] charity: an organization that helps people in need

Crowdfunding has become one of the most popular ways for people to raise money for a cause, project, or event. In 2017, $34 billion was raised globally. This number is expected to grow to more than $300 billion by 2025.

98-year-old Jiang Naijun used crowdfunding to start her supermarket and donates the profits to charity.

**COMPREHENSION** Based on the reading, write T for *true* or F for *false*.

1. _____ Sometimes strangers help fund a crowdfunding project.
2. _____ The idea of crowdfunding is old, but it has become easier to do with the Internet.
3. _____ The "97 Supermarket" project didn't reach its financial goal.

**THINK ABOUT IT** Discuss the questions with a partner or in a small group.

1. What would you like to crowdfund for? Why?
2. What might be some challenges with crowdfunding? Explain.

## 9.4 The Present Perfect—Overview of Uses

| EXAMPLES | EXPLANATION |
| --- | --- |
| People **have used** crowdfunding since 2010.<br>Google **has been** in existence for over 20 years. | We use the present perfect to show that an action or state started in the past and continues to the present. |
| I **have used** my laptop in coffee shops many times.<br>How many articles about crowdfunding **have** you **read**? | We use the present perfect to show that an action repeated during a period of time that started in the past and includes the present. |
| **Have** you ever **asked** relatives for money? | We use the present perfect to show that an action occurred at an indefinite time in the past. |

**EXERCISE 7** Tell if the sentences show continuation from past to present (**C**), repetition from past to present (**R**), or an indefinite time in the past (**I**).

1. Larry Page has been interested in computers since he was a child. __C__
2. How many emails have you received today? _____
3. I've had my laptop for one year. _____
4. The word *crowdfunding* has been in existence since 2006. _____
5. Internet security has become a big problem. _____
6. Has your computer ever had a virus? _____
7. My cousin has used crowdfunding two times. _____
8. Have you ever used your laptop in a coffee shop? _____

> **GRAMMAR IN USE**
> When an event happened in the recent past, and the effect is still felt, we often use the present perfect. This is especially common for speakers of British English. In American English, we use either the present perfect or the simple past.
>
> *Someone **has** just **donated** $10,000!*  *Someone just donated $10,000.*
> *I **have forgotten** my password again.*  *I forgot my password again.*
> ***Have** you **heard** the news?*  *Did you hear the news?*

## 9.5 The Present Perfect with Continuation from Past to Present

We use the present perfect to show that an action or state started in the past and continues to the present.

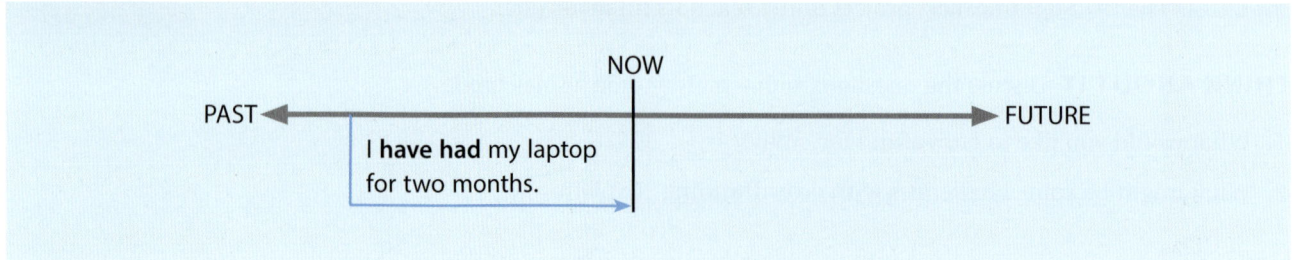

| EXAMPLES | EXPLANATION |
|---|---|
| Crowdfunding **has been** around **for about 10 years**. | We use *for* + an amount of time: *for two months, for three years, for a long time,* etc. |
| Crowdfunding sites **have been** on the Internet **since 2006**. | We use *since* with a date, month, year, etc., to show when the action began. |
| I **have been** interested in computers **(ever) since** I **was** a child. | We use *since* or *ever since* with the beginning of a continuous action or state. The verb in the *since* clause is simple past. |
| **How long have** you **had** your computer? | We use *how long* to ask about the amount of time from the past to the present. |
| I **have always dreamed** of starting a business. | We use the present perfect with *always* to show that an action or state began in the past and continues to the present. |
| I **have never heard** of crowdfunding. | We use the present perfect with *never* to show that something has not occurred any time before now. |

**EXERCISE 8** Fill in the blanks with the words from the box. You may use an item more than once.

| 've been interested | ever since | 've always wanted | had | since |
| how long | for | has never used | have | was |
| graduated | has | 've had | have been | has been |

1. I've been interested in computers _____*since*_____ I _____*was*_____ in high school.

2. I _____ to start my own business. Maybe now I can do it with crowdfunding.

3. The word *crowdfunding* _____ existed _____ 2006.

4. I _____ in crowdfunding _____ I read the article about it.

5. Crowdfunding websites _____ around _____ over 10 years.

6. My grandmother _____ a computer. She doesn't like computers.

7. I _____ my tablet _____ three months.

8. _____ _____ you _____ your tablet?

9. I've had my laptop ever since I _____ from high school.

10. _____ 1998, Google _____ one of the most popular search engines.

**ABOUT YOU** Write true statements using the present perfect form of the verbs given and *for, since, always,* or *never.* If possible, write about technology. Share your sentences with a partner.

    A: I've had my phone since March. How long have you had yours?
    B: Really? I've had mine for two years.

1. (*have*) I've had my smartphone since March.

2. (*like*) _____

3. (*be*) _____

4. (*want*) _____

5. (*know*) _____

6. (*have*) _____

**EXERCISE 9** Fill in the blanks with the present perfect and other missing words to complete this conversation. Use context clues to help you.

**A:** I see you have a new tablet. How ___long___ ___have you had___ it?
                                                              1.                    2.

**B:** I _____3._____ it _____4._____ just one week. I love it. What kind of tablet do you have?

**A:** I don't have a tablet. I _____5._____ never _____6._____ one. I don't like them.

**B:** Why not? I think they're wonderful.

**A:** They're great for some things, but they're not computers. I need a real computer. I'm a writer, and I need a good word processing program.

**B:** A writer? _____7._____ long _____8._____ a writer?

**A:** I _____9._____ a writer ever _____10._____ I graduated from college.

**B:** What do you write? Novels?

**A:** No. I _____11._____ never _____12._____ a novel. I write poetry. Do you like poetry?

**B:** Yes. I _____13._____ always _____14._____ poetry.

**A:** I'll give you a copy of my latest book.

# 9.6 The Simple Past, the Present Perfect, the Simple Present

| EXAMPLES | EXPLANATION |
| --- | --- |
| Sergey Brin **came** to the U.S. in 1979.<br>Brin **has been** in the U.S. since 1979.<br>Brin **lives** in California. | We use the simple past with an action that is completely past.<br>We use the present perfect to connect the past to the present.<br>We use the simple present to refer only to the present. |
| When **did** you **learn** about crowdfunding?<br>How long **have** you **known** about crowdfunding? | We use *when* to ask about the past.<br>We use *how long* to ask about the connection of past to present. |

**EXERCISE 10** Fill in the blanks with the simple past, the present perfect, or the simple present form of the verb given. Include any other words you see.

**A:** I _____ *have* _____ a great idea for a business but no way of funding it.
  1. have

**B:** What about crowdfunding?

**A:** I _____ of it. What is it?
  2. never hear

**B:** It's a way of getting money from friends, relatives, and strangers. Look it up online, and you'll find a lot of crowdfunding websites.

**A:** This is terrific! How _____ about it?
  3. you/know

**B:** I _____ about it ever since I _____ an article about
  4. know                                              5. read
it a few years ago.

**A:** So it _____ around for a long time?
  6. be

**B:** The idea _____ around for a long time but on the Internet only since 2010. A
  7. be
friend of mine _____ it last year to start a small business. In a short time, he
  8. use
_____ $25,000.
  9. collect

**A:** Wow! I _____ so happy you told me about it. I'm going to look it up right now.
  10. be

> **GRAMMAR IN USE**
>
> The news is typically about things important today. Often, a news story begins with the present perfect to give important information, and then it continues in the simple past to tell what happened, or the simple present to describe current feelings or thoughts.
>
> *Twelve boys and their coach **have disappeared** in Thailand. No one **has seen** them since their soccer game on June 23rd. A bypasser **found** their bikes and bags near a cave entrance. A teammate **said** the boys **went** into the cave after their game. Unfortunately, it **rained** heavily soon after. Officials **fear** they **are** lost in the cave, unable to get out.*

**EXERCISE 11** Circle the correct word to complete this conversation between a teacher (A) and students (B) and (C).

**A:** I (*like*/*have liked*) to know about my students' lives. Let's start with Bernard. Where are you from?
   1.

**B:** I'm from Rwanda.

**A:** Maybe some of the other students (*never hear*/*have never heard*) of Rwanda. Let's google it so everyone
   2.

can see where it is in Africa. OK. Here it is. (*Have you been*/*Are you*) in the United States for a long time?
   3.

**B:** No, (*I'm not*/*I haven't*).
   4.

**A:** How long (*are you*/*have you been*) in the United States?
   5.

**B:** I (*came*/*have come*) to the United States in 2018.
   6.

**A:** Thanks, Bernard. What about you, Carlos? Where are you from?

**C:** I'm from Puerto Rico.

**A:** Can you tell us a little about your country?

**C:** Puerto Rico isn't a country. It(*'s*/*'s been*) a territory of the United States. Puerto Ricans (*are*/*have been*)
   7.                                                                                        8.

American citizens.

**A:** Let's google "Puerto Rico." When (*did Puerto Rico become*/*has Puerto Rico become*) a territory of
   9.

the United States?

**C:** In 1898. Puerto Rico used to belong to Spain. The U.S. (*fought*/*has fought*) a war with Spain
   10.

and the United States (*won*/*has won*).
   11.

**A:** Thank you for this information. Please tell the class what language you speak in Puerto Rico.

**C:** We speak Spanish, but I (*'ve had*/*had*) English lessons since I was in high school.
   12.

**A:** Thanks, Carlos.

---

**FUN WITH GRAMMAR**

Get to know your classmate. You have five minutes to practice a conversation with a partner similar to the one above, discussing where you are from, one interesting piece of information about your countries, and your length of time in the United States. When you are finished, try to perform your conversation for the class without any notes.

   *A: Where are you from?*
   *B: I'm from China. How about you?*
   *A: I'm from Peru.*

# Khan Academy

Salman Khan records one of his tutorials for the Khan Academy.

Read the following article. Pay special attention to the words in bold. 9.4

**Have** you ever **had** trouble keeping up with a class? **Have** you **been** bored because your class moves too slowly for you? Either way, learning in a group can sometimes be frustrating.

Khan Academy, created by Salman Khan in 2006, **has** quickly **become** the largest "school" in the world. Students learn online at their own pace with short videos. With over 10,000 lectures in many different subjects, it **has attracted** about 18 million students a month, from kindergarten through high school. Amazingly, Khan **has** never **charged** any money for his videos. They are available to anyone anywhere in the world with a computer and an Internet connection.

Salman Khan didn't start out to create a revolution in instruction. In 2004, his niece asked him for help in math. He started to create math videos for her to view online. Then he decided to make his videos available to anyone who wanted to get math help. One day, he received an email from a stranger who improved his math grade by using Khan's videos. The email said, "You **have changed** my life and the lives of everyone in my family."

Khan's life **has changed**, too. In 2009, he quit his job and started making more instructional videos. At first he focused on math, but over the past few years, he **has added** many other subjects, including history, science, and art. Volunteers **have helped** translate his videos into at least 25 different languages. Khan **has** personally **created** over 3,000 videos.

At first Khan had no funding for his project. Since he started to appear on TV, he **has attracted** financial support from many people, including Bill Gates. So far, he **has raised** more than 40 million dollars.

Many teachers **have started** to use Khan's lectures to supplement[1] their classroom instruction. Because most of today's students are digital natives, it is not surprising that Khan Academy **has become** so popular with today's students.

---

[1] to supplement: to add to

**COMPREHENSION** Based on the reading, write T for *true* or F for *false*.

1. _____ Khan Academy is available only in the United States.
2. _____ Khan Academy is mostly for elementary and high school students.
3. _____ Salman Khan has created many of the videos himself.

**THINK ABOUT IT** Discuss the questions with a partner or in a small group.

1. What video courses would you be interested in taking?
2. What is a challenge of studying alone?

## 9.7 The Present Perfect with Repetition from Past to Present

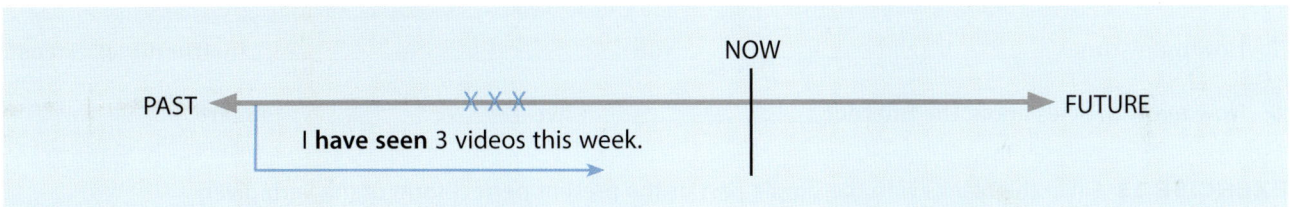

| EXAMPLES | EXPLANATION |
|---|---|
| Khan **has appeared** on TV many times.<br>**Up to now**, Khan Academy **has created** over 5,000 videos.<br>I **have watched** 10 videos on Khan Academy **so far**. | We use the present perfect to talk about repetition in a time period that includes the present. We expect more repetition. Adding the words *so far* and *up to now* indicate that we are counting up to the present moment. |
| How many times **has** Khan **been** on TV?<br>How much money **has** he **charged** for his videos?<br>He **hasn't charged** any money **at all** for his videos. | We can ask a question about repetition from past to present with *how much* and *how many*.<br>To indicate zero times, we can use a negative verb + *at all*. |

Notes:
We use the present perfect in a time period that is open. There is a possibility of more repetition.
   Khan **has made** over 3,000 videos so far. (possibility for more videos)
   Khan **has added** new subjects over the years. (possibility for adding more subjects)
We use the simple past with a time period that is finished or closed: *in 2004, 50 years ago, last week*, etc. There is no possibility of more repetition.
   Khan **made** a few videos in 2004 for his niece. (2004 ends the time period)

---

**GRAMMAR IN USE**

When you consider the action finished, use the simple past.

   I **read** many great books in high school.

When you know that the action might happen again in the future, use the present perfect.

   I**'ve read** many great books.

**EXERCISE 12** Fill in the blanks with the present perfect form of one of the verbs from the box.

| add | read | help ✓ | not charge | translate | use | attract | have | appear | be |

1. Salman Khan _____has helped_____ a lot of students improve their math skills.
2. Khan Academy _____ millions of students.
3. So far, Khan _____ any money for his instructional videos.
4. Khan started with math, but he _____ many other subjects.
5. Volunteers _____ Khan's lectures into about 25 different languages so far.
6. Khan _____ on many TV programs.
7. How many times _____ you _____ instructional videos?
8. How many articles about the Internet _____ we _____ so far?

**EXERCISE 13** Fill in the blanks with the simple past or the present perfect form of the verb given.

1. A magazine _____chose_____ Salman Khan as one of the 100 most influential people.
   choose
2. He _____has been_____ on the cover of several magazines.
   be
3. Several news programs _____ Salman Khan over the past few years.
   interview
4. Khan _____ Khan Academy in 2006.
   start
5. Sergey Brin and Larry Page _____ each other in graduate school in 1995.
   meet
6. So far they _____ Google's clean home page.
   not change
7. I _____ my laptop in coffee shops many times.
   use
8. Yesterday I _____ to a coffee shop to work on my laptop.
   go
9. So far my cousin _____ 80 percent of his crowdfunding goal.
   receive

**EXERCISE 14** Fill in the blanks with the simple past or the present perfect form of the verb given. Use contractions wherever possible.

**A:** Do you have any hobbies?

**B:** Yes. I love to read.

**A:** How many books __have you read__ this year?
                    1. you/read

**B:** I _____ about 20 books so far this year. Last month I
       2. read

_____ on vacation, and I _____ 10 books while I
3. go                                    4. read

_____ at the beach.
5. be

242  Unit 9

**A:** How _____ so many books on your vacation? They're heavy.
   **6.** you/carry

**B:** I _____ only one: my tablet. Before I left on my trip, I _____ 20 books.
   **7.** carry                                                              **8.** download

**A:** Are book downloads expensive?

**B:** I pay about $10 a book. But I _____ much more than that on print books over the
   **9.** spend

   years. My public library _____ about 5,000 books available for download so far, and
   **10.** make

   those are free. Every month, they add new electronic books.

**A:** I _____ to download books from my library.
   **11.** never/try

## 9.8 The Present Perfect with an Indefinite Time in the Past

| EXAMPLES | EXPLANATION |
|---|---|
| A: **Have** you **ever heard** of Khan Academy?<br>B: Yes, I **have**.<br>A: **Have** you **ever seen** Khan's history videos?<br>B: No, I never **have**. But I'**ve used** several of his math videos this semester. | We use the present perfect with *ever* to ask a question about any time from past to present.<br>We can answer an *ever* question with the present perfect when there is no reference to time. The time is indefinite or repeated in an open time frame. |
| A: I know your brother is using crowdfunding to raise money. **Has** he **raised** enough money **yet** for his project?<br>B: No, **not yet**. But he **has already raised** over $5,000. | We use the present perfect in a question with *yet* to ask about an expected action.<br>We use *yet* with questions and negative statements. We use *already* with affirmative statements. |
| A stranger wrote to Salman Khan, "You **have changed** my life."<br>Khan Academy **has become** the largest "school" in the world. | We can use the present perfect to talk about the past without any reference to time when the time is not important, not known, or imprecise. Using the present perfect, rather than the simple past, shows that the past is relevant to a present situation or discussion. |

**ABOUT YOU** Write questions in the present perfect. Use *How much* or *How many* and the words. Take turns asking and answering your questions with a partner.

1. (ebooks) How many ebooks have you bought?

2. (money) _____

3. (YouTube) _____

4. (online classes) _____

5. (smartphones) _____

**GRAMMAR IN USE**

The present perfect is commonly used to talk about accomplishments or achievements, especially when they were completed in the indefinite past. It is often necessary to talk about these things in job interviews or university applications.

I **have won** three awards for my work.

He **has produced** thousands of videos.

**Have** you **graduated** from high school?

She **has written** two novels, a dozen short stories, and numerous poems.

**EXERCISE 15** Fill in the blanks to complete each conversation using the correct form of the verb and *yet* or *already*.

1. **A:** ___Has your grandmother bought___ a computer _____yet_____ ?
   a. your grandmother/buy                                                      b.

   **B:** No, not ___yet___ . She _____ to several stores _____ , but she
   c.                          d. go                                     e.

   _____ _____ . She needs me to help her.
   f. not/decide    g.

2. **A:** The teacher gave us an assignment to write about crowdfunding. _____ it
   a. you/do

   _____ ?
   b.

   **B:** No, not _____ . But I _____ several articles about it.
   c.                          d. read

   I _____ what to write about _____ .
   e. not/decide                              f.

3. **A:** I just bought a new computer. My daughter helped me.

   **B:** _____ an anti-virus program for you _____ ?
   a. your daughter/install                              b.

   **A:** Yes. She _____ _____ .
   c.                  d.

4. **A:** I just read the article about Khan Academy. _____ it _____ ?
   a. you/read                          b.

   **B:** Yes, I _____ .
   c.

   **A:** I know Salman Khan _____ mostly math videos.
   d. make

   _____ any other kind of videos _____ ?
   e. he/make                              f.

   **B:** Yes. He _____ videos on many subjects. And volunteers
   g. create

   _____ them into many different languages.
   h. translate

   **A:** My language is Urdu. _____ videos into my language _____ ?
   i. they/translate                              j.

   **B:** Yes, they _____ .
   k.

5. **A:** I have trouble with math. I can't keep up with the teacher.

   **B:** _____ the teacher for help?
   a. you/ask

Unit 9

**A:** Yes, I _____ . But she only has time once a week. I need help after every class.
　　　　　　　　　b.

**B:** _____ Khan Academy _____ ?
　　　c. you/try　　　　　　　　　　　　d.

**A:** No. Where's Khan Academy? Is it in this city?

**B:** It's not a physical location. It's on the Internet.

**A:** I've _____ looked for help on the Internet, but it wasn't very good.
　　　　　　e.

**B:** But you _____ Khan Academy _____ . Try it.
　　　　　　f. not/try　　　　　　　　　　g.

I'm sure you'll get the help you need.

**ABOUT YOU** Write statements about yourself. Then find a partner and ask questions with *Have you ever...* Answer with: *Yes, I have; No, I haven't;* or *No, I never have.*

　A: *Have you ever studied computer programming?*
　B: *No, I never have.*

1. (*study*) computer programming

   *I've never studied computer programming.*

2. (*google*) your own name

   _____

3. (*use*) the Internet to look for a person you haven't seen in a long time

   _____

4. (*download*) music from the Internet

   _____

5. (*use*) a search engine in your native language

   _____

6. (*buy*) something online

   _____

7. (*edit*) photos on your computer

   _____

8. (*take*) a selfie with your a selfie stick

   _____

9. (*see*) the movie *The Social Network*

   _____

## 9.9 The Present Perfect vs. the Simple Past

| EXAMPLES | EXPLANATION |
| --- | --- |
| A: You were talking about getting a new computer. **Have** you **gotten** one **yet**?<br>B: Yes. I **got** a new one last week.<br>A: **Have** you **seen** any of Khan's videos?<br>B: Yes. I **saw** one this morning.<br>A: **Have** you **ever taken** a chemistry class?<br>B: Yes. Last semester, I **took** Chemistry 101. | We can answer a present perfect question with the simple past and a definite time. Some definite times expressions are:<br>• *last week, month, year, semester*<br>• *in 2008*<br>• *two weeks ago*<br>• *when I was 18 years old* |
| How long **have** you **had** your computer?<br><br>When **did** you **buy** your computer? | For a question with *how long* that connects the past to the present, we the use present perfect.<br>For a question with *when* about a specific time before now, we use the simple past. |

**EXERCISE 16** Fill in the blanks with the correct form of the verb given and any other words you see.

1. A: <u>Have you ever sent</u> money to help pay for a crowdfunding project?
         a. you/ever/send

   B: No, I _____. But last week, my sister _____ a project
                 b.                                                 c. see

   that she's interested in, so she _____ money to help fund it.
                                                     d. send

2. A: I need money for a new project I'm working on.

   B: _____ your friends for money?
      a. you/ever/ask

   A: No, I never _____. I don't like to borrow money from friends. Last year, a friend
                               b.

   of mine _____ money from me and never paid me back.
                    c. borrow

   B: _____ it to him?
      d. you/ever/mention

   A: No, I _____. I don't like to talk to friends about money.
           e.

   B: _____ of crowdfunding?
      f. you/ever/hear

   A: Yes, I _____. But I don't know how to use it.
             g.

3. A: You asked me for a suggestion for math help, and I told you about Khan Academy.

   _____ it yet?
      a. you/try

   B: Yes. Thanks for your suggestion. I _____ for it immediately.
                           b. look

   A: _____ you?
      c. help

**B:** Oh, yes. I _____ an A on my last calculus test. How long
d. get

_____ about Khan Academy?
e. you/know

**A:** For about a year. My cousin _____ me about it.
f. tell

4. **A:** _____ of Sergey Brin and Larry Page?
a. you/ever/hear

**B:** No, I never _____. Who are they?
b.

**A:** They're the creators of Google.

**B:** When _____ Google?
c. they/create

**A:** They _____ on it when they _____ in graduate
d. work                                                          e. be

school. They _____ it on the Internet in 1998.
f. put

**B:** "Sergey" sounds like a Russian name.

**A:** He is Russian. He _____ to the United States when he
g. come

_____ a child.
h. be

5. **A:** _____ a virus?
a. your computer/ever/get

**B:** Yes, it _____. Yesterday someone _____ my email to
b.                                                c. use

send a message to everyone in my address book. I don't know how that happened.

**A:** _____ your laptop or tablet in a coffee shop to connect to the Internet?
d. you/ever/use

**B:** Yes, I _____. In fact, I _____ to a coffee shop a few
e.                                         f. go

days ago to use the Wi-Fi there.

**A:** Maybe someone in the coffee shop _____ your personal information.
g. steal

**B:** Is that possible?

**A:** Yes, it is. Actually, it's not uncommon. I sent you an article about Internet security.

_____ it yet?
h. you/read

**B:** No, I _____. I _____ time.
i.                          j. have

**A:** I suggest you read it.

# Genealogy and the Genographic Project

Read the following article. Pay special attention to the words in bold. 9.5

Genealogy[1] is one of the most popular hobbies in the United States. The percentage of Americans interested in family history **has been increasing** steadily. This increase has to do with the ease of searching on the Internet.

Cyndi Howells quit her job in 1992 and **has been working** on her family tree ever since. To help other family historians, she created a website called Cyndi's List. Over the years, this site **has been growing**.

Although the Internet has made research easier, it is only the beginning for serious family historians. Genealogists[2] still need to go to libraries to find public records, such as the U.S. Census. Since 1790, the U.S. Census Bureau **has been conducting** a census every 10 years.

But genealogy research on the Internet and in libraries can only go back a couple of hundred years. Then it stops. In the past, that meant the end of one's family search. But since the beginning of the twenty-first century, serious family historians **have been using** genetics to trace their backgrounds. This technology shows the relationship between people, going back thousands of years.

In 2005, National Geographic started the Genographic Project. Since then, it **has been collecting** and **analyzing** DNA[3] from people all over the world. Dr. Spencer Wells, founder of the project, **has been using** this information to understand how we are all related to each other.

How does this project work? People get a DNA kit, put in a bit of saliva, and send it back. Dr. Wells has concluded that all humans alive today descended from early humans who lived in Eastern Africa around two hundred thousand years ago. Dr. Wells **has been studying** human migration[4] from Africa to other parts of the world. Dr. Wells thinks that by understanding who we are and where we came from, we will have a better sense of where we are going.

---

[1] genealogy: the study of family history
[2] genealogist: family historian
[3] DNA: the molecules that carry genetic information and define the traits of a person, plant, or animal
[4] migration: movement from one place to another, usually in large groups

Dr. Spencer Wells, director of National Geographic's Genographic Project

**COMPREHENSION** Based on the reading, write T for *true* or F for *false*.

1. _____ Library and Internet research for genealogy can help us find family information from thousands of years ago.
2. _____ DNA analysis can show us the relationship of people all over the world.
3. _____ The U.S. Census provides family historians with useful information.

**THINK ABOUT IT** Discuss the questions with a partner or in a small group.

1. What do you know about your family's genealogy? How did you learn what you know?
2. What more would you like to know about it?

## 9.10 The Present Perfect Continuous—Forms

| SUBJECT | HAVE/HAS (+ NOT) | BEEN | PRESENT PARTICIPLE | |
|---|---|---|---|---|
| Cyndi Howells | has | been | working | on her family history since 1992. |
| The Genographic Project | has | been | analyzing | information since 2005. |
| Family historians | have | been | using | DNA to trace their backgrounds. |
| The U.S. Census Bureau | hasn't | been | keeping | detailed records for more than 150 years. |

Observe statements, *yes/no* questions, short answers, and *wh-* questions.

| STATEMENT | YES/NO QUESTION & SHORT ANSWER | WH- QUESTION |
|---|---|---|
| Dr. Wells **has been studying** DNA for several years. | **Has** he **been studying** the DNA of people all over the world? Yes, he **has**. | How long **has** he **been studying** human DNA? |
| You **have been thinking** about researching your family history. | **Have** you **been thinking** about DNA testing? No, I **haven't**. | Why **haven't** you **been thinking** about DNA testing? |
| Cyndi Howells **has been working** on her family history. | **Have** you **been working** on your family history? No, I **haven't**. | Who **has been working** on your family history? |

**Note:**
The present perfect continuous is sometimes called the present perfect progressive.

**EXERCISE 17** Listen to the information about the U.S. Census. Write T for *true*, F for *false*, or NS for *not stated*. 🎧 9.6

1. _____ At first, children were not counted in the census.
2. _____ All census information is available to everyone.
3. _____ Most Americans complete the census questionnaire.

**EXERCISE 18** Listen to the information again. Fill in the blanks with the words you hear. 🎧 9.6

The U.S. Census ___has been collecting___ information every 10 years since 1790.
                         1.
Family historians _____ advantage of census records to trace their family history.
                              2.
What is the difference between the early census and the census today?

In 1790, when the population was less than four million, the government wanted to find out how many men were eligible for military service, so census workers didn't even count children. In more recent years, the government _____ this information to give citizens representation in Congress and
                    3.
to decide how to use federal money for schools, hospitals, roads, and more.

At first the census results were available to everyone. More recently, the government
_____ the privacy of individuals. Census information is only available after
          4.
72 years. Genealogists were excited when the 1940 census information became available in 2012.

Since 1950, the government _____ computers to compile census data, making
                                      5.
the information available much faster.

Before 1960, census takers went door to door. Since 1960, the government _____
                                                                                  6.
census forms to people through the U.S. mail.

For many years, the census forms were only in English. In recent years, the U.S. government
_____ census forms available in several languages besides English.
          7.

The government found that it needed data between the 10-year intervals. Since 2005, the census bureau
_____ information every year from a sample of Americans. Each year, 3.5 million
          8.
households receive a questionnaire.

**EXERCISE 19** Fill in the blanks with the present perfect continuous form of the verb given. Include any other words you see.

1. How long ___has Cyndi been managing___ a genealogy website?
                    Cyndi/manage
2. Interest in genealogy _____.
                                grow
3. Cyndi Howells _____ on her family history since 1992.
                        work
4. Cyndi _____ all over the United States to genealogy groups.
                lecture
5. The number of genealogy websites _____.
                                            increase
6. How long _____ records?
                U.S. Census Bureau/keep

250  Unit 9

7. How _____ information?
   *U.S. Census Bureau/collect*

8. _____ on a family tree? Yes, I _____.
   *you/work*

9. Family historians _____ the Internet to do family research since the 1990s.
   *use*

10. How long _____ human DNA?
    *Dr. Wells/study*

## 9.11 The Present Perfect Continuous—Use

We use the present perfect continuous to show that an action started in the past and continues to the present.

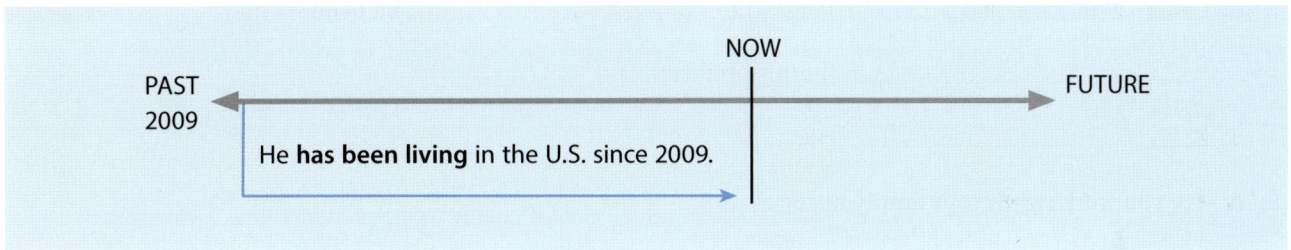

| EXAMPLES | EXPLANATION |
|---|---|
| The U.S. Census **has been collecting** information **for** over 200 years. | We use *for* with the amount of time. |
| Cyndi's website **has been helping** family historians **since** 1996. | We use *since* with the beginning time. |
| Cyndi **has been working** full-time on her website **since** she **quit** her job. | We use the simple past in the *since*-clause. |
| I **have been studying** my family history since 2010. OR I **have studied** my family history since 2010. | With some verbs (*live, work, study, teach,* and *wear*), we can use either the present perfect or the present perfect continuous with actions that began in the past and continue to the present. The meaning is the same. |
| My father is working on our family tree right now. He **has been working** on it since 9 a.m. | If an action is still happening, we use the present perfect continuous, not the present perfect. |
| I **have been** interested in genealogy for 10 years. She **has wanted** to learn about her family history since she was in high school. | We do not use the continuous form with nonaction verbs, such as *be, like, want, have, know, remember,* and *see*. |
| I **have been** *thinking about* sending my DNA for anaylsis. I **have** always *thought that* genealogy is an interesting hobby. | *Think* can be an action or nonaction verb, depending on its meaning. *Think about* = action verb *Think that* = nonaction verb |

**Note:**
We do not use the continuous form with *always* and *never*.

> I have **always** lived in this country.
> NOT: I have always been living in this country.

**EXERCISE 20** Fill in the blanks to complete the conversations.

1. **A:** _____Are_____ you studying your family history?
   a.

   **B:** Yes, I _____.
   b.

   **A:** How long _____ your family history?
   c.

   **B:** _____ about five years.
   d.

2. **A:** _____ Spencer Wells working on the Genographic Project?
   a.

   **B:** Yes, he _____.
   b.

   **A:** _____ long _____ he been
   c.                d.

   _____ on this project?
   e.

   **B:** _____ 2005.
   f.

3. **A:** Are you working on your family history?

   **B:** Yes, I _____.
   a.

   **A:** How long _____ you _____ on your family history?
   b.                     c.

   **B:** I _____ on it _____ about 10 years.
   d.              e.

4. **A:** Is your sister using your computer now?

   **B:** Yes, she _____.
   a.

   **A:** _____ long _____ it?
   b.              c.

   **B:** _____ she woke up this morning!
   d.

5. **A:** _____ the U.S. Census Bureau collect information about Americans?
   a.

   **B:** Yes, it _____.
   b.

   **A:** How _____ the U.S. Census Bureau _____
   c.                                      d.

   information about Americans?

   **B:** _____ over 200 years.
   e.

6. **A:** _____ your grandparents live in the U.S.?
   a.

   **B:** Yes, they _____.
   b.

   **A:** How _____ in the U.S.?
   c.

   **B:** Since they _____ born.
   d.

252   Unit 9

**ABOUT YOU** Write true statements using the present perfect with the words given and *for* or *since*. Share your sentences with a partner.

1. work <u>My brother has been working as an engineer for six years.</u>
2. study _____
3. live _____
4. use _____
5. try _____

**EXERCISE 21** Fill in the blanks with the correct form of the verb given. Use the present perfect, present perfect continuous, or the simple past. Fill in any other missing words.

**A:** Hi. My name is Ana. I'm from Guatemala.

**B:** Hi, Ana. My name is Jimmy. My family is from Cuba. How <u>long have you been living</u> here?
                                                                                    **1.** you/live

**A:** I _____ here for about six months. What about you?
     **2.** only/be

**B:** I _____ born in the U.S. My family _____ Cuba in
     **3.** be                                 **4.** leave

1962. Lately I _____ to trace my family history.
                **5.** try

**A:** Me, too. I've been _____ on a family tree _____ many years.
                       **6.** work                        **7.**

**B:** When _____ ?
         **8.** you/start

**A:** I _____ when I _____ 16 years old. Over the
     **9.** start                         **10.** be

years, I _____ a lot of interesting information about my family. Some of my
          **11.** find

ancestors were Mayans, and some were from Spain and France.

**B:** Where _____ all that information?
         **12.** you/find

**A:** There's a wonderful site called Cyndi's List. I _____ it
                                          **13.** use

_____ around 2001. Last summer, I _____
     **14.**                                             **15.** go

to Spain to look for information there.

**B:** How many ancestors _____ so far?
                     **16.** you/find

**A:** So far, I _____ about 50 in four generations. I'm still looking.
         **17.** find

**B:** _____ of the Genographic Project?
    **18.** you/ever/hear

**A:** No, I _____ . What is it?
         **19.**

**B:** It connects people from all over the world, going back thousands of years.

# SUMMARY OF UNIT 9

## The Present Perfect and the Simple Past

| PRESENT PERFECT | SIMPLE PAST |
| --- | --- |
| The action of the sentence began in the past and includes the present. | The action of the sentence is completely past. |
| Sergey Brin **has been** in the U.S. since 1979. | Sergey Brin **came** to the U.S. in 1979. |
| Khan's videos **have been** available for many years. | Khan **created** his first math videos in 2004. |
| I've always **wanted** to learn more about my family's history. | When I was a child, I always **wanted** to spend time with my grandparents. |
| How long **have** you **been** interested in genealogy? | When **did** you **start** your family tree? |

| PRESENT PERFECT | SIMPLE PAST |
| --- | --- |
| Repetition from past to present | Repetition in a past time period |
| Khan Academy **has created** over 5,000 videos so far. | Khan **created** several videos for his niece in 2004. |

| PRESENT PERFECT | SIMPLE PAST |
| --- | --- |
| The action took place at an indefinite time between the past and the present. | The action took place at a definite time in the past. |
| **Have** you ever **used** Cyndi's list? | **Did** you **use** the 1940 census in 2012? |
| My brother **has raised** $5,000 on a crowdfunding site already. | He **put** his project on a crowdfunding site six months ago. |
| I'm interested in the DNA project. I've **received** my kit, but I **haven't sent** the sample back yet. | My friend **sent** her DNA sample to the Genographic Project last month. |

## The Present Perfect and the Present Perfect Continuous

| PRESENT PERFECT | PRESENT PERFECT CONTINUOUS |
| --- | --- |
| A continuous action (nonaction verbs) | A continuous action (action verbs) |
| I **have been** interested in genealogy for five years. | I've **been working** on my family tree for five years. |
| A repeated action | A nonstop action |
| Cyndi Howell's website **has won** several awards. | The U.S. Census Bureau **has been keeping** records since the 1880s. |
| Question with *how many/how much* | Question with *how long* |
| How many times **has** Khan **been** on the cover of a magazine?<br>How much time **has** he **spent** on Khan Academy? | How long **has** Khan **been living** in Boston? |
| An action that is at an indefinite time, completely in the past | An action that started in the past and is still happening |
| Many teachers **have started** to use Khan lectures in their classrooms. | Dr. Wells **has been collecting** DNA for several years. |

# REVIEW

Fill in the blanks with the simple present, the simple past, the present perfect, or the present perfect continuous form of the verbs given. Include any other words you see. In some cases, more than one answer is possible.

**A:** What do you do for a living?

**B:** I ___work___ as a programmer. I ___'ve been working___ as a
  1. work                                           2. work

programmer for five years. But my job is boring.

**A:** _____ about changing jobs?
   3. you/think/ever

**B:** Yes. Since I _____ a child, I _____ to be an actor.
   4. be                          5. always/want

When I was in college, I _____ in a few plays. But since I
   6. be

_____, I _____ time to act. What about you?
   7. graduate      8. not/have

**A:** I _____ in computer security.
   9. work

**B:** How long _____ that?
   10. you/do

**A:** For about six years.

**B:** I _____ the field of computer security is very important.
   11. think

**A:** Yes, it is. But lately I _____ the computer for other things, too. My hobby is
   12. use

genealogy. I _____ on my family tree for about a year. Last month, I
   13. work

_____ information about my father's ancestors. My grandfather
   14. find

_____ with us now, and he likes to tell us about his past. He
   15. live

_____ born in Italy, but he _____ here when he
   16. be                                17. come

was very young, so he _____ here most of his life. He
   18. live

_____ much about Italy. I _____ any information
   19. not/remember              20. not/find

about my mother's ancestors yet.

# FROM GRAMMAR TO WRITING

## PART 1 Editing Advice

1. Don't confuse the *-ing* form and the past participle.

   I've been ~~taken~~ **taking** a course in genealogy.

   My parents have ~~giving~~ **given** me family photos.

2. Use the present perfect, not the simple present or present continuous, to describe an action or state that started in the past and continues to the present.

   He has **had** his laptop for two years.    How long ~~are you~~ **have you been** studying math?

3. Use *for*, not *since*, with the amount of time.

   I've been interested in my family's history ~~since~~ **for** three years.

4. Use the simple past, not the present perfect, with a specific past time.

   He ~~has studied~~ **studied** algebra when he was in high school.

   When ~~have~~ **did** you ~~studied~~ **study** algebra?

5. Use the simple past, not the present perfect, in a *since* clause.

   He has collected $5,000 since he ~~has put~~ **put** his project on a crowdfunding site.

6. Use the correct word order with adverbs.

   I have ~~studied never~~ **never studied** my family history. Have you ~~heard ever~~ **ever heard** of Dr. Spencer Wells?

7. Use the correct word order in questions.

   How long ~~your family has~~ **has your family** been in this country?

8. Use *yet* for negative statements; use *already* for affirmative statements.

   I haven't taken advanced algebra ~~already~~ **yet**.

9. Don't forget the verb *have* in the present perfect (continuous).

   I **have** been studying my family history for two years.

10. Don't forget the *-ed* of the past participle.

    He's watch**ed** a math video several times.

## PART 2 Editing Practice

Some of the shaded words and phrases have mistakes. Find the mistakes and correct them. If the shaded words are correct, write C.

How many changes ~~you have~~ **have you** made since you came (**C**) to the U.S.? For our journal, our teacher
                        1.                                    2.
asked us to answer this question. I have come to the U.S. two and a half years ago. Things have
                                    3.
change a lot for me since I've come here. Here are some of the changes:
   4.                       5.

256 Unit 9

First, since the past two years, I am studying to be a software engineer. I knew a little about
   6.                    7.                                          8.
this subject before I came here, but my knowledge has improve a lot. I started to work part-time
                     9.                                    10.              11.
in a computer company three months ago. Since I have started my job, I haven't have much time
                                                  12.    13.              14.
for fun.

Second, I have a driver's permit, and I'm learning how to drive. I haven't took the driver's test
                                                                       15.
yet because I'm not ready. I haven't practiced enough already.
16.                                    17.               18.

Third, I've been eaten a lot of different foods like hamburgers and pizza. I never ate those in
             19.                                                                 20.
my country. Unfortunately, I been gaining weight.
                              21.

Fourth, I've gone to several museums in this city. But I've taken never a trip to another
         22.                                             23.
American city. I'd like to visit New York, but I haven't saved enough money yet.
                                                 24.              25.

Fifth, I've been living in three apartments so far. In my country, I lived in the same house
       26.                                                          27.
with my family all my life.

One thing that bothers me is this: I've answered the following questions about a thousand
                                    28.
times so far: "Where do you come from?" and "How long time you have been in the U.S.?" I'm
                                              29.            30.
getting tired of always answering the same question. But in general, I been happy since I came to
                                                                      31.                32.
the U.S.

---

### WRITING TIP

When you write a paragraph or essay about a change in your life, start your paper with a sentence that states how the new situation (technology, for example) has changed your life.

*Since I got a cell phone, my life **has** greatly **improved**.*

Then use the simple past to talk about what you used to do and the simple present to talk about what you do habitually now.

*Before I got a cell phone, I **went** to work in the morning and only **talked** to my family at night. Now, I **call** before I **go** home to **ask** if they need anything.*

## PART 3 Write

Read the prompts. Choose one and write a paragraph or two about it.

1. Write about the changes that you have made since you came to this country, city, or school.
2. Write about new technology that you've started using recently. How has that made your life different?

## PART 4 Edit

Reread the Summary of Unit 9 and the editing advice. Edit your writing from Part 3.

# UNIT 10
## Gerunds
## Infinitives

A worker maintains the paint on a ship at sea.

# JOBS

Choose a job you love, and you will never have to work a day in your life.
CONFUCIUS

Job seekers attend the Big East Career Fair at Madison Square Garden in New York, U.S. The fair is for students and alumni from ten specific schools on the east coast.

# FINDING a JOB

Read the following article. Pay special attention to the words in bold. 10.1

**Finding** a job in the United States takes time and effort. Here are some tips[1] to help you:

- Write a good résumé. Include only relevant[2] experience. Describe your accomplishments[3]. Avoid **including** unnecessary information. Consider **asking** a friend to read your résumé to check it for grammar and spelling mistakes.

- Find out about available jobs. One way is by **looking** on the Internet. Another way is by **networking**. **Networking** means **exchanging** information with anyone you know who might know of a job. These people might be able to give you insider information about a company, such as who is in charge of **hiring** and what it is like to work at their company. You can find out about a job before it is even advertised. *The Wall Street Journal* reports that 94 percent of people who succeed in **finding** a job say that **networking** was a big help.

- Practice before you go for an interview. The more prepared you are, the more relaxed you will feel and the more you will convey[4] confidence. If you are worried about **saying** or **doing** the wrong thing, practice will help.

- Learn something about the company by **going** to the company's website.

- Arrive at least 15 minutes before the scheduled time of your interview. **Feeling** relaxed is important. **Arriving** on time or just a few minutes before the interview doesn't give you time to relax.

---

[1] tip: useful information
[2] relevant: closely connected
[3] accomplishment: a difficult thing done well
[4] to convey: to communicate

- Behave professionally during the interview. Avoid **chewing** gum. Turn off your cell phone completely.

- Avoid **saying** anything negative about your current job or employer.

- One question might be, "Tell me something about yourself." Instead of **talking** about your personal life, focus on your skills and work experience. Answer each question concisely[5]. Avoid **giving** long answers.

- At the end of the interview, offer a firm handshake. **Thanking** the interviewer by letter or email a few days later is a good idea.

Some people send out hundreds of résumés and go on dozens of interviews before **finding** a job. **Looking** for a job isn't something you do just once or twice in your lifetime.

---

[5] concisely: using few words to communicate

**COMPREHENSION** Based on the reading, write T for *true* or F for *false*.

1. _____ *Networking* means getting information from the Internet.
2. _____ Arriving right on time to an interview is a good idea.
3. _____ Thanking the interviewer with a handshake is enough.

**THINK ABOUT IT** Discuss the questions with a partner or in a small group.

1. What networking opportunities exist today for people who are looking for work?
2. If an interviewer asked you to describe your greatest weakness, what could you say that would also show something positive about you?

## 10.1 Gerunds—An Overview

A gerund is the *–ing* form of a verb.

| EXAMPLES | EXPLANATION |
|---|---|
| **Finding** a job is hard.<br>I recommend **talking** to a job counselor.<br>Are you thinking about **changing** careers? | A gerund (phrase) can be:<br>• the subject of a sentence.<br>• the object of the verb.<br>• the object of a preposition. |
| I'm worried about **not getting** a good job. | We put *not* in front of a gerund to make it negative. |

**Note:**
A gerund phrase is a gerund + a noun or noun phrase.
- *finding a job*
- *exchanging information*
- *preparing for a job interview*

**EXERCISE 1** Listen to these tips about how to be successful at your job. Then write T for *true* or F for *false*. 🎧 10.2

1. _____ You should speak up if you are unhappy about working on a project.

2. _____ If you practice talking confidently, you can become better at it.

3. _____ You should be direct about your weaknesses.

**EXERCISE 2** Listen to the tips again. Fill in the blanks with the words you hear. 🎧 10.2

You care ___about keeping___ your job. You may not be aware _____ things that
                    1.                                                            2.

can make your supervisor think less of you. So here are a few tips:

- Avoid _____ about things you have to do. If you dislike _____ on
                 3.                                                             4.

  a project, keep it to yourself. Don't say, "It's not my job." Even if you don't like _____
                                                                                                              5.

  it, do it anyway _____.
                                  6.

- Practice _____ positive words to show confidence and a good attitude.
                        7.

  _____ "It's not fair" makes you sound like a child.
          8.

- Get used _____ strong words. Instead _____, "I think I
                      9.                                                10.

  can do the job," simply say, "I can do the job. When do you need the work done?" Most people don't

  know how they sound. Consider _____ a friend listen to the way you talk. Or
                                                  11.

  try _____ yourself and analyzing what you say.
       12.

- Don't point out your weaknesses. "I'm not good _____ reports" sounds bad. Instead
                                                               13.

  say, "I want to do a good job. I'd like to work with someone who can help me learn to write better reports."

- _____ a coworker that you don't like a supervisor is not a good idea. You never
      14.

  know what this person might say to the supervisor.

- If you're interested _____ more tips on good job behavior, there are books and
                                15.

  online sources that can give you more information.

## 10.2 Gerunds as Subjects

| EXAMPLES | EXPLANATION |
|---|---|
| **Using** positive words conveys confidence.<br>**Not dressing** appropriately gives a bad impression. | We can use a gerund or gerund phrase as the subject of the sentence. |
| **Exchanging** ideas with friends **is** helpful.<br>**Visiting** company websites **pays** off. | A gerund subject takes a singular verb. |

**EXERCISE 3** Use the gerund form of one of the verbs from the box to complete each sentence.

| arrive | wear | feel | know | get ✓ | network | prepare | select |

1. _____Getting_____ a good night's sleep will help you feel rested and alert for an interview.
2. _____ with other people will improve your chances of finding a job.
3. _____ your clothes the night before the interview is a good idea.
4. _____ a good résumé is very important. Some people use a résumé service.
5. _____ something about the company will help you make a good impression.
6. Not _____ serious clothes to the interview will give a very bad impression.
7. _____ early for an interview will give you time to relax.
8. _____ relaxed before an interview is important.

**ABOUT YOU** Fill in the blanks with the gerund form of the verb given. Then tell if this behavior is or isn't common in a work situation in your country.

1. _____Socializing_____ with the boss (is/*isn't*) common.
   <sub>socialize</sub>
2. _____ the boss by his or her first name (*is/isn't*) acceptable.
   <sub>call</sub>
3. _____ with coworkers (*is/isn't*) common.
   <sub>socialize</sub>
4. _____ on time (*is/isn't*) very important.
   <sub>arrive</sub>
5. _____ a personal computer at a job (*is/isn't*) common.
   <sub>use</sub>
6. _____ jeans to the office (*is/isn't*) acceptable.
   <sub>wear</sub>
7. _____ a long lunch break (*is/isn't*) the custom.
   <sub>take</sub>
8. _____ from home (*is/isn't*) common.
   <sub>work</sub>
9. _____ coffee or tea while working (*is/isn't*) acceptable.
   <sub>drink</sub>
10. _____ early on Friday afternoons (*is/isn't*) common.
    <sub>leave</sub>

**ABOUT YOU** In preparing for an interview, it is good to think about the following questions. Give some thought to your answers and compare them with a partner's answers.

1. What are your strengths?

   working well with others; learning quickly; thinking fast in difficult situations

2. What are some of your weaknesses?

3. List your accomplishments and achievements. (They can be achievements in jobs, sports, school, etc.)

4. What are your short-term goals?

5. What are your long-term goals?

6. What are some things you like in a job situation? (personalities, tasks, environments, types of work)

7. What are some things you dislike? (personalities, tasks, environments, types of work)

**EXERCISE 4** Work with a partner to write sentences about behaviors during an interview that would hurt your chances of getting a job.

1. Chewing gum during the interview looks bad.
2. 
3. 
4. 
5. 
6. 

**264** Unit 10

## 10.3 Gerunds as Objects

| EXAMPLES | EXPLANATION |
|---|---|
| Do you **enjoy working** on a team?<br>**Avoid complaining** about your supervisor. | A gerund (phrase) can be the object of many verbs. |
| I **went shopping** for work clothes last weekend.<br>After work, I like to **go swimming**. | We use *go* + gerund in expressions of recreational activities. |

A gerund (phrase) can follow these verbs:

| | | | |
|---|---|---|---|
| admit | dislike | love | quit |
| appreciate | enjoy | mind | recommend |
| avoid | finish | miss | start |
| begin | hate | postpone | stop |
| consider | imagine | practice | suggest |
| continue | keep (on) | prefer | |
| discuss | like | put off | |

We use *go* + gerund in the following expressions:

| | | | |
|---|---|---|---|
| go boating | go camping | go fishing | go hunting |
| go jogging | go shopping | go skating | go swimming |
| go bowling | go dancing | go hiking | go skiing |

**Notes:**

1. *I mind* means that something bothers me. *I don't mind* means that something is OK with me; it doesn't bother me.

    *Do you **mind wearing** a suit to work? No, I don't **mind**.*

2. *Put off* means "postpone."

    *Don't **put off writing** your résumé. Do it now.*

*For a list of verbs followed by gerunds, see Appendix D.

**EXERCISE 5** Use the gerund form of a verb from the box to complete each conversation.

| answer | shop | find | say | get | be | do ✓ |
|---|---|---|---|---|---|---|
| work | wear | go | act | discuss | talk | read |

1. **A:** I want to quit my boring job. I dislike _____*doing*_____ the same thing every day.
   <br>                                                                       a.

   **B:** I suggest _____ another job before you quit. I can't imagine _____
   <br>                           b.                                                                                  c.

   without a job.

2. **A:** Interviewing for a job scares me. I hate _____ about my strengths.
   <br>                                                                                    a.

   **B:** Have you considered _____ help from a job counselor? You can practice _____
   <br>                                                                              b.                                                      c.

   common interview questions. I have a good book about job hunting. When I finish _____
   <br>                                                                                                                                            d.

   it, you can borrow it.

*continued*

3. **A:** I have to wear a suit for my new job.

   **B:** I dislike _____ anything but jeans.
   <br>a.

   **A:** Me, too. I have to go _____ for some new clothes. Can you help me pick something out?
   <br>b.

   **B:** Sorry. I don't have time. I suggest _____ to a store and asking the salesperson to help you.
   <br>c.

4. **A:** I really like my job.

   **B:** What do you like about it?

   **A:** I enjoy _____ on a team. The people on my team are smart and creative. I like
   <br>a.

   _____ how to do a project with them.
   <br>b.

5. **A:** My boss always asks me to do something that isn't my job. Sometimes I have to tell her, "It's not fair."

   **B:** Stop _____ "It's not fair" and just do it. Quit _____ like a child.
   <br>a.     b.

**ABOUT YOU** Use the words below to make statements about yourself regarding jobs. Share your answers with a partner.

1. I hate <u>getting up every morning at 5 for my job.</u>
2. I enjoy _____
3. I don't mind _____
4. I've considered _____
5. I can't imagine _____
6. I avoid _____
7. I began _____

**EXERCISE 6** Make a list of suggestions and recommendations for someone looking for a job or about to go on a job interview. Discuss your list with a partner.

1. <u>I recommend getting a good night's sleep the night before the interview.</u>
2. _____
3. _____
4. _____
5. _____
6. _____

266   Unit 10

## 10.4 Preposition + Gerund

A gerund can follow certain verb + preposition or adjective + preposition combinations.

| COMMON VERB + PREPOSITION COMBINATIONS | | EXAMPLES |
|---|---|---|
| verb + *about* | care about<br>complain about<br>dream about<br>forget about<br>know about<br>talk about<br>think about<br>worry about | My sister **dreams about becoming** an engineer. |
| verb + *to* | look forward to<br>object to | I **look forward to getting** a job and **saving** money. |
| verb + *on* | depend on<br>insist on<br>plan on | I **plan on going** to a career counselor. |
| verb + *in* | believe in<br>succeed in | My father **succeeded in finding** a good job. |
| verb + object + *from* | stop + . . . + from | No one can **stop** you **from following** your dream. |
| **COMMON ADJECTIVE + PREPOSITION COMBINATIONS** | | **EXAMPLES** |
| adjective + *of* | afraid of<br>capable of<br>guilty of<br>proud of<br>tired of | I'm **afraid of losing** my job. |
| adjective + *about* | concerned about<br>excited about<br>upset about<br>worried about<br>sad about | He is **upset about not getting** the job. |
| adjective + *for* | responsible for<br>famous for | Who is **responsible for hiring** in this company? |
| adjective + *to* + object + *for* | grateful to . . . for | I'm **grateful to** you **for helping** me find a job. |
| adjective + *at* | good at<br>successful at | I'm not very **good at writing** a résumé. |
| adjective + *to* | accustomed to<br>used to | I'm not **accustomed to talking** about my strengths. |
| adjective + *in* | interested in<br>successful in | Are you **interested in getting** a better job? |

**Note:**

In general, you can use a gerund after any preposition.

*What is your method **of preparing** for an interview?*

*It's hard to do well at an interview **without practicing**.*

---

*For a list of verbs and adjectives followed by a preposition, see Appendix E.

**EXERCISE 7** Fill in the blanks with a preposition and the gerund form of a verb from the box.

| talk | do | work | complain | get | help |
|------|------|------|----------|-----|------|
| be | practice | tell | hear | go ✓ | connect |

1. **A:** I plan ___on going___ to India for a year to work in a clinic as a physician assistant.
   a.

   **B:** That's great. You've talked a lot _____ other people. This is your chance.
   b.

   **A:** When I get back, I'd like to go to medical school, but it's so expensive. I'm worried _____ not
   c.
   _____ financial aid.
   d.

   **B:** With your experience in India, you're a good candidate for financial aid.

2. **A:** I have an interview next week. I'm afraid _____ not _____ well.
   a.                    b.

   **B:** Have you thought _____ for the interview?
   c.

   **A:** No, I haven't. I don't know how to do that.

   **B:** I have a friend who has a lot of experience with job interviews. Are you interested _____
   d.
   with her? She can give you good tips. I can set up a meeting for you. (*A few weeks later…*)

   **A:** I'm grateful to you _____ me with your friend. She helped me a lot.
   e.

3. **A:** Some people complain _____ long hours. But I don't even have a job.
   a.

   I'm upset _____ unemployed for so long.
   b.

   **B:** How long have you been unemployed?

   **A:** For almost six months. I'm worried _____ the interviewer about my long
   c.
   unemployment. It might hurt my chances of getting a job.

4. **A:** A coworker of mine always insists _____ about the boss. She hates the boss.
   a.

   **B:** Tell her you're not interested _____ her complaints.
   b.

**ABOUT YOU** Fill in the blanks with a preposition + gerund or noun phrase to complete each statement about jobs. Share your answers with a partner.

1. I'm afraid ___of losing my job.___

2. I'm not accustomed _____

3. Coworkers often talk _____

4. After work, I'm (not) interested _____

268 Unit 10

5. I worry _____

6. I'm proud _____

7. I'm not used _____

8. On Fridays, most workers look forward _____

**EXERCISE 8** Fill in the blanks with the gerund form of the verb given. Some of the blanks need a preposition before the gerund. If so, add the preposition.

**A:** I need to find a job. I've had 10 interviews, but so far no job.

**B:** Have you thought <u>about practicing</u> for the interview? You can practice _____
                      **1.** practice                                                         **2.** answer

questions that the interviewer might ask you. Many interviewers ask the same general questions. For

example, the interviewer will probably ask you to name your strengths.

**A:** I dislike _____ about myself.
               **3.** talk

**B:** But it's necessary. And she'll probably ask you to name your weaknesses, too.

**A:** What should I say? I'm afraid _____ the truth about my weaknesses.
                                **4.** tell

**B:** There's a way to make your answer sound positive. For example, "I'm a perfectionist. I worry

_____ in a project with mistakes. But I plan _____ careful so that
**5.** turn                                                                               **6.** be

I meet deadlines."

**A:** Wow! That sounds more like a strength than a weakness.

**B:** That's the idea. Here's another possible question: "Do you mind _____ overtime to finish
                                                                                                    **7.** stay

a project?"

**A:** Will I have to work overtime? I'll have to get a babysitter for my son.

**B:** Don't complain _____ a babysitter. Don't mention personal problems.
                             **8.** get

**A:** It feels like I'm never going to find a job. I'm tired _____ .
                                                                       **9.** look

**B:** Be patient. If you keep _____ , you'll succeed _____ a job.
                                 **10.** try                                **11.** find

I suggest _____ a book that gives you sample interview questions.
             **12.** get

**A:** Thanks so much. I'm grateful to you _____ me so much help.
                                              **13.** give

Employees gather for a group cheer just before opening a store during a busy holiday shopping weekend.

# EMPLOYEE ENGAGEMENT

Read the following article. Pay special attention to the words in bold. 10.3

Do you like **to go** to work? Or are you glad **to leave** at the end of the day? If you have a full-time job, you probably spend most of your waking hours at work. It would be nice **to spend** that time in a pleasant atmosphere, right?

According to a survey, 70 percent of Americans are not happy at work. They often feel job burnout: physical and mental stress. Some of them can't wait **to get** home, but they often take their stress home with them to their families.

When workers are happy, they do a better job, and the company gains from this. What makes workers happy? The answer is "employee engagement." Researchers have been studying what makes a worker feel engaged. Engaged employees are enthusiastic about their work. Researchers have found that it takes a combination of things **to build** an engaged workforce:

1. Employees need **to feel** that the boss appreciates their work.
2. Workers need **to take** breaks during the day. When people work continuously, they feel worse physically. More work is not necessarily better work. Some experts believe that workers need a break every 90 minutes. Some companies have fitness facilities and nap rooms for their employees.
3. Workers want **to be** able to focus on one thing at a time. Too often, managers want them **to do** several things at once. The result is workers get stressed out, and their work suffers.
4. Workers want **to feel** that they are doing something meaningful. They want **to be** excited about what they're doing.

Employers need **to choose** a job candidate who fits the company's mission[1]. A worker who doesn't fit in is likely[2] **to quit**. It takes time and costs money **to train** a new employee. So it's important for a company **to hire** the right people and **make** the work atmosphere fun and meaningful.

---
[1] mission: purpose
[2] is likely: is probably going to

**COMPREHENSION** Based on the reading, write T for *true* or F for *false*.

1. _____ One way to promote employee engagement is for the employer to show the employee appreciation.
2. _____ The majority of Americans are happy to go to work.
3. _____ It is expensive for a company to train a new employee.

**THINK ABOUT IT** Discuss the questions with a partner or in a small group.

1. What type of job do you think would make you feel engaged? For example, would you like a job that encourages teamwork? Or would you feel more engaged in a job that requires mostly independent work?
2. Reread point 2 in the reading. What are some creative ways employers could offer employees breaks at work?

## 10.5 Infinitives—An Overview

An infinitive is *to* + the base form of a verb.

| EXAMPLES | EXPLANATION |
| --- | --- |
| Are you happy **to go** to work?<br>I need **to take** a break.<br>It's important **to hire** the right people. | We can use an infinitive after:<br>• certain adjectives.<br>• certain verbs.<br>• expressions beginning with *it*. |
| They decided **not to hire** me. | To make an infinitive negative, we put *not* before the infinitive. |

**Note:**
When we connect two infinitives with *and*, we usually omit *to* after *and*.
  He wants **to take** a break and **rest**.

**EXERCISE 9** Fill in the blanks with the words you hear. 🎧 10.4

It's important ___to write___ a good, clear résumé. It's only necessary
1.

_____ your most recent and related work. Employers are busy people. Don't
2.

expect them _____ long résumés.
3.

You need _____ your abilities in your résumé. Employers expect you
4.

_____ action verbs _____ your experience. Don't begin your
5. 6.

sentences with *I*. Use past-tense verbs such as: *managed, designed, created,* and *developed*. It's

not enough _____ you improved something. Be specific. How did you improve it?
7.

Before making copies of your résumé, it's important _____ the grammar and
8.

spelling. Employers want _____ if you have good communication skills. Ask a
9.

friend or teacher _____ your résumé and check for mistakes.
10.

*continued*

It isn't necessary _____ references. If the employer wants you
                        11.

_____ references, he or she will ask you _____ so during or
      12.                                              13.

after the interview.

Don't include personal information such as marital status, age, race, family information, or

hobbies.

Be honest in your résumé. Employers can check your information. No one wants

_____ a liar.
      14.

## 10.6 Infinitives after Expressions with *It*

| EXAMPLES | EXPLANATION |
|---|---|
| **It's important to write** a good résumé.<br>**It isn't necessary to include** all your experience.<br>**It's a good idea to practice** before an interview. | An infinitive phrase can follow certain expressions beginning with *it*. |
| It's important **for managers to show** appreciation.<br>It was hard **for me to leave** my last job. | We use *for* + a noun or object pronoun to make a statement that is true of a specific person or people. |
| It **takes patience to find** a job.<br>It **took me** three weeks **to finish** my project. | We can use an infinitive after *take* + *time*, *patience*, or *money*. We can add an object before the infinitive. |
| It **costs** a lot of money **to train** a new worker.<br>It **cost me** $100 **to use** a résumé service. | We can use an infinitive after *cost* + (object) + money. |
| It's important **to do** a good job.<br>**Doing** a good job is important. | There is no difference in meaning between an infinitive after an *it* expression and a gerund subject. |

We often use an infinitive after *it* + *be* + these words:

| dangerous | expensive | a good/bad idea | impossible/possible |
| difficult | fun | hard | necessary |
| easy | a good/bad experience | important | a pleasure |

**EXERCISE 10** Fill in the blanks with the infinitive form of a verb from the box.

| practice | check | have ✓ | describe | arrive | write | include | dress |

1. It's necessary _____*to have*_____ a Social Security card.

2. When you write a résumé, it isn't necessary _____ all your previous experience.

   Choose only the most recent and related experience.

272  Unit 10

3. It's important _____ your spelling and grammar before sending a résumé.

4. It's important _____ your past work experience in detail, using words like *managed*, *designed*, *supervised*, and *built*.

5. It takes time _____ a good résumé.

6. It's a good idea _____ interview questions before going to an interview.

7. It's important _____ your best when you go to an interview, so choose your clothes carefully.

8. It's a good idea _____ early for your interview.

**EXERCISE 11** Complete each statement with an infinitive phrase to talk about work. You can add an object, if you like.

1. It's easy <u>to get information about a company online.</u>

2. It's necessary <u>for me to work overtime once a month.</u>

3. It's important _____

4. It's impossible _____

5. It's possible _____

6. It's a pleasure _____

7. It isn't a good idea _____

8. It's hard _____

## 10.7 Infinitives after Adjectives

| EXAMPLES | EXPLANATION |
|---|---|
| Are you **available to work** overtime?<br>A happy worker is **likely to stay** with the company. | An infinitive (phrase) can follow certain adjectives. |

An infinitive can follow these adjectives:

| | | | | |
|---|---|---|---|---|
| afraid | glad | lucky | proud | sorry |
| available | happy | prepared | ready | surprised |

*For a list of adjectives followed by infinitives, see Appendix D.

**EXERCISE 12** Complete the conversation with the appropriate infinitive form of a verb from the box.

| help | talk | show | go ✓ | have | answer | wait | say |

**A:** I have my first interview tomorrow. I'm afraid ___to go___ alone. Would you go with me?
                                                1.

**B:** I'd be happy _____ in the car. But nobody can go with you to an interview.
                       2.

You have to do it alone. It sounds like you're not ready _____ a job interview.
                                                               3.

You should see a job counselor and get some practice before you have an interview.

**A:** I don't have time. Maybe you can help me.

**B:** I'd be happy _____ you. We can go over some basic questions. Here's one question you
                       4.

should be ready _____: "Why are you leaving your present job?"
                    5.

**A:** I'm afraid _____ anything about my present job. I don't like my supervisor.
                    6.

**B:** Never say that! I'd be happy _____ you a few good websites that will give you typical
                                        7.

questions and good answers.

**A:** Thanks. I'm glad you were available _____ to me this afternoon. I feel better already.
                                                8.

## 10.8 Infinitives after Verbs

| EXAMPLES | EXPLANATION |
|---|---|
| I **need to find** a better job.<br>I **want to make** more money. | An infinitive (phrase) can follow certain verbs. |

An infinitive can follow these verbs:

| agree | decide | learn | remember | begin* | love* |
| attempt | expect | need | try | continue* | prefer* |
| begin | forget | plan | want | hate* | start* |
| choose | hope | promise | would like | like* | |

**Notes:**
1. A gerund can also follow these verbs* with little or no difference in meaning. See chart 10.3.
    *I* **love to work** *with children.* = *I* **love working** *with children.*
2. *Plan on* + gerund is the same as *plan* + infinitive.
    *I* **plan on seeing** *a counselor.* = *I* **plan to see** *a counselor.*
3. Remember that in some expressions, *to* is part of a verb phrase, not part of an infinitive.
    *I* **look forward to starting** *my new job. (verb + to + gerund)*
    *I* **need to write** *a résumé. (verb + infinitive)*

*For a list of verbs followed by infinitives, see Appendix D.

**EXERCISE 13** Fill in the blanks with the infinitive form of a verb from the box.

| feel | take | go | ask | find | sleep ✓ |
| work | get | be | hear | have | |

**A:** How's your new job?

**B:** I really like it. It's a great company. We can take a break every two hours. And we even have a nap room. Sometimes people need ____to sleep____ for a few minutes.
                                                          1.

**A:** I've never heard of a nap room. I would like _____ a nap in the middle of the
                                                        2.
day. I usually start _____ tired around two o'clock, but I have to keep working.
                          3.
How's your boss?

**B:** She's wonderful. She includes us on company decisions. Employees want _____
                                                                                    4.
like their opinion is important, don't you think?

**A:** Yes, I do.

**B:** It's fun for me _____ to work. After six months on the job, we can choose
                          5.
_____ from home, too. But I prefer _____
       6.                                              7.
with my team members at the office.

**A:** You're lucky _____ such a good job. My job is terrible.
                        8.

**B:** I'm sorry _____ that.
                      9.

**A:** I need _____ a new job. Do you know if your company is hiring?
                   10.

**B:** I don't know. But I promise _____ on Monday morning.
                                           11.

**ABOUT YOU** Work with a partner who has a job. Use the phrases to ask a question. Your partner will answer.

1. afraid/give your boss your opinion

   A: *Are you afraid to give your boss your opinion?*

   B: *Yes, I am.* OR *No, I'm not.*

2. like/go to work every day
3. plan/stay at your job for a long time
4. expect/make a lot of money
5. need/work at home
6. hope/get a better position within the company

*continued*

7. like/socialize with your coworkers
8. try/keep up with changes in technology
9. want/work overtime
10. hate/get up in the morning to go to work

## 10.9 Objects before Infinitives

| EXAMPLES | EXPLANATION |
| --- | --- |
| I **want my boss to appreciate** my work.<br>My boss **expects me to work** overtime. | We can use an object noun or pronoun between some verbs and an infinitive. |

We can use an object between these verbs and an infinitive:

| advise | expect | need | want |
| allow | help | permit | would like |
| ask | invite | tell | |

**Note:**
We can follow *help* by either an object + base form or an object + infinitive.
  He helped me **find** a job.
  He helped me **to find** a job.

**EXERCISE 14** Fill in the blanks with pronouns and infinitives to complete the conversation.

**A:** I want to quit my job.

**B:** Why?

**A:** I don't like my supervisor. He expects ___me to work___ at night and on weekends.
  1. work

**B:** But you get extra pay for that, don't you?

**A:** No. I asked _____ me a raise, but he said the company can't afford it.
  2. give

**B:** Is that the only problem?

**A:** No. My coworkers and I like to go out for lunch. But he doesn't want _____ out. He
  3. go
  expects _____ in the company cafeteria.
  4. eat

**B:** That's awful. He should permit _____ wherever you want to.
  5. eat

**A:** That's what I think. I also have a problem with my team manager. She never gives anyone a compliment. When I do a good job, I expect _____ something nice. But she
  6. say
  only says something when I make a mistake.

## 10.10 Infinitives to Show Purpose

| EXAMPLES | EXPLANATION |
|---|---|
| You can use the Internet **in order to find** job information. <br> I need a car **in order to get** to work. | We use *in order to* + verb to show purpose. |
| You can use the Internet **to find** job information. <br> I need a car **to get** to work. | *To* is the short form of *in order to*. |

**Note:**
The purpose phrase can come before the main clause. If so, we often use a comma after the purpose phrase.
> I need a car **to get** to work.
> **To get** to work, I need a car.

### GRAMMAR IN USE

*To* + verb is used to say why we do something. It gives the reason or purpose for an action. It can be used in any tense.

> Marilyn is calling **to invite** us for dinner.
> Jeff has gone to the store **to buy** some milk.
> I will call you tomorrow **to see** how you are.

All these statements answer the question *Why?*

**EXERCISE 15** Fill in the blanks with an infinitive to show purpose. Answers will vary.

1. I bought the Sunday newspaper _____(in order) to look for_____ a job.
2. I called the company _____ an appointment.
3. She wants to work overtime _____ more money.
4. You can use a résumé writing service _____ your résumé.
5. My job is in a distant suburb. I need a car _____ to work.
6. In the United States, you need experience _____ a job, and you need a job _____ experience.
7. You need to practice _____ well in an interview.
8. You should ask someone to read your résumé for you _____ sure you didn't make any mistakes in grammar or spelling.
9. You should try networking _____ your chances of finding a job.

# 10.11 Infinitives or Gerunds after Verbs

| EXAMPLES | EXPLANATION |
|---|---|
| I started **looking** for a job a month ago.<br>I started **to look** for a job a month ago. | We can follow these verbs with either a gerund or an infinitive with almost no difference in meaning: *begin, continue, like, love, prefer,* and *start*. |
| I was sleepy, so I **stopped (in order) to get** a cup of coffee.<br><br>I **stopped driving** to work. Now I take public transportation. | Following *stop* with a gerund or infinitive affects the meaning.<br>*Stop* + infinitive means "stop one activity in order to start something different."<br>*Stop* + gerund means "quit." |
| I **used to be** a teacher. Now I work in a hotel.<br><br>I'm **not used to talking** about my strengths, but that's what you have to do to find a job.<br><br>At first it was hard for me, but I finally **got used to working** at night. | *Used to* + base form tells about a past habit or custom. This habit or custom has been discontinued.<br>*Be used to* + gerund, noun, or pronoun means *be accustomed to.* Something is or was familiar to a person.<br>*Get used to* + gerund, noun, or pronoun means "become accustomed to." |

**Notes:**

1. The negative of *used to* + base form is *didn't use to.* (We remove the *d.*)

    I **didn't use to** drive to work.

2. The negative of *be* + *used to* + gerund, noun, or pronoun is *isn't/aren't/wasn't/weren't used to.* (We do not remove the *d.*)

    I'**m not used to** working on Saturdays.

3. The negative of *get/got used to* is usually *can't/couldn't get used to.*

    He **can't get used to** working at night.

---

\* For a list of verbs followed by either gerunds or infinitives, see Appendix D.

**EXERCISE 16** Circle the correct words to complete this story. In some cases, both choices are possible. If that's the case, circle both choices.

I was tired of driving to the office every day, so I started (*to use/using*) public transportation.
                                                                                            1.

But I was still wasting two hours a day. So my boss agreed to let me work from home a few days a

week. At first I had some difficulty. I (*wasn't used to being/didn't use to be*) alone all day, so I felt
                                                              2.

a bit lonely.

I had to get used to (*stick/sticking*) to a schedule. Every time the phone rang, I stopped
                                3.

(*to answer/answering*) it. Because I had a lot of work to do, I had to find a way to deal with
        4.

**278** Unit 10

personal phone calls. I decided to stop (*to answer/answering*) the phone completely until I was
5.
finished with my day's work. Now I return calls only in the evening.

I had the same problem with email and text messages. I usually prefer (*to answer/answering*) an
6.
email or text as soon as it comes in. But I was losing concentration. Now I stop (*to work/working*)
7.
every two hours, get a little exercise, answer my personal emails and texts, and then get back
to work.

Now (*I used to work/I'm used to working*) at home. I save time by not traveling, I save money
8.
on gas or public transportation, and I love (*to set/setting*) my own schedule.
9.

> ### FUN WITH GRAMMAR
>
> Write sentences with infinitives and gerunds. Get into teams. Your teacher will say a verb. Write a sentence using the verb + an infinitive or the verb + a gerund. The team with the most creative sentence wins the point.
>
> *stop* — We **stopped** on the way to school **to get** donuts for everyone.
> **Stop eating** my fries and get your own!

Working from home requires discipline, but can save you time and money.

# SUMMARY OF UNIT 10

## Gerunds

| EXAMPLES | USE OF GERUNDS |
|---|---|
| **Working** all day is hard. | As the subject of the sentence |
| I **like working** on a team. | As the object of the verb |
| I don't **enjoy working** as a taxi driver. | After certain verbs |
| I **go shopping** after work. | In many idiomatic expressions with *go* |
| I'm worried **about losing** my job. | After prepositions |

## Infinitives

| EXAMPLES | USE OF INFINITIVES |
|---|---|
| I **need to find** a new job. | After certain verbs |
| My boss wants **me to work** overtime. | After an object |
| I'm **ready to quit**. | After certain adjectives |
| It's **important to have** some free time. | After certain expressions beginning with *it* |
| I work **(in order) to support** my family. | To show purpose |

## Gerund or Infinitive—No Difference in Meaning

| GERUND | INFINITIVE |
|---|---|
| I like **working** with computers.<br>She began **working** at 8:30. | I like **to work** with computers.<br>She began **to work** at 8:30. |
| **Writing** a good résumé is important. | It's important **to write** a good résumé. |

## Gerund or Infinitive—Difference in Meaning

| EXAMPLES | USES |
|---|---|
| I **used to work** at night. Now I work in the day. | Past habit |
| I'**m used to working** at night. It's not a problem for me. | Customary activity |
| I stopped **to make** a personal phone call. | Stop in order to do something else |
| Stop **making** personal phone calls at work. The boss won't like it. | Quit completely |

# REVIEW

Fill in the blanks with the gerund or infinitive form of the verb given. In some cases, both a gerund and an infinitive are possible. Add a preposition where needed.

**A:** Hi, Molly. I haven't seen you in ages. What's going on in your life?

**B:** I've made many changes. First, I quit __working__ in a factory. I disliked
   1. work

__doing__ the same thing every day. And I wasn't used
   2. do

__to standing__ on my feet all day. My boss often wanted me __to work__
   3. stand                                                    4. work

overtime on Saturdays. I need __to be__ with my children on Saturdays.
   5. be

**A:** So what do you plan __to do__?
   6. do

**B:** I've started __taking__ some general courses at the community college.
   7. take

**A:** What career are you planning?

**B:** I'm not sure. I'm interested __in working__ with children. Maybe I'll become a teacher's
   8. work

aide. I've also thought __about working__ in a day-care center. I care
   9. work

__about helping__ people.
   10. help

**A:** It's important __to have__ a job that you like. So you're starting a whole new career.
   11. have

**B:** It's not new, really. I used __to be__ a kindergarten teacher back in my country.
   12. be

But my English wasn't very good when I came here, so I found a job in a factory. I look

forward __to going__ back to my former profession.
   13. go

**A:** How did you learn English so fast?

**B:** By __talking__ with people at work and __watching__ TV. But it
   14. talk                                         15. watch

hasn't been easy for me __to understand__ English. I studied formal English in my country,
   16. understand

but here I have to get used __to saying__ things like "gonna" and "wanna." I've had to
   17. say

make a lot of changes.

**A:** Let's get together sometime and talk some more.

**B:** I'd love to. Maybe we can go __shopping__ together sometime.
   18. shop

# FROM GRAMMAR TO WRITING

## PART 1  Editing Advice

1. Use a gerund after a preposition.

    He succeeded in ~~to get~~ *getting* a good job.

2. Use the correct preposition.

    She insisted ~~in~~ *on* helping me with my résumé.

3. Use a gerund after certain verbs.

    I enjoy ~~to~~ work*ing* with children.

4. Use an infinitive after certain verbs.

    I decided *to* quit my job.

5. Use a gerund, not a base form, as a subject.

    ~~Find~~ *Finding* a good job is important.

6. Don't forget to include *it* before certain adjectives.

    ~~Is~~ *It's* important to find a good job.

7. Don't use the past form after *to*.

    I decided to ~~saw~~ *see* a job counselor.

8. After *want, expect, need, advise,* and *ask*, use an object pronoun, not a subject pronoun, before the infinitive. Don't use *that* as a connector.

    He wants ~~that I~~ *me to* check the spelling on his résumé.

9. Use *for*, not *to*, when introducing an object after impersonal expressions beginning with *it*. Use the object pronoun after *for*.

    It's important ~~to they~~ *for them* to finish their project on time.

10. Use *to* + base form, not *for*, to show purpose.

    I called the company ~~for~~ *to* make an appointment.

11. Don't put *be* before *used to* for the habitual past.

    I ~~am~~ used to work in an office. Now I work in a hospital.

12. Don't use the *-ing* form after *used to* for the habitual past.

    She used to work~~ing~~ on Saturdays, but now she has Saturdays off.

13. Don't forget the *d* in *used to*.

    I use*d* to drive to work. Now I take public transportation.

## PART 2 Editing Practice

Some of the shaded words and phrases have mistakes. Find the mistakes and correct them. If the shaded words are correct, write C.

I'm planning **be** [to] a nurse. I'd love **to be** [C] a doctor, but I don't **want be** in school for so many
     1.                                    2.                              3.

years. My mother is a doctor, and she wanted **that I study** medicine, too. I know that you're never
                                              4.

too old to learn something new, but I'm 35 years old, and **start** something new at my age is not
                                                            5.

easy. **Study** medicine takes too long. It would take me eight years **become** a doctor. I went to my
       6.                                                               7.

college counselor **to get** advice. She **advised me take** biology and chemistry this semester as well
                    8.                    9.

as English and math. It's hard **to** me to take so many courses, but I have no choice.
                                10.

In my country, **I'm used to** work in a nursing home. I enjoyed **to help** older people, but I
                 11.                                                12.

didn't make enough money. When I decided **to came** to the U.S., I had to think about my future.
                                           13.

People say that **is not hard** **to find** a job as a nurse in the U.S. It's important **for** me to be in a
                  14.           15.                                                        16.

profession where I can help people. I can do that more quickly **by going** into a nursing program.
                                                                 17.

---

### WRITING TIP

Gerunds and infinitives are very common in writing. Gerunds are used as subjects and as objects of prepositions. Infinitives are most often used as objects of verbs. Be sure to include them in your writing.

If you choose prompt 1 below, you may use a gerund subject for your topic sentence and use prepositions + gerunds in your examples.

*Working in Italy is very different from working in the United States. In the U.S., people are **used to working** all the time. In Italy, people are **good about leaving** work at work and relaxing when home.*

For prompt 2, recall that *like/not like* can take a gerund or infinitive.

*At my last job, the work day started at 6:00 a.m. I **didn't like waking up** at 5:00 every morning, but I **liked to walk** to work while the city was still quiet.*

Incorporate a variety of verbs to express preferences (*enjoy, hate, dislike, prefer, appreciate*) but remember to check whether gerunds or infinitives or both can follow.

---

## PART 3 Write

Read the prompts. Choose one and write a paragraph about it.

1. Write about the differences between working in the U.S. and working in another country. You may write about coworkers, salary, vacation time, relationships with superiors, punctuality, or another topic about work that interests you.
2. Write about your current job or a job you had in the past. Tell what you like(d) or don't (didn't) like about that job.

## PART 4 Edit

Reread the Summary of Unit 10 and the editing advice. Edit your writing from Part 3.

UNIT
# 11
### Adjective Clauses

# MAKING CONNECTIONS

Participants of the Millennial Trains Project ride from Chicago to New York City, U.S.

> Many people will walk in and out of your life, but only true friends will leave footprints in your heart.
>
> ELEANOR ROOSEVELT

The North High School class of 1936 gathered for their 75th reunion in St. Louis Park, Minnesota, U.S.

# Reconnecting with Old Friends

**Read the following article. Pay special attention to the words in bold.** 11.1

Estimates show that Americans move about 11.3 times in their lifetimes. As a result, they often lose touch with old friends. Usually, during their twenties and thirties, people are too busy building their careers and starting their families to think much about the past. However, as people get older, they often start to wonder about the best friend **they had in high school**, the soldier **with whom they served in the military**, or the person **who lived next door** when they were growing up.

Before the Internet, finding an old friend required going to libraries to search through old phone books of different cities. It was hard work, and you needed a lot of luck. It was especially hard to find women **who changed their names when they got married**.

Then came the Web, **which made it possible to find someone in seconds**. A quick search on various social media sites, such as Facebook or Instagram, can help you find that old classmate or neighbor. In addition, there are several sites **where alumni[1] of a specific high school can include themselves according to the year they graduated**. Married women **who chose to change their names** list themselves by their maiden names[2] so that others can find them easily.

Another way **that people make connections with old friends** is through class reunions. Often people come from out of town for a reunion, **which can last for a whole weekend**: Friday evening in the high school **that they attended**, Saturday evening for a dinner in a restaurant or hotel, and a Sunday brunch. They remember the time **when they were young** and exchange information about what they are doing today. They sometimes bring their high school yearbooks, **which have photos of the graduates**, other students, and school activities.

It takes some effort to connect with old friends. Looking back at fond memories, renewing old friendships, making new friends, and even starting a new romance with an old love can be the reward.

---

[1] alumni: graduates or former students of a school
[2] maiden name: a woman's family name which she may or may not change when she marries

**COMPREHENSION** Based on the reading, write T for *true* or F for *false*.

1. _____ Americans in their twenties and thirties often reconnect with old friends.
2. _____ Women usually list their maiden names on high school websites.
3. _____ A yearbook is a book that shows the people who attended the reunion.

**THINK ABOUT IT** Discuss the questions with a partner or in a small group.

1. Think of a close friend from childhood that you have lost touch with. How could you find him or her again?
2. In your culture, do you have organized reunions with former classmates? Do you enjoy such events? Or would you enjoy such events if your schools had them?

## 11.1 Adjective Clauses—Overview

| EXAMPLES | EXPLANATION |
| --- | --- |
| Today it is common to find married women **who have not changed their names**.<br>What is the name of the high school **that you attended**? | An adjective clause is a group of words that contains a subject and verb. It describes or identifies the noun before it (*women, high school*). |

Notes:

1. *Who, whom, that, which, whose, where,* and *when* mark the beginning of an adjective clause.
   Sometimes an adjective clause begins with no marker.
   
   I have a lot of friends **who moved away after we graduated**.
   
   The friends **I had in high school** are married now. (no marker)

2. Some adjective clauses are set apart from the rest of the sentence with commas.
   
   I like to look at my yearbook, **which has photos of my classmates**.

3. An adjective clause can identify any noun in a sentence.
   
   Von Steuben High School, **which is located in Chicago**, is a science academy.
   
   I attended Von Steuben High School, **which is located in Chicago**.

4. Compare adjectives and adjective clauses. An adjective precedes a noun. An adjective clause follows a noun.
   
   I attended a **big** high school.
   
   I attended a high school **that has over 5,000 students**.

**EXERCISE 1** Listen to the article. Then write T for *true* or F for *false*. 🎧 11.2

1. _____ Americans don't typically move from location to location.
2. _____ Older people prefer to live in states with warmer climates.
3. _____ San Francisco doesn't need lower paid workers.

**EXERCISE 2** Listen again. Fill in the blanks with the words you hear. 🎧 11.2

Why do so many Americans lose touch with old friends ___that___ they had when they were
                                                        1.
younger? One reason is mobility. The average American will probably move more than 11 times in his or

her lifetime. Even though the number of people _____ move to a different state has gone
                                                    2.
down considerably since the 1950s, _____ 3.5 percent of households moved from state to
                                        3.
state, there are still a lot of people _____ move across state lines.
                                           4.

Some people move to states _____ the climate is better. The states _____
                                5.                                              6.
are losing the most population are in cold climates: New York, Illinois, New Jersey, and Connecticut. One

exception to this is North Dakota, _____ has very cold winter weather. It has a growing oil
                                       7.
industry and low unemployment, so it attracts young people who are looking for jobs. However, older

people usually want to live in states _____ have a good climate.
                                          8.

Some cities, such as San Francisco, attract high-paid professionals, _____ drive up the
                                                                         9.
cost of living. This makes it hard to attract lower-paid workers, such as construction workers,

_____ skills are just as important, but _____ don't earn enough to live in cities
    10.                                            11.
like San Francisco.

Washington, DC, is another place _____ attracts new residents. Washington was the
                                      12.
number one city Americans moved to in 2018. Most of them were young professionals _____
                                                                                       13.
were looking for work.

## 11.2 Relative Pronouns as Subjects

A relative pronoun can be the subject of the adjective clause.

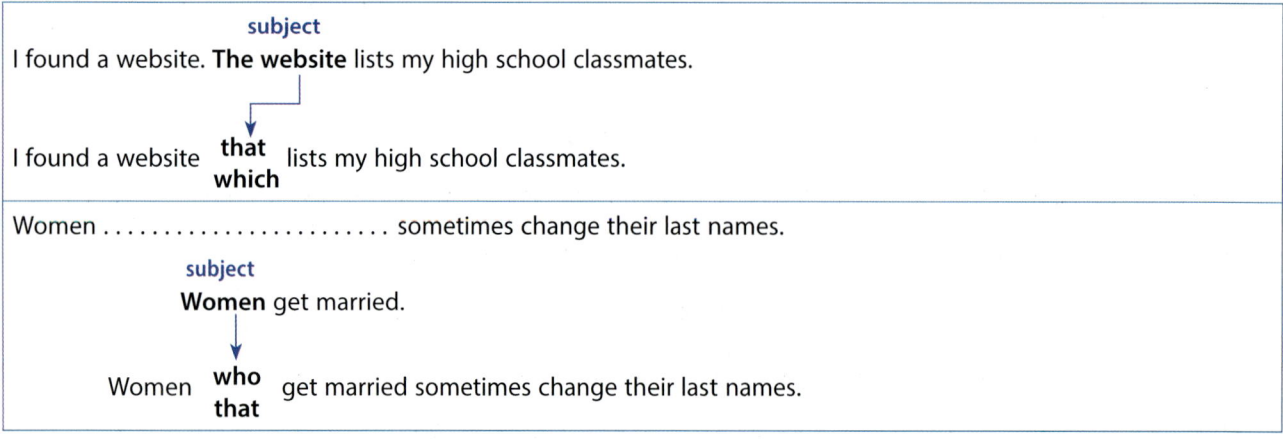

288   Unit 11

**Notes:**

1. The relative pronouns *who, that,* and *which* can be the subject of the adjective clause. Use *who* or *that* for people. Use *that* or *which* for things.
2. The verb in the adjective clause must agree in number with its subject.

   A **website** that **has** statistics needs to update its data frequently.

   **Websites** that **have** statistics need to update their data frequently.

**Punctuation Note:**

When the noun is unique, we set the adjective clause apart from the rest of the sentence with commas. We use only *who* and *which*; we don't use *that*.

   I want to move to a state **that has low unemployment**. (no comma)

   I want to move to North Dakota, **which has low unemployment**. (North Dakota is unique.)

---

### GRAMMAR IN USE

Adjective clauses are common in both written and spoken English. They make your writing and speech more fluent. Instead of using short, simple sentences to express an idea, try to combine ideas using adjective clauses. For example:

   *Juan comes from a small village. The village has only 210 residents.*
   ↓
   *Juan comes from a small village that has only 210 residents.*

---

**EXERCISE 3** Fill in the blanks with an adjective clause from the box.

| who have moved | that allows | who plan ✓ | who live | who have changed |
|---|---|---|---|---|
| who plays | that is convenient | that was popular | that will cover | |
| that is different | who can create | who have died | who graduated | |

Planning a reunion takes time and effort. People ___who plan___ a reunion start at least a
                                                      1.
year in advance. They form a committee of about 10 people. Each committee member has a task

_____ from the tasks of other committee members. For example, one
           2.

committe member needs to calculate a budget for the reunion activities. The reunion committee

will charge an amount of money _____ the cost of attending the various
                                                3.

activities. Another committee member is in charge of locating classmates. This is the hardest part,

so all members of the committee help. To find classmates, the committee uses phone books, word

of mouth, social media sites, and other websites to search. It is especially hard to find women

_____ their names. The committee has to find classmates
           4.

_____ nearby and classmates _____ away. Sadly,
           5.                                              6.

sometimes they even find some classmates _____.
                                                      7.

*continued*

The committee chooses someone _____8._____ a reunion website. A reunion website is something _____9._____ classmates to read about each others' lives.

The committee tries to set a date _____10._____ for most people. The committee hopes to find about 50 percent of the people _____11._____ with their class, but 25 percent is a more realistic number.

At the reunion dinner, there's often a DJ. This is a person _____12._____ recorded music. The DJ plays music _____13._____ when the students were in high school.

**ABOUT YOU** Fill in the blanks with *who* or *that* + a form of the verb given. Then complete the statement. Answers will vary.

1. most of the students __who graduated__ from my high school
   graduate
   Most of the students who graduated from my high school went to college.

2. friends __who moved__ to another state
   move
   I have several friends who moved to another state.

3. a classmate of mine _____ in life
   succeed
   _____

4. a social media site _____ photos of my friends
   have
   _____

5. the music _____ popular when I was in high school
   be
   _____

6. a person _____ next door to me when I was growing up
   live
   _____

7. classmates _____ to college
   go
   _____

8. a teacher _____ me
   inspire
   _____

## 11.3 Relative Pronouns as Objects

The relative pronoun can be the object of the adjective clause.

| |
|---|
| I contacted an old friend.<br>     **object**<br>  I found **my friend** on a social media site.<br>        who<br>I contacted an old friend **whom** I found on a social media site.<br>        that<br>        Ø |
|      **object**<br>  She attended **a high school**.<br>The high school . . . . . . . . . . . . . . is in New York City.<br>    which<br>The high school **that** she attended is in New York City.<br>    Ø |

**Notes:**

1. The relative pronouns *who(m), that,* and *which* can be the object of the adjective clause. In conversation, we usually omit the relative pronoun when it is the object of the adjective clause.

    *I contacted an old friend I found on a social media site.*
    *The high school she attended is in New York City.*

2. *Whom* is more formal than *who*. However, the relative pronoun is usually omitted altogether in conversation.

    *I reconnected with an old friend **who(m)** I saw at the reunion.*
    *I reconnected with an old friend I saw at the reunion.*

**Punctuation Note:**
When the noun is unique, we set the adjective clause apart from the rest of the sentence with commas. We use only *who* and *which*; we don't use *that*.

 *The high school **(that) she attended** is very small.* (no comma)
 *Taft High School, **which I attended from 1998–2002**, is very small.* (Taft High School is unique.)

---

**EXERCISE 4** Underline the adjective clause in each sentence.

1. I've lost touch with some of the friends <u>I had in high school</u>.

2. The high school I attended is in another city.

3. The teachers I had in high school are all old now.

4. We didn't have to buy the textbooks we used in high school.

5. My best friend married a man she met in college.

6. The friends I've made in this country don't know much about my country.

7. At the reunion, she saw a guy she dated in high school.

**EXERCISE 5** Fill in the blanks with a phrase from the box to complete the conversation between a mother and her teenage daughter.

| she hasn't seen | I had ✓ | she put | she wrote | she married | I have for them |
| they attended | we had | I made | you take | they graduated | |

**A:** I'd like to contact an old friend ____I had____ in high school. I wish I could find her. I'll never
                                            1.
forget the good times _____ back then. When we graduated, we said we'd always
                              2.
stay in touch. But then we went to different colleges.

**B:** Didn't you keep in touch by email?

**A:** When I was in college, email didn't exist. At first we wrote letters. But little by little, we wrote less and less
until, eventually, we stopped writing. I still have the letters _____ to me in a box in
                                                                          3.
the basement.

**B:** Why don't you write to the address on the letters?

**A:** That wouldn't work. The address _____ on the letters was of the college town where
                                              4.
she lived. I don't know what happened to her after she left college.

**B:** Have you tried calling her parents?

**A:** The phone number _____ is now disconnected. Maybe her parents have died.
                                5.

**B:** Why don't you try one of those classmates websites? There are websites with names of students categorized
by the high school _____ and the date _____.
                          6.                                          7.

**A:** But my friend probably got married. I don't know the last name of the man _____.
                                                                                              8.

**B:** That's not a problem. You can search for her by her maiden name on these sites.

**A:** If I find her, she'll probably think I'm crazy for contacting her almost 25 years later.

**B:** I'm sure she'll be happy to receive communication from a good friend _____ in
                                                                                          9.
years. When I graduate from high school, I'm never going to lose contact with the friends
_____. We'll always stay in touch.
        10.

**A:** That's what you think. But as time passes, your lives go in different directions, and you lose touch.

**B:** But today we have all kinds of social media.

**A:** Well, that's a help. Even so, the direction _____ in life is different from the direction
                                                              11.
your friends choose.

**EXERCISE 6** Fill in the blanks with appropriate words to complete the conversation. Answers may vary. You may use both subject and object relative pronouns. Remember: You can omit an object relative pronoun.

**A:** I'm lonely. I have a lot of friends in my native country, but I don't have enough friends here. The friends <u>(that) I have there</u> send me email and photos all the time, but that's not enough. I need to make
               **1.**

new friends here.

**B:** Haven't you met any people here?

**A:** Of course. But the people _____ here don't share my interests. I like reading,
                             **2.**

meditating, and going for quiet walks. Americans seem to like parties, TV, sports, movies, and going to

restaurants.

**B:** You're never going to meet people with the interests _____. Your interests don't
                                                **3.**

include other people. You need some interests _____ other people, like tennis or
                                       **4.**

dancing, to mention just a few.

**A:** The activities _____ cost money, and I don't have much.
                  **5.**

**B:** There are many parks in this city _____ free tennis courts. If you like to dance, I
                                 **6.**

know of a park district near here _____ free dance classes. In fact, there are a lot of
                                **7.**

things _____ in this city. I can give you a list, if you want.
        **8.**

**A:** Thanks. I appreciate the suggestions _____ me.
                              **9.**

**B:** Tomorrow I'll email you a list of interesting activities. I'm sure you'll find something

_____ on that list.
      **10.**

**ABOUT YOU** Use the words given to write a sentence. Discuss your answers with a partner.

1. the high school I attended

   <u>The high school I attended was very small.</u>

   OR

   <u>I can show you a photo of the high school I attended.</u>

2. the kids I knew in high school

   _____

*continued*

3. the teachers I had in high school

   _____

4. the subject I liked best in high school

   _____

5. the way I stay in touch with old friends

   _____

6. the best friend I had in high school

   _____

7. the social media I use

   _____

8. the friends I had when I was a child

   _____

9. the activities I liked in high school

   _____

10. the way I meet people now

    _____

### FUN WITH GRAMMAR

Define people, places, and things. Form two teams. Team A thinks of a person, place, or thing. Team B works together to define it using an adjective clause. Then switch roles. For each correct sentence, the team earns a point. The team with the most points wins.

*Team A: a giraffe*

*Team B: A giraffe is an animal that has a long neck and eats leaves.*

Members of a Meetup group gather to watch birds.

# MAKING CONNECTIONS USING MEETUP

Read the following article. Pay special attention to the words in bold.

Would you like to meet people **whose** interests are the same as yours? Maybe you like to knit and would like to meet with other knitters. Or maybe you're interested in the theater and want to find people **with whom** you can attend a play. A website called Meetup lets you do that. Unlike most social networking groups, **whose** members communicate with each other online, Meetup members actually meet each other in person. Most Meetup members want to get together just for fun: to play chess, discuss books, ride their bikes, practice French, etc. Some Meetups are support groups: people get together with others who have the same problem. For example, there are Meetups of people who have lost a spouse, or parents **whose** children have a serious disease. Other Meetup groups are for the purpose of career networking. As of 2019, there were about 39 million Meetup members in almost 200 countries.

Meetup was the brainchild[1] of Scott Heiferman, **whose** idea for creating these communities came as a result of the September 11, 2001 attacks in the United States. Heiferman stated that the manner **in which** the people of New York City came together in the aftermath[2] of that traumatic[3] event inspired him. He wanted to make it easy for people to connect with strangers in their own community. He created Meetup in 2002.

Meetup connects people online so that they can meet offline. Anyone can start a Meetup. Meetup believes that "people can change their personal world, or the whole world, by organizing themselves into groups that are powerful enough to make a difference."

---

[1] brainchild: an important idea or project of a person
[2] aftermath: the result of a tragic event
[3] traumatic: psychologically harmful

Adjective Clauses

**COMPREHENSION** Based on the reading, write T for *true* or F for *false*.

1. _____ Meetup members first make contact online.
2. _____ All Meetup groups are for the purpose of having fun together.
3. _____ Scott Heiferman got his idea for Meetup after the tragedy of September 11, 2001.

**THINK ABOUT IT** Discuss the questions with a partner or in a small group.

1. Think of an interest or hobby you have. Do you think there is a Meetup for that? Would you be interested in joining such a Meetup? If there isn't such a Meetup, would you like to create such a group? Why or why not?
2. Read the quote at the end of the article. In what ways do you think Meetup members are able to make a difference?

## 11.4 Relative Pronouns as Objects of Prepositions

A relative pronoun can be the object of a preposition.

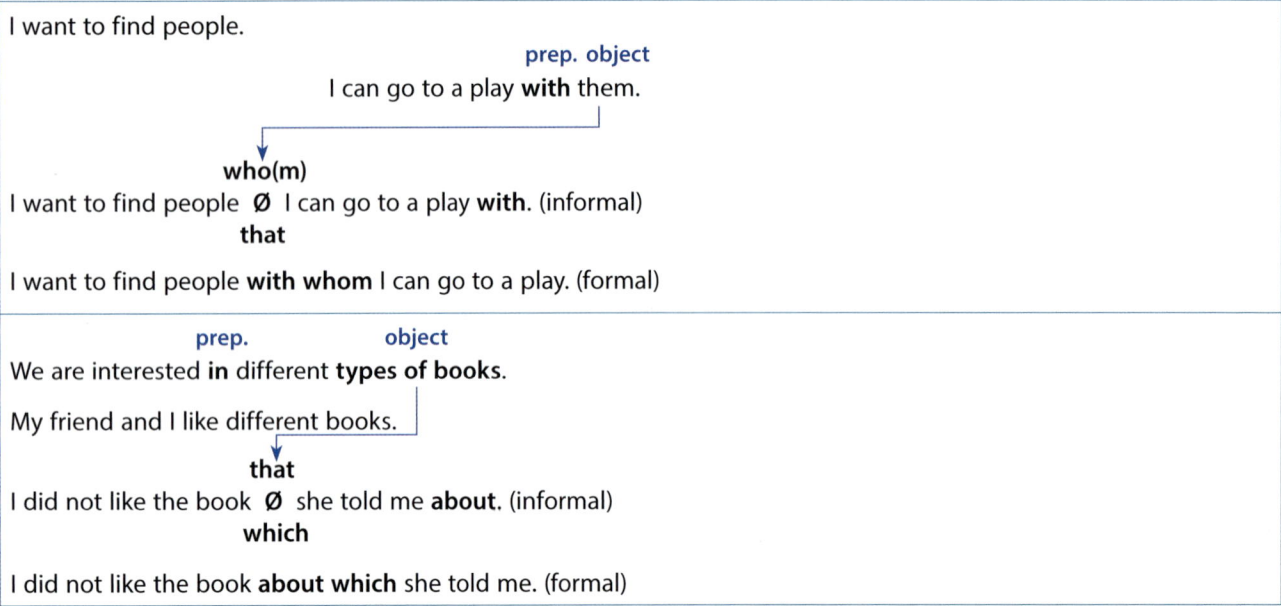

**Notes:**

1. Informally, we put the preposition at the end of the adjective clause. The relative pronoun is usually omitted. The most common way to say the above sentences is:

    *I want to find people I can go to a play **with**.*    *I did not enjoy the book you told me **about**.*

2. In very formal English, the preposition comes before the relative pronoun, and only *whom* and *which* may be used. *That* and *who* are not used directly after a preposition.

    *I want to find people **with whom** I can go to a play.* (NOT *with who* or *with that*)
    *I did not enjoy the book **about which** you told me.* (NOT *about that*)

**Punctuation Notes:**

1. When the adjective clause is not essential to identify the noun, we set it apart from the rest of the sentence with commas.

    *Heiferman, **who(m) we read about**, is a member of a Meetup.* (We know who Heiferman is without the adjective clause.)

2. A nonessential adjective clause begins with *who, whom, which, where, when,* or *whose*. We don't use *that*.

**EXERCISE 7** Change these sentences to make them more informal.

1. I'd like to find people with whom I can go hiking.

   I'd like to find people I can go hiking with.

2. A woman with whom I work started a Meetup for young Hispanic professionals.

3. Scott Heiferman, about whom we read, is a member of a parents' Meetup.

4. He pays attention to the Meetups for which people are signing up.

5. People want to get together with others with whom they share a common interest.

6. The office in which Scott works is located in New York City.

**EXERCISE 8** Change these sentences to make them more formal.

1. What is the name of the high school you graduated from?

   What is the name of the high school from which you graduated?

2. He found a friend that he served in the military with.

3. I can't find the friend I was looking for.

4. The high school she graduated from was torn down.

5. Do you remember the teacher I was talking about?

6. In high school, the activities I was interested in were baseball and band.

## 11.5 Whose + Noun

*Whose* is the possessive form of *who*. It represents *his, her, its, their,* or the possessive form of the noun.

| |
|---|
| I want to meet people. |
|                         **Their** interests are the same as mine. |
| I want to meet people **whose** interests are the same as mine. |
| Scott . . . . . . . . . . . . . . . . . . . . . gets together with other parents of small children. |
|     **Scott's** children are small. |
| Scott, **whose** children are small, gets together with other parents of small children. |

**Note:**
We use *who* to substitute for a person. We use *whose* for possession or relationship.
    *I want to meet people **who** are interested in sports.*
    *I want to meet people **whose** interests are the same as mine.*

**Punctuation Note:**
When the adjective clause is not essential to identify the noun, we set it apart from the rest of the sentence with commas.
    *Heiferman, **whose office is in New York**, created Meetup after September 11th.* (We know who Heiferman is without the adjective clause.)

---

**EXERCISE 9** Fill in the blanks with *whose* + a word from the box.

| | | |
|---|---|---|
| jobs | last name | inspiration |
| family | interests ✓ | members |

1. Do you want to meet people ___whose interests___ are the same as yours?

2. I joined a French Meetup _____ speak French very well.

3. People _____ keep them busy don't always have the time or energy to get together with friends.

4. I lost touch with an old friend _____ moved to another state.

5. I'm looking for a woman _____ used to be Carter. She changed it when she got married.

6. Scott Heiferman, _____ came from the way people came together after the 9/11 tragedy, started Meetup in 2002.

**EXERCISE 10** Some people were asked what kind of friends they'd like to meet. Fill in the blanks with a response, using the words given.

1. I'd like to meet people <u>whose values are the same as mine</u>.
   Their values are the same as mine.

2. My math group is a club _____.
   I found it through Meetup.

3. I'd like to find a friend _____.
   I can trust that friend.

4. I don't want to be with people _____.
   They don't take life seriously.

5. I want to meet people _____.
   They like to play soccer.

6. I joined a Spanish Meetup _____.
   Its members speak Spanish very well.

7. We meet in a coffee shop _____.
   It isn't crowded in the morning.

8. I go to a book club Meetup _____.
   It meets at my local library.

9. There's a Meetup for divorced people _____.
   They have children.

10. I go to a Meetup for parents _____.
    Their children are deaf.

11. The Meetup _____ has about 50 members.
    I go to it.

12. The person _____ is a nice woman I met at a Meetup.
    I play tennis with her.

13. People _____ interest me.
    Their political views are similar to mine.

14. Neighbors _____ have a lot in common with me.
    The neighbors have small children.

---

**GRAMMAR IN USE**

We don't use an adjective clause when we can simply use an adjective.

*I like books **that are educational**.* (not needed: *I like educational books*.)

*We met many people **who were interesting**.* (not needed: *We met many interesting people*.)

When you cannot use an adjective, use an adjective clause.

*I like books **that have beautiful photos**.* (needed)

# The SCIENCE of FRIENDSHIP

Read the following article. Pay special attention to the words in bold. 🎧 11.4

"I still remember the day **when we met**," says Alexa Martinez of her best friend Gabby Rivero. "It was in 2014, **when we were in high school**. Gabby sat in front of me in math class. At first, we didn't talk much. But later that year, **when we were both in the school play**, we became friends."

Like many people, Alexa and Gabby became friends for two main reasons. One was proximity. Research shows that we make friends with people who are nearby. (The person might be in a class with you at school or in the same office **where you work**.) Later, Alexa and Gabby were both in the school play, and they discovered a shared interest: acting. If two people have something in common[1], this also increases the possibility that they will be friends.

To become *close* friends with another person, though, two other factors are important. First, the two people should be able to share personal feelings and information with each other. A good friend will also be there to listen and offer help at times **when the other person needs it**.

Alexa recalls how she and Gabby became close friends. "Acting in the play was really hard," she says. "There were times **when I thought about quitting**. I never told other people this, but I could always talk to Gabby. She was very supportive[2]. She said things like, 'Acting is hard, but you're really good at it. I get nervous, too.'"

Both Alexa and Gabby needed extra practice, so they decided to meet and study their lines together after school. "There was a café **where we went** every day," Alexa recalls. "In time, we became good friends. After the school play ended, we continued to hang out[3]—and even now, we're still very close."

---

[1] to have something in common: to have similar interests or beliefs as another person
[2] supportive: helpful and kind
[3] to hang out: to spend time relaxing and enjoying oneself

**COMPREHENSION** Based on the reading, write T for *true* or F for *false*.

1. _____ Alexa and Gabby met and became friends in a high school math class.
2. _____ Most people become friends with another person because they don't want to be alone.
3. _____ According to the reading, a *close friend* is someone that we can talk to about personal things and who helps us in hard times.

**THINK ABOUT IT** Discuss the questions with a partner or in a small group.

1. Think of one of your good friends. How did you meet and become friends?
2. How does this person fit the definition of a close friend given in the passage? Give an example.

## 11.6 Adjective Clauses with *Where* and *When*

Some adjective clauses begin with the relative adverbs *where* and *when*.

| EXAMPLES | EXPLANATION |
| --- | --- |
| Alexa met Gabby at Woodside High, **where they went to high school**.<br>There was a café **where they went every day**. | *Where* means "in that place." |
| "I still remember the day **(when) we met**," says Alexa.<br>"It was in 2014, **when we were in high school**." | *When* means "at that time." |

**Punctuation Note:**
When the adjective clause is not essential to identify the noun, we set it apart from the rest of the sentence with commas.

> They went to Java House, **where they studied**. (We don't need the adjective clause to identify the place.)
>
> We met on the first day of school, **when we were in high school**. (We don't need the adjective clause to identify the day.)

We can omit *when* in a sentence with no comma. We cannot omit *where*.

---

**EXERCISE 11** Two friends are talking about how they met. Write each adjective clause in the correct place to complete the dialogue.

when we were studying      when we met ✓
where we took that class      where we could buy hot tea
when it was very cold      when I passed the TOEFL
where we're going to college

**A:** I still remember the day ___when we met___.
                                                   1.

**B:** Me, too. It was in 2016, _____ for the TOEFL. You sat next to me in a test prep class.
                                                       2.

*continued*

**A:** That's right! Do you remember the school _____?
3.

**B:** Yeah, it was terrible. The rooms had no heating, and we were there in the winter, _____.
4.

**A:** I know. Luckily the school had a café _____. It was the only way to stay warm.
5.

**B:** You know, I'll never forget the day _____. I was so happy.
6.

**A:** I know. And now we're both in the U.S. _____!
7.

**EXERCISE 12** Fill in the blanks with *who, whom, that, which, when, where, whose,* or Ø for no word. Sometimes more than one answer is possible.

**A:** I'm getting married next month.

**B:** Congratulations! Are you marrying the woman ___that or Ø___ you met at Mark's party last year?
1.

**A:** Oh, no. My fiancée is the woman _____ I introduced you to last week.
2.

**B:** Oh, yeah. Now I remember. What's her name again?

**A:** Sara Liston.

**B:** I know someone _____ last name is Liston. I wonder if they're related. So how did you meet?
3.

**A:** Actually, we met in 2012 _____ we were in college. We were just friends.
4.

Then earlier this year, I saw Sara at a Meetup _____ we reconnected.
5.

**B:** What kind of Meetup was it?

**A:** It's for people _____ like movies. We watch a film, and then we have a meal after and discuss it.
6.

**B:** Sounds fun.

**A:** You should join. I'll send you a text _____ has information about the next movie _____ we're going to see and the time _____ we're going to get together.
7.     8.     9.

302  Unit 11

**ABOUT YOU** Use the words given to form an adjective clause. Then tell a partner if you agree or disagree. Give your reasons.

1. My friends are people _(whom) I can trust with all my secrets_.
   I can trust them with all my secrets.

2. A good friend is a person _____ almost every day.
   I see him.

3. My best friend is a person _____.
   He knows everything about me.

4. Most of my friends are people _____.
   They speak my native language.

5. This school is a place _____.
   I can make many new friends easily here.

6. It is hard to be friends with a person _____.
   His political views are different from mine.

7. Childhood is the only time _____.
   It is easy to make friends then.

8. I still remember the place _____.
   I met my best friend there.

9. I don't remember the day _____.
   I met my best friend then.

10. I want to return to the country _____.
    I was born there.

> **FUN WITH GRAMMAR**
>
> Play *Find Someone Who*… Complete these sentences using adjective clauses. Then go around your classroom and find someone who agrees with each statement. Write his or her name on the line under the statement. The person to finish first wins the game.
>
> 1. My closest friends are people _____.
>
> 2. My favorite activity is one _____.
>
> 3. My favorite childhood memory is one _____.
>
> 4. The café I go to most often is one _____.
>
> 5. I like a school _____.
>
> 6. My favorite kind of movies are ones _____.

# SUMMARY OF UNIT 11

**Adjective Clauses with:**

### RELATIVE PRONOUNS AS SUBJECTS

I lost touch with a friend **who/that moved to Alaska**.
A high school **that/which has a strong science program** attracts good students.
Scott Heiferman, **who created Meetup**, wants to connect people.
North Dakota, **which has cold winters**, has attracted people looking for jobs.

### RELATIVE PRONOUNS AS OBJECTS

I have a new friend **who/whom/that/Ø I met at a Meetup**.
The high school **that/which/Ø I attended** is not very big.
My wife, **who/whom I met at a math Meetup**, is a teacher.
My tenth high school reunion, **which I attended last year**, was at a hotel.

### RELATIVE PRONOUNS AS OBJECTS OF PREPOSITIONS

| | |
|---|---|
| FORMAL: | Some of the friends **with whom I went to high school** moved away. |
| INFORMAL: | Some of the friends **who(m)/that/Ø I went to high school with** moved away. |
| FORMAL: | The Meetup **about which I told you** meets at a neighborhood café. |
| INFORMAL: | The Meetup **that/which/Ø I told you about** meets at a neighborhood café. |

### RELATIVE PRONOUNS FOR POSSESSION

I have a friend **whose brother lives in Japan**.
Scott Heiferman, **whose inspiration came from the aftermath of 9/11**, created Meetup to bring people together.

### RELATIVE ADVERBS FOR PLACE

I like to visit the city **where I went** to college.
Boston, **where I went to college**, is cold in the winter.

### RELATIVE ADVERBS FOR TIME

My friends and I get together in a café at a time **when/Ø it isn't crowded**.
We get together on Monday at 4 o'clock, **when the café isn't crowded**.

# REVIEW

Fill in the blanks with *who, whom, that, which, whose, where, when,* or Ø. In some cases, more than one answer is possible.

1. I'm still friends with the people  <u>who or whom or that or Ø</u>  I met in high school.

2. The high school _____ I attended is in Poland.

3. Most of the people with _____ I went to high school still live in our hometown.

4. Childhood is the time _____ it's easiest to make friends.

5. There are some teachers _____ names I've forgotten.

6. A coffee shop near my house is the place _____ my chess Meetup gets together.

7. I use several social networking sites _____ allow me to exchange information with my friends.

8. Scott Heiferman, _____ started his first company when he was 23, worked at a fast-food restaurant to get back in touch with real people.

9. Heiferman started Meetup in 2002, _____ he was 30 years old.

10. Silicon Valley, _____ is the center of technology, is in California.

11. The high school from _____ I graduated has around 5,000 students.

12. My sister married Mark Peters, _____ she met at a Meetup.

# FROM GRAMMAR TO WRITING

## PART 1  Editing Advice

1. Use *who* or *that* to introduce a person. Use *that* or *which* to introduce a thing.

    The states ~~what~~ **that** are losing the most population are in cold climates.

    I have many friends ~~which~~ **who** go to Meetups.

2. If the relative pronoun is the subject of the adjective clause, don't omit it.

    She started a group ∧**that** now has 100 members.

3. Use *whose* to substitute for a possessive form.

    Gabby, ~~her~~ **whose** father was an actor, hopes to find work in movies.

4. If the relative pronoun is used as the object of the adjective clause, don't put an object after the verb of the adjective clause.

    There are a lot of interesting Meetups that I found ~~them~~.

5. Use subject-verb agreement in the adjective clause.

    I have a friend who live**s** in Madrid.

6. Put a noun before an adjective clause.

    **A person who** ~~Who~~ has a few good friends is lucky.

7. Use *where*, not *that*, to mean "in a place."

    She moved to North Dakota, ~~that~~ **where** she found a good job.

8. Use *whom* and *which*, not *who* and *that*, if the preposition precedes the relative pronoun.

    He found a group in ~~that~~ **which** he's interested.

    I've never met the person about ~~who~~ **whom** you are talking.

9. Use the correct word order in an adjective clause (subject before verb).

    The first play that ~~acted in Gabby~~ **Gabby acted in** was at her high school.

10. Don't confuse *whose* (possessive form) and *who's* (*who is*).

    A woman ~~whose~~ **who's** in my science Meetup teaches biology at a high school.

## PART 2  Editing Practice

Some of the shaded words and phrases have mistakes. Find the mistakes and correct them. If the shaded words are correct, write C.

I would like to find one of the friends that **C** I had in college. I found a website ~~that~~ **where** I can look
                                                        **1.**                                                **2.**
for old friends. My friend, whose name is Linda Gast, got married shortly after we graduated.
                              **3.**
The man which she married is Bart Reed. I tried googling the names "Linda Gast" and "Linda
         **4.**
Reed," but I had no luck. I found a woman with who she shared a room in college, and she gave
                                                **5.**

306  Unit 11

me a phone number. The phone number **that gave me her roommate** is not in service anymore.
6.  7.

I called a man **what** used to be her neighbor, but he said that she moved away a long time ago.
8.

The last reunion **that** I attended **it** was four years ago, but she wasn't there. The **people were** our
9.  10.  11.

friends in high school didn't know anything about her. I looked in the phone book and found

some people **their** name is the same as hers, but they weren't the right people. I went back to the
12.

high school **that** she was a student, but they had no information about her.
13.

    Because of the Internet, now is a time **when** it's easier than ever to find people. But my
14.

search, **which have** taken me almost five years, has produced no result. Recently I met someone
15.  16.

**whose** a friend of her brother, and he told me that Linda's now living in South America. He's
17.

going to try to find Linda's current address. Looking for Linda is hard, but I'm determined to find

her. **Who** tries hard enough usually succeeds.
18.

> ### WRITING TIP
> Using a variety of adjectives and adjective clauses to describe nouns will make your writing more interesting. If you are writing about friendships (prompt 1), you might want to describe the kinds of people you were friends with when you were younger compared to now:
>
> > When I was younger, my friends were people **who were in the drama club**. Now my friends are people **who have young children like me**.
>
> If you are writing about two types of relationships (prompt 2), you could describe the differences between the two:
>
> > At work, I'm friendly with people **who are serious and reliable**. When I'm away from work, I prefer to spend time with people **who are relaxed and fun to be around**.

## PART 3  Write
Read the prompts. Choose one and write a paragraph about it.

1. Compare the friendships you have today with the friendships you had when you were younger.
2. Compare your social relationships with your work relationships.

## PART 4  Edit
Reread the Summary of Unit 11 and the editing advice. Edit your writing from Part 3.

UNIT
# 12
**Superlatives
Comparatives**

# SPORTS and ATHLETES

2,300 athletes, and one green sea turtle, await the start of the 140.6-mile race at the Ironman World Championship triathlon in Kailua Kona, Hawaii, U.S.

> Obstacles don't have to stop you. If you run into a wall, don't turn around and give up. Figure out how to climb it, go through it, or work around it.
>
> MICHAEL JORDAN

# GREGG TREINISH  Extreme Athlete and Conservationist

Read the following article. Pay special attention to the words in bold.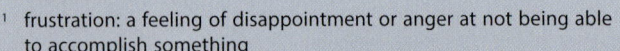

Gregg Treinish is an adventurer who turned his love of physical challenges into something more.

In 2004, Treinish hiked the Appalachian Trail, one of **the longest** footpaths in the world, measuring about 2,180 miles (3,508 km) in length. This path follows through 14 states from Maine to Georgia. Maryland and West Virginia are **the easiest** states to hike. New Hampshire and Maine are **the most difficult**. While Treinish was hiking one of **the hardest** parts, he kept slipping and cutting his legs on the sharp rock. In frustration[1], he picked up a rock and threw it at a tree. "I felt like **the lowest** person on earth," he said, for being on this adventure purely for his own experience. He knew he wanted to do something more, but he didn't know what that was.

Then he and his friend, Deia Schlosberg, spent two years hiking 7,800 miles from Ecuador to Tierra del Fuego, following along the Andes Mountains, **the longest** mountain chain in the world. When they arrived, they commented that Tierra del Fuego was one of **the most spectacular** places on Earth.

In 2008, National Geographic named Gregg Treinish Adventurer of the Year. But he wasn't fulfilled[2]. He felt his **biggest** challenge was in his mind. He began asking himself: Is it enough to hike **the longest, most difficult** trails? Am I doing anything to help the world? How can I turn my adventures into something more beneficial?

Treinish had an idea: He thought that scientists might need information from hard-to-reach places where only **the bravest** adventurers go. And he was right. Scientists want data, samples, and photographs from **the most remote** places on Earth—places that they can't go to themselves. Treinish founded Adventurers and Scientists for Conservation (ASC) to connect scientists with extreme adventurers. Now, when athletes go to these unusual places, they can do something to benefit the world by collecting information for scientists. Several thousand adventurers have collected data with ASC.

ASC mountain climbers have discovered Earth's **highest** known plant life on Mount Everest and have brought back samples for researchers to study. These samples help farmers learn to grow crops in extreme conditions.

For Treinish, connecting science and outdoor adventure is **the most satisfying** kind of adventure. "Adventurers tell me these chances to give back have changed their whole perspective[3]. Now, being **the strongest** or summiting **the coolest** peak[4] isn't what's important. Trying to contribute and make a difference is what matters. And there's so much more we can do."

---

[1] frustration: a feeling of disappointment or anger at not being able to accomplish something
[2] fulfilled: satisfied
[3] perspective: a way of seeing things; point of view
[4] to summit a peak: to reach the top of a mountain

Gregg Treinish takes measurements while Jason Wilmot records them. They concluded that these tracks in Mongolia were made by a snow leopard.

**COMPREHENSION** Based on the reading, write T for *true* or F for *false*.

1. _____ The difficulty of the Appalachian Trail changes as a hiker goes from state to state.
2. _____ Gregg Treinish hiked along the Andes Mountains alone.
3. _____ Gregg's goal is to connect adventurers with each other.

**THINK ABOUT IT** Discuss the questions with a partner or in a small group.

1. Reread Gregg's questions: "Am I doing anything to help the world? How can I turn my adventures into something more beneficial?" Is there something in your life you could do to benefit the world?
2. What jobs might Gregg's organization have? Which ones would you be interested in?

## 12.1 The Superlative Forms of Adjectives and Adverbs

|  | SIMPLE | SUPERLATIVE |
|---|---|---|
| One-syllable adjectives and adverbs | long<br>big | the longest<br>the biggest |
| Two-syllable adjectives that end in *y* | easy<br>happy | the easiest<br>the happiest |
| Other two-syllable adjectives | remote<br>extreme | the most remote<br>the most extreme |
| Some two-syllable adjectives have two forms | simple<br><br>polite | the simplest<br>the most simple<br>the politest<br>the most polite |
| Adjectives with three or more syllables | spectacular<br>difficult | the most spectacular<br>the most difficult |
| *-ly* adverbs | quickly<br>directly | the most quickly<br>the most directly |
| Irregular superlatives | good/well<br>bad/badly<br>far | the best<br>the worst<br>the farthest |
| Quantity words | little<br>few | the least<br>the fewest |
|  | a lot<br>much<br>many | the most |

**Notes:**

1. Other two-syllable adjectives that have two forms are:
   *handsome, quiet, gentle, narrow, clever, friendly, angry, common, stupid*
2. Adjectives that are past participles use *the most*.
   *tired—the most tired*
   *fulfilled—the most fulfilled*
   *worried—the most worried*

**EXERCISE 1** Listen to the conversation about Emma Gatewood, another amazing athlete. Then write T for *true* or F for *false*. 🎧 12.2

1. _____ Emma Gatewood was never in the Olympics.

2. _____ Emma Gatewood's grandmother hiked the Appalachian trail.

3. _____ Emma Gatewood relied on wild food in addition to the dried food she carried with her.

**EXERCISE 2** Listen to the conversation again. Fill in the blanks with the words you hear. 🎧 12.2

A: I just read an article about one of _the most interesting_ athletes.
                                            1.

B: Was it about Michael Phelps? He's one of _____ swimmers in the world.
                                              2.

A: No. It was about a woman.

B: Was it Katie Ledecky? She was one of _____ female swimmers at the 2016
                                           3.
Olympics. I liked her _____ of all the female swimmers that year.
                         4.

A: No. This woman was never at the Olympics. Her name was Emma Gatewood. She was the first woman to hike the Appalachian Trail solo—at the age of 67! People often called her "Grandma Gatewood." She believed that hikers should carry _____ equipment possible. She wasn't
                                                   5.
interested in taking _____ equipment for her hike. She took a homemade bag
                        6.
and carried a blanket, a raincoat, and a shower curtain.

B: A shower curtain? What for?

A: She used it to make a tent.

B: That's _____ thing I've ever heard!
             7.

A: She believed in doing things _____ way possible.
                                   8.

B: And _____ way possible, too. What about food?
          9.

A: She carried some dried food, but she did _____ she could to find wild food.
                                                10.

B: She was quite a woman!

A: Yes, she was. She hiked the Appalachian Trail again at the age of 75. At that time, she was
_____ woman to hike the trail.
   11.

B: I've read stories of several athletes, but I like her story _____.
                                                                   12.
She inspires me _____.
                    13.

A: Me, too. She's one of _____ athletes I've ever read about.
                            14.

**EXERCISE 3** Write the superlative of each word.

1. fat — _the fattest_
2. important — _the most important_
3. interesting — _____
4. good — _____
5. responsible — _____
6. thin — _____
7. carefully — _____
8. bad — _____
9. famous — _____
10. lucky — _____
11. simple — _____
12. extreme — _____
13. far — _____
14. bored — _____

## 12.2 Superlatives—Use

| EXAMPLES | EXPLANATION |
| --- | --- |
| The Andes is **the longest** mountain chain in the world. What is **the most difficult** part of the Appalachian Trail? | We use the superlative form to point out the number one item(s) of a group of three or more. |
| Treinish hiked **some of the most difficult** trails. Gatewood was **one of the most remarkable** hikers. | We often say *one/some of the* before a superlative form. The noun that follows is plural. |
| Mt. Everest is **the highest** mountain **in the world**. The Appalachian Trail is not **the longest** trail **in the United States**. | We often put a prepositional phrase after a superlative phrase: *in the world, of all time, in the U.S.*, etc. |
| The north part of the Appalachian Trail is **the least challenging**. | You can use *the least* to make a superlative. |
| What is the most spectacular place **(that) you've ever seen**? | An adjective clause with the present perfect and *ever* often completes a superlative statement. |
| In 2016, **one of the fastest swimmers** in the world was Katie Ledecky. Michael Phelps won **the most medals** at the 2016 Olympics. | A superlative form can precede any noun in the sentence. |
| Grandma Gatewood inspires me **the most**. I like her story **the best**. | A superlative form can follow a verb (phrase). |

**Notes:**

1. Use *the* before a superlative form. Omit *the* if there is a possessive form before a superlative.
   
   What was *your most challenging* adventure? (NOT: *your the most challenging*)

2. When the verb *be* connects a noun to a superlative adjective + noun, there are two possible word orders:
   
   *Football is the most popular sport in the U.S.*
   
   *The most popular sport in the U.S. is football.*

**EXERCISE 4** Write the superlative form of the word given.

1. At age 15, Michael Phelps was  __the youngest__  American male swimmer in 68 years to make
   <sub>young</sub>
   an Olympic team.

2. At the 2008 Olympics, he broke a record set in 1972, making him _____ swimmer
   <sub>fast</sub>
   ever for that event.

3. Many people think Michael Phelps was _____ athlete at the 2012 Olympics.
   <sub>exciting</sub>

4. A popular sports magazine named Phelps _____ sportsman of the year in 2008.
   <sub>good</sub>

5. At the 2012 Olympics in London, he was _____ swimmer.
   <sub>successful</sub>

6. He won _____ medals at the 2012 Olympics.
   <sub>a lot</sub>

7. Will anyone take his place? Or will he always be _____ swimmer of all time?
   <sub>great</sub>

**ABOUT YOU** Give your opinion. Write a superlative sentence about each of the following items. Then compare your answers to a partner's.

1. popular athlete in my country

   Manny Pacquiao is one of the most popular athletes in my country.

2. boring sport

   _____

3. interesting sport

   _____

4. good athlete

   _____

5. bad thing about (*name a sport*)

   _____

6. popular sport in my country

   _____

7. easy sport for children

   _____

8. challenging sport

   _____

9. dangerous adventure

   _____

**ABOUT YOU** Use the words to write superlative sentences about your experiences. Use the present perfect form with *ever* after the superlative. Share your answers with a partner.

1. long/distance/walk

   <u>My hike through the Alps was the longest distance I've ever walked.</u>

2. interesting/sporting event/see

3. dangerous/thing/do

4. difficult/sport/play

5. good/athlete/see

6. challenging/thing/do

> **FUN WITH GRAMMAR**
>
> Describe your classmates. Form groups of at least three. Take five minutes to write as many superlative sentences as you can to describe the people in your group (e.g., *This person is the most adventurous. This person is the tallest. This person is the funniest.*). Then share them with the class. The class will try to guess which person each sentence describes.

At age 35, Norway's Aksel Lund Svindal became the oldest Olympic alpine skiing champion with his win in 2018. Norway won the most medals (39) at the 2018 Winter Olympics in PyeongChang, South Korea.

# Americans' Attitude toward Soccer

Fans cheer on the U.S. Women's National Team in Los Angeles, California. This was the seventh "Countdown to the Cup" game ahead of the 2019 FIFA Women's World Cup in France.

Read the following article. Pay special attention to the words in bold. 12.3

Almost everyone in the world calls it "football." Americans call it "soccer." Whatever you call it, it is by far the most popular sport in the world. In many countries, top international soccer players are as well-known as rock stars or actors—but not in the United States.

In 1999, when the Women's World Cup was played in the United States, there was **more excitement** about soccer **than** ever before. It seemed as if the United States might start to become **more interested** in this international sport. In 2014, when the World Cup was held in Brazil, a record number of people in the United States (an average of 24.7 million), watched the game in which the U.S. team tied with Portugal in the first round. Soccer seemed to be getting **more popular**. But for the next World Cup in 2018, the men's team did not even qualify to play. The number of viewers in the United States went down by nearly one half.

Some statistics show that interest in soccer is **higher than** before. Certainly, during the World Cup, there is a **larger** audience for soccer **than** at other times. But soccer is still much **less popular** in the United States **than** in the rest of the world.

Experts believe that to increase interest in soccer, professional teams have to produce **better** players and capture kids' interest at a **younger** age. Many American parents enroll their kids in soccer programs because they consider soccer **safer than** other sports, such as football or hockey. Between 1990 and 2010, the number of young soccer players doubled. **More recently**, however, that number has been dropping. Between 2015 and 2018, the percentage of 6- to 12-year-olds playing soccer dropped nearly 14 percent. With **more** time spent on electronics, **fewer** American kids are playing youth sports **than** ever before. But while soccer numbers are down, baseball and basketball numbers are up. For American soccer to be on a level with the rest of the world, **a lot more** children need to play, and these developmental programs need to be **more rigorous**[1].

The record number of viewers who tuned in to watch the women play in 2019 is encouraging. Will the 2019 World Cup win by the United States' women's national team lead to **more** interest in the sport? Only time will tell.

---

[1] rigorous: difficult; having high standards

**COMPREHENSION** Based on the reading, write T for *true* or F for *false*.

1. _____ American soccer players are as well-known as movie stars.
2. _____ Interest in soccer is slowly increasing in the United States.
3. _____ Most Americans watch soccer during the World Cup.

**THINK ABOUT IT** Discuss the questions with a partner or in a small group.

1. Is soccer popular in your country? When you were a child, did you dream of becoming a successful soccer player?
2. Discuss the dangers of playing soccer. Do you agree that soccer is safer than American football and ice hockey? Explain.

## 12.3 The Comparative Forms of Adjectives and Adverbs

|  | SIMPLE | COMPARATIVE |
|---|---|---|
| One-syllable adjectives and adverbs | high<br>large | higher<br>larger |
| Two-syllable adjectives that end in *y* | easy<br>happy | easier<br>happier |
| Other two-syllable adjectives | remote<br>extreme | more remote<br>more extreme |
| Some two-syllable adjectives have two forms | simple<br><br>polite | simpler<br>more simple<br>politer<br>more polite |
| Adjectives with three or more syllables | popular<br>demanding | more popular<br>more demanding |
| *-ly* adverbs | quickly<br>directly | more quickly<br>more directly |
| Irregular comparatives | good/well<br>bad/badly<br>far | better<br>worse<br>farther |
| Quantity words | little<br>few | less<br>fewer |
|  | a lot<br>much<br>many | more |

**Notes:**

1. Other two-syllable adjectives that have two forms are:
   handsome, quiet, gentle, narrow, clever, friendly, angry, stupid
2. Adjectives that are past participles use *more*.
   tired—more tired
   fulfilled—more fulfilled
   worried—more worried
3. We use *than* before the second item of comparison.
   *Football is more popular **than** soccer in the U.S.*

**EXERCISE 5** Listen to the following article. Fill in the blanks with the words you hear. 12.4

What are the differences between college sports and professional sports? Of course, professional athletes are __more experienced than__ college athletes, but college athletes are
<u>        1.        </u>

_____ and sometimes _____. The ticket prices are
        2.                                  3.

_____ for professional sports _____ they are for college sports. In
        4.                                  5.

professional sports, athletes make a lot of money, but college athletes don't. So college athletes are

_____ about the sport _____ they are about
        6.                                  7.

financial gain.

In college baseball, players use aluminum bats; in professional baseball, players use wooden bats. Fans like the sound the wooden bat makes _____ the sound of the aluminum
                                                        8.

bat. The baseball stadium for professional baseball is _____ than the baseball stadium
                                                        9.

for college baseball.

Some fans think that college basketball is _____ professional basketball. The
                                            10.

atmosphere of college basketball is _____ because college students cheer on their
                                     11.

favorite team _____ after a score. The fans of professional basketball are
                12.

_____ the fans of college basketball.
        13.

College basketball is _____ either college baseball or football. The fans are
                        14.

_____ to the action. College football has a _____ crowd if the
        15.                                                      16.

home team is good that year.

In professional sports, fans are sometimes _____ in their favorite players
                                            17.

_____ the whole team. In college sports, the team gets _____ than
        18.                                                              19.

the individual players.

Which do you think is _____ ?
                        20.

**EXERCISE 6** Write the comparative form of each word.

1. fat          _____fatter_____           4. low          _____

2. important   _____more important_____           5. beautifully  _____

3. exciting    _____           6. good         _____

318   Unit 12

7. remarkable _____        12. surprised _____

8. athletic _____          13. high _____

9. bad _____               14. large _____

10. rigorous _____         15. far _____

11. challenging _____      16. enthusiastically _____

## 12.4 Comparatives—Use

| EXAMPLES | EXPLANATION |
|---|---|
| Basketball is **livelier than** baseball.<br>Soccer is **more popular than** boxing. | We use the comparative form to show the difference between two people or things. |
| European children train **more rigorously** in soccer **than** American children. | We use *than* before the second item of comparison. |
| Soccer is **less popular than** football in the U.S. | We can use *less* to make a comparison. |
| College athletes have **less experience than** professional athletes.<br>Soccer players have **fewer injuries than** football players. | We can put *more, less, fewer, better, worse,* and other comparative forms before a noun.<br>We use *less* with noncount nouns; we use *fewer* with count nouns. |
| My sister **likes soccer more than** I do.<br>You **play basketball better than** your brother does. | We can put *more, less, better, worse,* and other comparative forms after a verb (phrase). |
| Interest in soccer is **much lower** in the U.S. **than** it is in other countries.<br>I like soccer **a little better than** I like baseball. | *Much, a lot,* or *a little* can come before a comparative form. |
| **The more** they practice, **the better** they play.<br>**The older** you are, **the harder** it is to learn a new sport. | We can use two comparisons in one sentence to show cause and result. |

**Notes:**
1. Omit *than* if the second item of comparison is not included.
    *Basketball is popular in the U.S., but football is **more popular**.*
2. When a pronoun follows *than*, the correct form is the subject pronoun (*he, she, I,* etc.). Usually an auxiliary verb follows (*is, do, did, can,* etc.). Informally, many Americans use the object pronoun (*him, her, me,* etc.) after *than* without an auxiliary verb.
    FORMAL: *You are taller than **I am**.*       FORMAL: *I can play soccer better than **he can**.*
    INFORMAL: *You are taller than **me**.*       INFORMAL: *I can play soccer better than **him**.*

**EXERCISE 7** Circle the correct words to complete each statement.

1. Professional athletes make (**much more**/more much) money than college athletes.

2. A basketball player is (*more tall/taller*) than a gymnast.

3. A baseball game has (*little/less*) action than a soccer game.

*continued*

4. Football players use (*more padding/padding more*) than soccer players.

5. Football players are (*much/more*) heavier than soccer players.

6. A football team has (*much/more*) players than a baseball team.

7. Americans are (*enthusiastic less/less enthusiastic*) about soccer than Europeans.

8. Michael Phelps (*faster swims/swims faster*) than other swimmers.

9. Who plays (*better/more better*), college athletes or professional athletes?

10. College baseball has (*fewer/less*) fans than college basketball.

11. I think football is exciting, but soccer is (*more exciting/more exciting than*).

**EXERCISE 8** Fill in the blank with the comparative of a word from the box. Include *than* when necessary.

| easily | tall | strong | slow | popular✓ | active | large | good |

1. In the United States, basketball is _____more popular than_____ soccer.

2. Basketball players are usually _____ football players.

3. A golf game (18 holes) takes about three or four hours. It is much _____ most other sports.

4. A soccer ball is _____ a tennis ball.

5. Children learn sports _____ adults.

6. People who lift weights are _____ people who don't.

7. Soccer players are always moving. Soccer players are _____ baseball players.

8. Professional athletes are usually _____ college athletes.

**EXERCISE 9** Use the information in the chart to write sentences that compare these two female Olympic swimmers. Answers may vary.

|  | MISSY FRANKLIN | NATALIE COUGHLIN |
| --- | --- | --- |
| year born | 1995 | 1982 |
| height | 6 feet 1 inches tall | 5 feet 8 inches tall |
| weight | 165 pounds | 139 pounds |
| education | didn't finish college | graduated from college |
| age when she started to swim competitively | 7 | 6 |
| participation in Olympic Games | 2012 and 2016 | 2004, 2008, and 2012 |
| number of Olympic medals won | 6 | 12 |

1. <u>Missy is younger than Natalie. OR Natalie is older than Missy.</u>
2. 
3. 
4. 
5. 
6. 
7. 

American gold medal swimmers Megan Romano, Shannon Vreeland, Natalie Coughlin, and Missy Franklin at the 2013 World Aquatics Championships in Barcelona, Spain.

**ABOUT YOU** Compare yourself to a family member or friend. Share your answers with a partner.

1. interested in baseball

   <u>My brother is more interested in baseball than I am.</u>

2. tall

3. strong

*continued*

4. athletic

5. competitive

6. enthusiastic about sports

7. a good swimmer

8. knowledgeable about soccer

**EXERCISE 10** Fill in the blanks with the comparative or superlative form of the word given. Include *than* or *the* when necessary.

1. In the United States, baseball is ___more popular than___ soccer.
   <br>popular
2. Baseball is one of ___the most popular___ sports in the United States.
   <br>popular
3. A tennis ball is _____ a baseball.
   <br>soft
4. An athlete who wins the gold medal is _____ athlete in his or her sport.
   <br>good
5. Who is _____ basketball player in the world?
   <br>tall
6. I am _____ in baseball _____ in basketball.
   <br>interested
7. In my opinion, soccer is _____ sport in the world.
   <br>exciting
8. Weightlifters are _____ golfers.
   <br>muscular
9. Soccer is a _____ sport _____ baseball.
   <br>fast
10. A basketball team has _____ players _____ a baseball team.
    <br>few
11. My friend and I both jog. I run _____ my friend.
    <br>far
12. Who's a _____ soccer player—you or your brother?
    <br>good
13. In golf, the player who has _____ score wins.
    <br>low
14. European soccer players are _____ American soccer players.
    <br>well-known

# An Amazing Athlete

Read the following article. Pay special attention to the words in bold. 12.5

Erik Weihenmayer is **as tough as** any mountain climber. In 2001, he made his way to the top of the highest mountain in the world—Mount Everest—at the age of 33. But Erik is different from other mountain climbers in one important way: he is completely blind. He is the only blind person to reach the top of the tallest mountain.

Erik was an athletic child who lost his vision in his early teens. At first, he refused to use a cane or learn braille[1], insisting he could do **as well as** any teenager. But he finally came to accept his disability. He couldn't play **the same** sports **as** he used to. He would never be able to play basketball or catch a football again. At 16, he became interested in rock climbing. Rock climbing led to mountain climbing, the greatest challenge of his life.

The members of his climbing team say that Erik isn't different from a sighted climber. He has **as much training as** the others. He is **as strong as** the rest. He is like any other climber: flexible, mentally tough, and able to tolerate physical pain.

Climbing Mount Everest was a challenge for every climber on Erik's team. The reaction to the mountain air for Erik was **the same as** it was for his teammates: lack of oxygen causes the heart to beat more slowly than usual, and the brain does not function **as clearly as** normal. To climb Mount Everest is an achievement for any athlete. Erik Weihenmayer showed that his disability wasn't **as important as** his ability.

---

[1] braille: a system of reading and writing for the blind that uses raised dots for letters, numbers, and symbols

Erik Weihenmayer on Mount Everest

**COMPREHENSION** Based on the reading, write T for *true* or F for *false*.

1. _____ When Erik became blind, he used a cane to get around.
2. _____ Erik doesn't have as much training as his teammates.
3. _____ At the highest altitudes, the brain functions as clearly as normal.

**THINK ABOUT IT** Discuss the questions with a partner or in a small group.

1. Reread the last line of the article. Can you give an example from your life or someone else's life where a disability wasn't as important as an ability?
2. Can you give an example of another amazing athlete? What did he or she do that was unusual?

## 12.5 As...As

| EXAMPLES | EXPLANATION |
| --- | --- |
| Erik is **as strong as** his teammates.<br>At high altitudes, the brain does**n't** function **as clearly as** normal. | We can show that two things are equal or unequal in some way by using:<br>    (not) as + adjective/adverb + as |
| Skiing is **not as difficult as** mountain climbing. | When we make a comparison of unequal items, we put the lesser item first. |

**Note:**
Omit the second *as* if the second item of comparison is omitted.
    Baseball is popular in the United States. Soccer is not **as popular**.

**EXERCISE 11** Fill in the blanks with a word from the box and *as...as*.

| strong | well | dangerous✓ | clearly | prepared |

1. Rock climbing is not _____*as dangerous as*_____ mountain climbing.
2. At high altitudes, you can't think _____ you can at lower altitudes.
3. Erik trained well, and he was _____ his teammates.
4. When Erik became blind, he wanted to do _____ any other teenager.
5. Erik is _____ other climbers.

**EXERCISE 12** Change these comparative sentences to sentences using *not as...as*.

1. Europeans are more interested in soccer than Americans.

    *Americans are not as interested in soccer as Europeans.*

2. Soccer is more popular in Latin America than it is in the United States.

    _____

324  Unit 12

3. Football is more dangerous than soccer for children.

4. Missy Franklin is younger than Natalie Coughlin.

5. Missy Franklin is taller than Natalie Coughlin.

6. Professional European soccer players are more famous than professional American soccer players.

**ABOUT YOU** Compare yourself to another person. (Or compare two people you know.) Use the following words and *as . . . as*. You may add a comparative statement if there is inequality. Discuss your answers with a partner.

1. athletic

   *I'm not as athletic as my uncle. He's much more athletic than I am.*

2. interested in basketball

3. good at sports

4. walk fast

5. strong

6. excited about soccer

7. smart

8. good at languages

## 12.6 As Many/Much . . . As

| EXAMPLES | EXPLANATION |
|---|---|
| Soccer players don't usually have **as many injuries as** football players.<br>Erik had **as much training as** his teammates. | We can show that two things are equal or unequal in quantity by using:<br>    (*not*) *as many* + count noun + *as*<br>    (*not*) *as much* + noncount noun + *as* |
| I don't play soccer **as much as** I used to. | We can use *as much as* after a verb phrase. |

**EXERCISE 13** Fill in the blanks with *as much/many. . . as*.

1. Does Gregg Treinish get ____as much____ satisfaction from extreme sports ____as____ he used to?

2. Nancy Coughlin didn't win _____ medals in the 2012 Olympics _____ she did in the 2008 Olympics.

3. You don't hear about Michael Jordan _____ you used to.

4. Grandma Gatewood didn't carry _____ equipment on the Appalachian Trail _____ other hikers.

5. She didn't spend _____ money on equipment _____ other hikers.

6. Michael Phelps didn't win _____ gold medals in 2012 _____ he did in 2008.

7. American soccer teams don't win _____ games at the World Cup _____ European teams.

8. Americans don't show _____ interest in soccer _____ Latin Americans.

9. Americans don't know _____ about soccer _____ Europeans.

**ABOUT YOU** Fill in information about yourself. Then find a partner and compare your answers.

*I don't spend as much time in nature as my partner does.*

|  | NOT AT ALL | OCCASIONALLY | FREQUENTLY |
|---|---|---|---|
| 1. I spend time in nature. | ○ | ● | ○ |
| 2. I exercise. | ○ | ○ | ○ |
| 3. I read sports magazines. | ○ | ○ | ○ |
| 4. I attend sporting events. | ○ | ○ | ○ |
| 5. I watch basketball games. | ○ | ○ | ○ |
| 6. I watch soccer on TV. | ○ | ○ | ○ |

**ABOUT YOU** Compare yourself today to the way you were five years ago. Use *as . . . as, as much/many . . . as*, or a comparative form. Share your answers with a partner.

1. thin

   I'm not as thin as I was five years ago. OR I'm heavier than I was five years ago.

2. strong

   _____

3. physically fit

   _____

4. interested in sports

   _____

5. exercise

   _____

6. have time to relax

   _____

7. watch sports programs on TV

   _____

## 12.7 The Same . . . As

We can show that two things are equal or not with *the same . . . (as)*.

| EXAMPLES | EXPLANATION |
| --- | --- |
| **Pattern A:**<br>Erik had **the same ability as** his teammates. | **Pattern A:**<br>Noun 1 + verb + *the same* noun *as* + noun 2. |
| **Pattern B:**<br>Erik and his teammates had **the same ability**. | **Pattern B:**<br>Noun 1 and noun 2 + verb + *the same* noun. |

**Note:**
We can make statements of equality or inequality with many types of nouns, such as *size, shape, color, value, religion, age, height*, or *nationality*.

   He is **the same height as** his teammate. (height = noun)

   He is **as tall as** his teammate. (tall = adjective)

   Missy **isn't the same age as** Natalie. (age = noun)

   Missy **isn't as old as** Natalie. (old = adjective)

**EXERCISE 14** Use the words to make statements with *(not) the same (. . . as)*.

1. a golf ball/a tennis ball (*size*)

   <u>A golf ball isn't the same size as a tennis ball.</u>

2. a basketball team/a soccer team (*number of players*)

   <u>A basketball team and a soccer team don't have the same number of players.</u>

3. a soccer ball/a football (*shape*)

   _____

4. a soccer player/a basketball player (*height*)

   _____

5. a college athlete/a professional athlete (*experience*)

   _____

6. a baseball/a softball (*size*)

   _____

7. football players/soccer players (*uniforms*)

   _____

8. a female athlete/a male athlete (*amount of money*)

   _____

**EXERCISE 15** Use the information in the chart to compare two Olympic swimmers. Use two methods of comparison.

|  | MICHAEL PHELPS | NATHAN ADRIAN |
|---|---|---|
| year born | 1985 | 1988 |
| height | 6 feet 4 inches tall | 6 feet 6 inches tall |
| weight | 185 pounds | 225 pounds |
| education | received bachelor's degree | received bachelor's degree |
| age when he started swimming | 7 | 2 |
| participation in Olympic games | 2000, 2004, 2008, 2012, and 2016 | 2008, 2012, and 2016 |
| number of Olympic medals won | 28 | 8 |

1. <u>Michael is older than Nathan.</u>

   <u>Nathan and Michael weren't born in the same year.</u>

2. _____

3. _____

4. _____

5. _____

6. _____

7. _____

Gold medalists Nathan Adrian and Michael Phelps thank the crowd at the 2016 Olympic Games in Rio de Janeiro, Brazil.

Superlatives, Comparatives

Tom Brady of the New England Patriots runs with the ball during a football game against the Buffalo Bills in Buffalo, New York, U.S.

# FOOTBALL and SOCCER

Read the following article. Pay special attention to the words in bold. 🎧 12.6

It may seem strange that Americans give the name "football" to a game played mostly by throwing and carrying a ball with one's hands. Speakers of a language other than English usually refer to this sport as *American football*, but in the United States, it's simply *football*.

Many of the rules in soccer and football are the same. In both games, there are 11 players on each side, and a team scores its points by getting the ball past the goal of the other team. The playing fields for both sports **are** also very much **alike**.

When the action begins, the two games look very different. In addition to using their feet, soccer players are allowed to hit the ball with their heads. In football, the only person allowed to touch the ball with his feet is a special player known as the kicker. Also, in football, tackling[1] the player who has the ball is not only allowed but encouraged, whereas[2] tackling in soccer will get the tackler thrown out of the game.

Football players and soccer players **don't dress alike** or even **look alike** in many ways. Since blocking and tackling are a big part of American football, the players are often very large and muscular and wear heavy padding and helmets. Soccer players, on the other hand, are usually thinner and wear shorts and polo shirts. This gives them more freedom of movement so that they can show off the fancy footwork that makes soccer such a popular game around the world.

---

[1] tackling: knocking a player to the ground
[2] whereas: in contrast

**COMPREHENSION** Based on the reading, write T for *true* or F for *false*.

1. _____ A soccer team and a football team don't have the same number of players.
2. _____ It is common to see tackling in a football game.
3. _____ Football players need padding to protect their bodies.

**THINK ABOUT IT** Discuss the questions with a partner or in a small group.

1. Imagine that a soccer player wants to start playing football. Which rules or aspects of the game do you think could be most challenging to learn?
2. Which game do you prefer to watch? Why? Which would you prefer to play? Why?

## 12.8 Showing Similarity with *Like* and *Alike*

We can show that two things are similar (or not) with *like* and *alike*.

| EXAMPLES | EXPLANATION |
|---|---|
| **Pattern A:**<br>A soccer player **looks like** a rugby player.<br>A soccer player **doesn't look like** a football player. | **Pattern A:**<br>Noun 1 + verb + *like* + noun 2. |
| **Pattern B:**<br>A soccer player and a rugby player **look alike**.<br>A soccer player and a football player **don't look alike**. | **Pattern B:**<br>Noun 1 and noun 2 + verb + *alike*. |
| **Pattern A:**<br>He **is like** his brother in some ways. They both love soccer.<br>He **is not like** his sister. They have different interests. | **Pattern A:**<br>Noun 1 + *be like* + noun 2. |
| **Pattern B:**<br>He and his brother **are alike** in some ways.<br>He and his sister **are not alike**. | **Pattern B:**<br>Noun 1 and noun 2 + *be alike*. |

**Notes:**

1. We use the sense perception verbs (*look, sound, smell, taste, feel,* and *seem*) with *like* and *alike* to show an outward similarity or difference.
2. We can use other verbs with *like/alike*: *act, sing, dress, think,* etc.

    *A soccer player doesn't **dress like** a football player.*

    *A soccer player and a football player **don't dress alike**.*

3. We use *be like/be alike* to show an inward similarity or difference.

    *Erik **is like** his teammates. He's a strong climber.* (be like = an inward similarity)

---

### GRAMMAR IN USE

Questions with *What + like* or *What + look like* don't ask for comparisons. They ask for a description:

*What is he like?* (asks about personality) *He's funny and really smart.*

*What is it like?* (asks for a description) *It's challenging.*

*What does he look like?* (asks for a physical description) *He's tall with brown hair.*

When *Who* is used instead of *What* in these questions, similarities are asked for:

*Who is he like? He's like his brother. They are both athletic.*

*Who does he look like? He looks like his father. They are both tall and handsome.*

Superlatives, Comparatives

**EXERCISE 16** Fill in the blanks with an item from the box. You can use some items more than once.

| are alike | is like | don't look like | look like | aren't alike |
| dress alike | think alike | look alike | am not like | sound like |

1. **A:** You're so tall. You ____look like____ a basketball player.

   **B:** Everyone who sees me says the same thing.

2. **A:** _____ wrestling _____ boxing?

   **B:** In some ways, they _____ because they fight in a ring. But in many ways they're different.

3. **A:** My brother and I _____ in some ways.

   **B:** How?

   **A:** We're both very athletic.

4. **A:** Soccer players _____ football players at all.

   **B:** Football players are much bigger. And they wear completely different uniforms.

5. **A:** The swimming competition and the diving competition at the Olympics are very different.

   **B:** You're right. They _____ at all.

6. **A:** You _____ your brother.

   **B:** Everybody says that. We both talk about our favorite soccer team all the time.

7. **A:** My nieces are identical twins. They _____. Here's a picture of them.

   **B:** Oh, how cute. They're wearing the same outfit.

   **A:** Yes. They like to _____. But they _____ in all ways. One loves sports. The other doesn't.

8. **A:** I have a great idea. Let's take the day off and go to a baseball game.

   **B:** I had the exact same idea. You and I _____.

9. **A:** My sister is a great swimmer.

   **B:** What about you?

   **A:** When it comes to swimming, I _____ my sister at all. I'm afraid of the water.

   **B:** But you _____ in some ways. You're both interested in mountain climbing.

**ABOUT YOU** Compare yourself to someone in your family or compare two members of your family using the following words. Share your answers with a partner.

1. look like <u>I don't look like my mother. She's tall. I'm very short.</u>

2. be like _____

3. be alike _____

4. sing like _____

5. think alike _____

6. dress like _____

7. act like _____

**EXERCISE 17** Fill in the blanks in the conversation. Use different methods of comparison from this unit. Use context clues to help you.

**A:** I heard that you have a twin brother. Do you and your brother look ____<u>alike</u>____ ?
                                                                              1.

**B:** No. He _____ look _____ me at all.
              2.            3.

**A:** But you're twins.

**B:** We're fraternal twins. That's different from identical twins. We're not even _____ height.
                                                                                        4.

He's not _____ I am. He's 5'8". I'm 6'2".
          5.

**A:** But you're _____ in some ways, aren't you?
                    6.

**B:** No. We're completely different. I'm athletic and I'm on the high school football team, but David hates sports. He's a much _____ student than I am. He gets all A's. He's more
                                   7.

_____ our mother, who loves to read and learn new things, and I _____ our
    8.                                                                   9.

father, who's athletic and loves to build things. Also, I'm outgoing, but he's very shy. And we don't dress

_____ at all. He likes to wear neat, conservative clothes, but I prefer torn jeans and
   10.

T-shirts. There's only one similarity: over the phone, people don't know if it's my brother or me. We

sound _____ .
        11.

# SUMMARY OF UNIT 12

## Simple, Comparative, and Superlative Forms

### SHORT WORDS

Jacob is **tall**.
Mark is **taller than** Jacob.
Bart is **the tallest** member of the basketball team.

### LONG WORDS

Basketball is **popular** in the United States.
Basketball is **more popular than** soccer in the United States.
Soccer is **the most popular** sport in the world.

## Comparisons with *As . . . As* and *The Same . . . As*

Soccer players aren't **as tall as** basketball players.
Soccer players aren't **the same height as** basketball players.
Soccer players and basketball players aren't **the same height**.

I didn't swim **as many minutes as** you did.
I didn't spend **as much time** in the pool **as** you did.
I don't work out **as much as** you do.

## Comparisons with *Like* and *Alike*

She**'s like** her mother. They're both interested in sports.
She and her mother **are alike**. They're both interested in sports.
She **looks like** her mother. They're both tall and strong.
She and her mother **look alike**. They're both tall and strong.

# REVIEW

Fill in the blanks to complete the conversation. In some cases, answers may vary.

**A:** It's football season, and my husband doesn't pay as ____much____ attention to me
                                                              **1.**
_____as_____ he does to his football games. Many women have _____ problem
  **2.**                                                          **3.**

_____ I do. They call us "football widows" because we lose our husbands during football
  **4.**

season.

**B:** Your husband sounds _____ my husband. I feel _____ a widow, too. Most
                              **5.**                             **6.**

men act _____ during football season. My husband isn't _____ interested in me as
         **7.**                                                     **8.**

he is in watching TV. He looks _____ a robot in front of the TV. When I complain, he tells
                                  **9.**

me to sit down and join him. But I don't like football.

**A:** I think soccer is much _____ than football. My favorite team is the
                                       **10.**

Chicago Fire.

**B:** In my opinion, they're not _____ good _____ the Los Angeles Galaxy. I
                                      **11.**              **12.**

think the Galaxy is much _____. But _____ teams are from
                                **13.**              **14.**

Europe and Latin America.

**A:** Exactly! Soccer is _____ sport in the world. It's only in the U.S. that it
                                  **15.**

isn't very popular. Even during the World Cup, Americans don't pay _____
                                                                        **16.**

attention to the games as Europeans and Latin Americans.

**B:** It's crazy! I think the action in soccer is _____ the action in football. And it's
                                                        **17.**

_____ fun to watch soccer players. Football players look _____ big
     **18.**                                                            **19.**

monsters with their helmets and padding.

**A:** Did you watch the World Cup in 2016? The _____ game was between Germany and
                                                     **20.**

Argentina. I mentioned Lionel Messi to my husband, and he said, "Who's that?" I said,

"He's _____ player in the world."
         **21.**

**B:** I love Messi. He's a strong player. But Cristiano Ronaldo is even _____.
                                                                              **22.**

**A:** Well, let's do our favorite sport: shopping. We can spend _____ time shopping
                                                                     **23.**

_____ they do in front of the TV.
    **24.**

**B:** You and I think _____. We're football widows, so our husbands can be
                            **25.**

"shopping widowers."

# FROM GRAMMAR TO WRITING

## PART 1  Editing Advice

1. Don't use *more* and *-er* together.

    He plays baseball ~~more~~ better than his brother.

2. Use *than* before the second item of comparison.

    Soccer is more exciting ~~that~~ than baseball.

3. Use *the* before a superlative form.

    Mt. Everest is ^the tallest mountain in the world.

4. Use a plural noun in the phrase "one of the [superlative] [plural noun]."

    Lionel Messi is one of the best soccer player^s in the world.

5. Use the correct word order.

    I ~~more like sports~~ like sports more than you do.

    I have ~~interest more~~ more interest than you do in sports.

6. Use *be like* for inward similarity. Use *look like* for an outward similarity.

    He is ~~look~~ like his brother. They are both talented athletes.

    He ~~is~~ look^s like his brother. They are both tall and muscular.

7. Use the correct negative for *be like, look like, sound like, feel like*, etc.

    He ~~isn't~~ doesn't look like an athlete. He's not in good shape.

8. Use *the same* before nouns.

    A baseball isn't the same ~~big~~ size as a volleyball.

9. Use *as* before adjectives and adverbs.

    A baseball isn't ~~the same~~ as big as a volleyball.

10. With equality and inequality, use *as* with the second item.

    A football isn't the same shape ~~than~~ as a soccer ball.

11. Don't confuse *more* and *most*.

    Tierra del Fuego is the ~~more~~ most spectacular place he has ever seen.

## PART 2 Editing Practice

Some of the shaded words and phrases have mistakes. Find the mistakes and correct them. If the shaded words are correct, write C.

       most          C
Soccer is the ~~more~~ popular sport in the world. It is more popular than football, baseball, and
      1.              2.
basketball combined. I know Americans prefer football, but for me soccer is much more interesting that
                             3.      4.
football. In fact, I think soccer is the more exciting sport in the world. There are some good American
                5.
teams, but they aren't as good as some of the European teams. I think Italy has one of the best team.
          6.                      7.  8.

  The name "football" is confusing. "Football" is sounds like a game where you use your feet, but
                        9.
football players carry the ball. A football and a soccer ball don't look alike at all. A soccer ball is round, but
                             10.
a football isn't. The game of football isn't look like the game of soccer at all. These sports are completely
                   11.
different. The players are different, too. Soccer players are not the same big as football players. There is
                               12.
just one similarity: a soccer team has the same number of players as a football team.
                13.           14.

  I especially like Cristiano Ronaldo. In my opinion, he is one of the best player in the world. I love to
                            15.
watch soccer, but I like to play it even more. When I lived in my country, I played more better because I
                                 16.
more practiced. I played every weekend. But here I don't have time as much as before. I watch it on TV, but
  17.                        18.
it isn't as much fun as playing it.
   19.

---

**WRITING TIP**
When you write an essay, you need an introduction, a body, and a conclusion. The introduction includes your thesis statement, which expresses the central point of your essay. Each body paragraph introduces a main idea and supporting points. The conclusion is where you end your essay and restate your thesis. It is always good to create an outline to organize your ideas before you begin writing an essay.

---

## PART 3 Write

Read the prompts. Choose one and write an essay about it.

1. Compare two athletes from the same sport. If you don't follow sports, compare two famous people from the same field (politics, movies, art, etc.). If you use information from an outside source, attach that source to your essay.
2. Write about a person who accomplished something amazing. You can write about a famous person or a person you know. If you use information from an outside source, attach that source to your essay.

## PART 4 Edit

Reread the Summary of Unit 12 and the editing advice. Edit your writing from Part 3.

UNIT
# 13
**Active and Passive Voice**

# THE LAW

Lady Justice's scale symbolizes fairness and balance, and her sword represents punishment. Her statue is often outside courthouses in the U.S.

> Injustice anywhere is a threat to justice everywhere.
> DR. MARTIN LUTHER KING, JR.

# The Supreme Court

The U.S. Supreme Court Building, Washington, DC

**Read the following article. Pay special attention to the words in bold.** 13.1

You have probably heard of the Supreme Court of the United States. Why **was** this court **created**, how **are** the justices **selected**, and how is it different from other courts?

The Supreme Court **was created** by the U.S. Constitution to balance the power of the president and Congress. It has nine justices[1], one of whom is the Chief Justice. The president nominates a justice, but he doesn't have the final say. His choice has to **be confirmed**[2] by the Senate. Supreme Court justices **are** not **appointed** for a fixed number of years. According to the Constitution, they "shall hold their offices during good behavior." This usually means they serve for life or until they retire. Until 1981, all the justices were male. Then Sandra Day O'Connor, who **was nominated** by President Ronald Reagan, became the first female justice.

About 10,000 cases **are filed** every year, but the Supreme Court hears only about 75–80 cases. The Supreme Court hears cases that **are appealed**[3] from lower courts when these courts are not able to resolve a conflict. No new evidence[4] **is presented**, and no witnesses **are heard**. Attorneys[5] present their case in writing and orally. The judges listen to each side, review the evidence that **was presented** in the lower courts, and meet privately to decide the case. A simple majority of five justices is all that **is needed** to decide a case.

Once a case **is heard** on the Supreme Court, it **cannot be heard** in any other court. The justices' decision is final.

---

[1] justice: a judge in a court of law
[2] confirmed: formally accepted
[3] appealed: brought from a lower court to a higher court for review
[4] evidence: words or objects that support the truth of something
[5] attorney: a lawyer

**COMPREHENSION** Based on the reading, write T for *true* or F for *false*.

1. _____ The president has the final word in selecting a Supreme Court justice.
2. _____ To decide a case, all the justices must agree.
3. _____ A Supreme Court justice can serve for life.

### GRAMMAR IN USE

The passive voice is useful in reporting facts objectively. The passive puts emphasis on the receiver or object of the action (e.g., *Two people **were injured** in the accident.*). It also takes emphasis away from an unknown subject (e.g., *The painting **was stolen** from the museum.*).

The passive also allows a writer or speaker to adjust the focus. For example:

*Judge Brown **sentenced** Mel Simon to 10 years in prison.* (active)

*Mel Simon **was sentenced** to 10 years in prison.* (passive)

In the active voice, focus is placed on the judge. In the passive voice, Mel Simon is the focus.

---

**EXERCISE 3** Change each sentence to passive voice. Use the same tense. Do not include the agent.

1. They **take** a vote. _A vote is taken._
2. They **made** a decision. _____
3. They **will take** a vote. _____
4. They **are going to change** the law. _____
5. We **have paid** the attorneys. _____
6. We **must find** a good lawyer. _____
7. They **need to write** a report. _____

**EXERCISE 4** Underline the verb. Then write *A* if the sentence is active or *P* if the sentence is passive.

1. The justices <u>discussed</u> the case in private. __A__
2. A decision <u>was made</u> to change the law. __P__
3. Sandra Day O'Connor became the first female justice on the Supreme Court. _____
4. About 75 cases are heard in the Supreme Court each year. _____
5. Some laws need to be changed. _____
6. The justices sometimes interrupt the attorneys. _____
7. Some justices will retire soon. _____
8. In many court cases, witnesses are brought in. _____
9. In criminal court, witnesses are questioned. _____
10. Schools in Kansas separated African-American children from other children. _____
11. The first African-American justice was appointed to the Supreme Court in 1967. _____
12. Things have changed a lot in the last 60 years. _____

Members of a jury listen to an attorney's argument.

# JURY DUTY

Read the following article. Pay special attention to the words in bold. 13.3

All Americans **are protected** by the Constitution. No one person can decide if a person is guilty of a crime. Every citizen has the right to a trial by jury. When a person **is charged** with a crime, he or she **is considered** innocent until the jury decides he or she is guilty.

Most American citizens **are chosen** for jury duty at some time in their lives. How **are** jurors **chosen**? The court gets the names of citizens from lists of taxpayers, licensed drivers, and voters. Many people **are called** to the courthouse for the selection of a jury. From this large group, a limited number of people **is chosen**. Alternates[1] are also chosen. The lawyers and the judge ask each person questions to see if the person is going to be fair. If the person has made any judgment about the case before hearing the facts presented in the trial, he or she **is not selected**. If the person doesn't understand enough English, he or she **is not selected**. The court needs jurors who can understand the facts and be open-minded. When the final jury selection **is made**, the jurors must promise to be fair in deciding the case.

Sometimes a trial goes on for several days or more. Jurors **are not permitted** to talk with family members and friends about the case. In some cases, jurors **are not permitted** to go home until the case is over. They stay in a hotel and **are not permitted** to watch TV or read newspapers that give information about the case.

After the jurors hear the case, they have to reach a decision, or a verdict. They go to a separate room and talk about what they heard and saw in the courtroom. When they are finished discussing the case, they take a vote.

Jurors **are paid** for their work. They receive a small amount of money per day. Employers must give a worker permission **to take off work** to be on a jury. Jury duty **is considered** a very serious responsibility.

---

[1] alternate: a person who takes the place of a juror who cannot serve for some reason, such as illness

**COMPREHENSION** Based on the reading, write T for *true* or F for *false*.

1. _____ Only American citizens are selected for a jury in the United States.
2. _____ People with limited English are often not selected for jury duty.
3. _____ Jurors receive a small amount of money for serving.

**THINK ABOUT IT** Discuss the questions with a partner or in a small group.

1. Do you agree that a person is considered innocent until proven guilty of a crime? Why or why not? Is this true in your home country?
2. Have you ever had jury duty in the United States? If yes, describe the experience. If not, would you be eager to perform jury duty? Why or why not?

## 13.3 The Passive Voice—Use

| EXAMPLES | EXPLANATION |
|---|---|
| Laws **should be obeyed**.<br>The jurors **will be paid** at the end of the trial.<br>A man **was charged** with a crime. | The passive voice is often used without an agent when:<br>• the action is done by people in general.<br>• the agent is unknown or unimportant.<br>• the agent is obvious. |
| **Active**: The lawyers **presented** the case yesterday.<br>**Passive**: The case **was presented** in two hours.<br>**Active**: The judge and the lawyers **choose** 12 people.<br>**Passive**: People who don't understand English **are not chosen**. | The passive voice is used to shift the emphasis from the agent to the receiver of the action. |
| A Supreme Court justice **is nominated** by the president. | The passive voice is sometimes used with an agent. |
| It **is considered** the responsibility of every citizen to serve on a jury. | Often the passive voice is used after *it* when talking about general beliefs, findings, and discoveries. |

**Notes:**
1. The active voice is much more commonly used than the passive voice. Do not overuse the passive voice.
2. Informally, *they* is often used as the subject in an active sentence when the subject is not a specific person.
   They **give** you instructions in court. (Informal)
   You **are given** instructions in court. (Formal)

---

**EXERCISE 5** Fill in the blanks with the passive voice of the verb given. Use the simple present.

1. Jurors ____are chosen____ from lists.
    <sub>choose</sub>
2. Only people over 18 years old _____ for jury duty.
    <sub>select</sub>
3. A questionnaire _____ out and _____.
    <sub>fill</sub>      <sub>return</sub>
4. Many people _____ to the courthouse.
    <sub>call</sub>
5. Not everyone _____.
    <sub>choose</sub>
6. The jurors _____ a lot of questions.
    <sub>ask</sub>
7. Jurors _____ time for lunch.
    <sub>permit</sub>
8. Jurors _____ a paycheck at the end of the trial if they are not employed.
    <sub>give</sub>

**EXERCISE 6** Fill in the blanks with the passive voice of the verb given. Use the simple past.

1. I _____was sent_____ a letter.
   <sub>send</sub>
2. I _____ to go to the courthouse on Fifth Street.
   <sub>tell</sub>
3. My name _____.
   <sub>call</sub>
4. I _____ a form to fill out.
   <sub>give</sub>
5. A video about jury duty _____ on a large TV.
   <sub>show</sub>
6. The jurors _____ to the third floor of the building.
   <sub>take</sub>
7. I _____ a lot of questions by the lawyers.
   <sub>ask</sub>
8. I _____ for the jury.
   <sub>choose</sub>

**EXERCISE 7** Fill in the blanks with the passive voice of the verb given. Use the present perfect.

1. The jurors _____have been given_____ a lot of information.
   <sub>give</sub>
2. Many books _____ about the courts.
   <sub>write</sub>
3. Many movies _____ about criminal trials.
   <sub>make</sub>
4. Many people _____ for jury duty.
   <sub>choose</sub>
5. Your name _____ for jury duty.
   <sub>select</sub>
6. The check _____ with the clerk.
   <sub>leave</sub>
7. The check _____ in an envelope.
   <sub>put</sub>
8. A notice about jury duty _____ to your house.
   <sub>send</sub>

**EXERCISE 8** Fill in the blanks with the passive voice of the verb given. Use the future with *will*.

1. You _____will be taken_____ to a courtroom.
   <sub>take</sub>
2. You _____ to stand up when the judge enters the room.
   <sub>tell</sub>
3. Each of you _____ a lot of questions.
   <sub>ask</sub>
4. The lawyers _____.
   <sub>introduce</sub>
5. Information about the case _____ to you.
   <sub>present</sub>
6. Twelve of you _____.
   <sub>select</sub>
7. Besides the 12 jurors, two alternates _____.
   <sub>choose</sub>
8. All of you _____.
   <sub>pay</sub>

**EXERCISE 9** Fill in the blanks with the passive voice for each of the underlined verbs.

1. The jury took a vote. The vote _____was taken_____ after three hours.

2. The lawyers asked a lot of questions. The questions _____ in order to find facts.

3. The court will pay us. We _____ $20 a day.

4. They told us to wait. We _____ to wait on the second floor.

5. They gave us instructions. We _____ instructions about the law.

6. People pay for the services of a lawyer. Lawyers _____ a lot of money for their services.

7. You should use a pen to fill out the form. A pen _____ for all legal documents.

8. They showed us a film about the court system. We _____ the film before we went into the courtroom.

9. Someone needs to tell us what to do. We _____ how the jury system works.

10. Many people consider *Brown v. The Board of Education* a very important case. It _____ an important step toward the end of inequalities.

## 13.4 Negatives and Questions with the Passive Voice

Compare statements, *yes/no* questions, short answers, *wh-* questions, and subject questions.

| | |
|---|---|
| AFFIRMATIVE STATEMENT: | They **are permitted** to talk to other jurors. |
| NEGATIVE STATEMENT: | They **aren't permitted** to talk to family members. |
| YES/NO QUESTION: | **Are** they **permitted** to eat in the courtroom? |
| SHORT ANSWER: | No, they **aren't**. /No, they**'re not**. |
| WH- QUESTION: | What **are** they **permitted** to do in the courtroom? |
| NEGATIVE WH- QUESTION: | Why **aren't** they **permitted** to talk to family members? |
| SUBJECT QUESTION: | Who **is permitted** in the courtroom? |

**EXERCISE 10** Write *A* if the sentence is active. Write *P* if the sentence is passive.

1. Did you go to court last week? _____A_____

2. Which courtroom were you sent to? _____

3. The jurors didn't agree with each other. _____

4. Jurors aren't paid a lot of money. _____

5. I haven't been selected for a jury. _____

*continued*

6. Some jurors won't be needed. _____

7. How many questions did the lawyers ask you? _____

8. Did you receive a letter for jury duty? _____

9. How are justices selected for the Supreme Court? _____

10. Which justice will resign next? _____

**EXERCISE 11** Fill in the blanks with the negative form of the underlined verbs.

1. I was selected for jury duty last year. I ____wasn't selected____ this year.

2. The jurors are paid. They _____ a lot of money.

3. Twelve people were chosen. People who don't understand English well _____.

4. We are allowed to eat in the waiting room. We _____ to eat in the courtroom.

5. We were told to keep an open mind. We _____ how to vote.

**EXERCISE 12** Change the statements to questions using the words given.

1. The jurors are paid. (*how much*)

   How much are the jurors paid?

2. The jurors are given a lunch break. (*when*)

   _____

3. I wasn't chosen for the jury. (*why*)

   _____

4. You were given information about the case. (*what kind of information*)

   _____

5. Several jurors have been sent home. (*which jurors*)

   _____

**FUN WITH GRAMMAR**

Be a news reporter. Work with a partner to prepare a short TV news report. The goal is to use the passive voice correctly and effectively. The news can be true or made up. You can talk about any news topic: the weather, famous people, crime, politics, personal interest stories, etc. The class will listen and write down uses of the passive. Then the class will vote on the most engaging news report.

# Who Owns the Photo?

Read the following article. Pay special attention to the bold and underlined verbs. 🎧 13.4

In 2011, wildlife photographer David Slater <u>traveled</u> to Indonesia to photograph an endangered type of monkey, the crested black macaque. For days, Slater followed a group of these animals through a forest. One afternoon, when the group stopped to rest, Slater put his camera on a stand and moved away. A few minutes later, several monkeys approached the camera and started to play with it. Some pressed buttons and began taking photos of themselves. By the end, Slater had hundreds of monkey selfies[1]. One **was taken** by a female macaque. In the photo, she <u>seems</u> to be smiling. The image **was published** by different news media and <u>became</u> famous worldwide.

In the summer of 2011, Slater's famous photo <u>appeared</u> on Wikipedia, a popular U.S. website. Slater contacted the company and <u>complained</u>. He asked the website to remove the photo, or to pay him for using it. His request **was rejected**. Why? Slater didn't hold the copyright[2], Wikipedia said. It **was owned** by the monkey—because she took the picture. But since a copyright **cannot be held** by an animal, Wikipedia argued, the photo **could be used** by anyone for free.

Today, the famous monkey selfie <u>remains</u> on Wikipedia—where it **can be downloaded** by anyone— and Slater's fight with the company continues. A photographer does more than just press a button on a camera, Slater has said. When this case **is heard** in court, he hopes a judge will agree.

Some good <u>has come</u> from this situation, though. The legal case has attracted a lot of international attention, and people have begun protecting the crested black macaque. Slater has also agreed to help. He is donating 10 percent of the money that **is made** from the sale of the monkey photos to a conservation group. "I only wanted to help these animals—and I still do," says Slater. Now he hopes the legal system will help him.

The monkey in the photo took this picture of herself.

Crested black macaques **are hunted** for their meat. Their environment **is also threatened** by human development. Because of this, there are only about 100,000 of them today.

[1] selfie: a photo that someone takes of himself or herself
[2] copyright: the legal ownership of a photo, book, song, etc., which gives a person the exclusive right to publish or sell the material and make money from it

**Active and Passive Voice**

**COMPREHENSION** Based on the reading, write T for *true* or F for *false*.

1. _____ The photo of the smiling monkey was taken by David Slater.
2. _____ In Wikipedia's opinion, the monkey photo isn't owned by David Slater.
3. _____ Because of David Slater's legal case, people have begun protecting the crested black macaque.

**THINK ABOUT IT**

1. Imagine that you are Wikipedia's lawyer. Why, in your opinion, can the monkey photo be used for free? Then imagine that you are David Slater's lawyer. Why, in your opinion, does your client own the photo?
2. Which side do you agree with and why?

## 13.5 Transitive and Intransitive Verbs

Transitive verbs have an object. Intransitive verbs have no object.

| EXAMPLES | EXPLANATION |
| --- | --- |
| (A) Wikipedia **published** the photo of the monkey.<br>(P) The photo of the monkey **was published** by Wikipedia. | Transitive verbs have an active (A) and a passive (P) form. |
| (A) A monkey **took** the photo.<br>(P) The photo **was taken** by a monkey. | The active voice is more common than the passive voice when there is a specific agent. |
| In the photo, the monkey **seems** to be smiling.<br>The photo **became** famous worldwide.<br>The photo **appeared** on Wikipedia.<br>Slater **complained** about this.<br>The famous photo **remains** on Wikipedia. | Intransitive verbs don't have a passive form. Some intransitive verbs are: *arrive, be, become, come, complain, depend, die, fall, go, grow* (in a natural way), *happen, laugh, leave* (a place), *occur, rain, recover* (from an illness), *remain, run, sleep, stay,* and *work*. The sense perception verbs are also usually intransitive: *appear, feel, look, seem, smell, sound,* and *taste*. |

Notes:

1. Even though *have* and *want* are followed by an object, these verbs are not usually used in the passive voice.

   Slater **has** a famous photo. (NOT: *A famous photo is had by Slater.*)

   He **wants** a new camera. (NOT: *A new camera is wanted by him.*)

2. Some verbs can be used both as transitive verbs and intransitive verbs.

   The monkeys **stopped** to rest. (intransitive)

   The reporter **stopped** Slater and asked a question. Slater **was stopped** by the reporter. (transitive)

**EXERCISE 13** Circle the correct word(s) to complete each sentence.

1. David Slater (**takes**/is taken) photos of endangered animals.
2. The photo of a smiling monkey (took/was taken) in Indonesia.
3. Wikipedia (used/was used) the photo without Slater's permission.
4. Slater contacted Wikipedia. He said the photo (should remove/should be removed) from the website.
5. Slater said, "An artist's work (cannot use/cannot be used) for free."
6. Wikipedia (rejected/was rejected) Slater's request.
7. Now the case (will go/will be gone) to court.
8. Some good things (have happened/have been happened) because of this case.
9. For years, crested black macaques (have hunted/have been hunted) for their meat or (have kept/have been kept) as pets.
10. As a result, many of these animals (have died/have been died).
11. But now, the monkeys (protected/are protected) in some places.
12. Conservationists hope that more of the monkeys (can save/can be saved).

**EXERCISE 14** Look at each underlined verb in the conversation. If it is correct, put a check (✓). If it is incorrect, write the correct active or passive form.

A: Why weren't you in school yesterday?

B: I _was had_ (had) jury duty. It _was_ (✓) interesting.
     1.                           2.

A: What _was happened_ ?
                3.

B: A woman _was sued_ her employer.
                4.

A: Why?

B: The woman _was injured_ on the job. She _complained_ , but the company _wasn't helped_
                     5.                             6.                           7.

her. The case _went_ to court, and the woman _won_ a lot of money.
                    8.                               9.

A: How much _was_ she _paid_ ?
                10.           11.

B: She _gave_ three million dollars by the court.
       12.

A: Wow! Was the woman happy?

B: Yes. She _was appeared_ to be very happy.
             13.

A: Now that jury duty is over, you don't have to do it again. Right?

B: No, that's not true. A person _can chosen_ for jury duty more than once.
                                  14.

**EXERCISE 15** Find and underline the verb in each sentence. Then identify which sentences can be changed to the passive voice and change those sentences. If no change is possible, write *NC* (*no change*).

1. In the photo, the monkey <u>appears</u> to be smiling.

   NC

2. Wikipedia <u>used</u> the photo without Slater's permission.

   The photo was used (by Wikipedia) without Slater's permission.

3. Slater became angry about this.

   _____

4. Wikipedia didn't pay Slater for his work.

   _____

5. Anyone can download the photo of the smiling monkey.

   _____

6. In the future, a judge will decide Slater's case.

   _____

7. Laws protect us.

   _____

8. Some court cases seem silly.

   _____

9. The Supreme Court has decided important cases.

   _____

10. Jurors should arrive on time to court.

    _____

**ABOUT YOU** Read the sentences in the chart. Write the correct active or passive form of the verb in parentheses. Think about a country's legal system you know about. For each sentence, check *yes* or *no*. Then work with a partner. Use the sentences in the chart to ask and answer questions.

Country: _____

|  | YES | NO |
|---|---|---|
| 1. Citizens (select) _____are selected_____ to be on a jury. | | |
| 2. People (represent) _____ by lawyers in court. | | |
| 3. Jurors (pay) _____ for their service in court. | | |
| 4. The laws (be) _____ fair. | | |
| 5. Famous trials (show) _____ on TV. | | |
| 6. The death penalty (use) _____ in some cases. | | |
| 7. The country (have) _____ a Supreme Court. | | |
| 8. Lawyers (respect) _____, and they make good money, so many people (become) _____ attorneys. | | |

A: I know about the legal system in Spain.
B: In Spain, are citizens selected to be on a jury?
A: Yes. In some cases, people are selected to be on a jury.

Among major law schools in the U.S., Yale University had the lowest acceptance rate for the fall of 2018.

# SUMMARY OF UNIT 13

## Active and Passive Voice—Forms

| ACTIVE | PASSIVE |
| --- | --- |
| Sam **drove** the car. | The car **was driven** (by Sam). |
| Sam **didn't drive** the car. | The car **wasn't driven** (by Sam). |
| Sam **will drive** the car. | The car **will be driven** (by Sam). |
| Sam **has driven** the car. | The car **has been driven** (by Sam). |
| Sam often **drives** the car. | The car **is** often **driven** (by Sam). |
| Sam **should drive** the car. | The car **should be driven** (by Sam). |
| Sam **needs to drive** the car. | The car **needs to be driven** (by Sam). |
| **Did** Sam **drive** the car? | **Was** the car **driven** (by Sam)? |
| When **did** Sam **drive** the car? | When **was** the car **driven** (by Sam)? |
| Why **didn't** Sam **drive** the car? | Why **wasn't** the car **driven** (by Sam)? |

## The Active Voice—Use

| EXAMPLES | EXPLANATION |
| --- | --- |
| I **hired** an attorney.<br>The attorney **prepared** the evidence.<br>She **will present** the evidence in court. | In most cases, when either the active or passive can be used, we use the active voice. |
| The accident **happened** last month.<br>She **went** to court. | When the verb is intransitive (it has no object), the active voice must be used. There is no choice. |

## The Passive Voice—Use

| EXAMPLES | EXPLANATION |
| --- | --- |
| I **was chosen** for jury duty. | The agent is not known or is not important. |
| The criminal **was taken** to jail. | The agent is obvious. |
| Jury duty **is considered** a responsibility of every citizen. | The agent is everybody or people in general. |
| The court paid me. I **was paid** at the end of the day. | The emphasis is shifted from the agent to the receiver of the action. |
| It **was discovered** that many accidents are the result of driver distraction. | When talking about general beliefs and findings, we begin with *It*. |
| Accidents **are caused** by distracted drivers. | The emphasis is on the receiver of the action more than on the agent. (In this case, the agent is included in a *by* phrase.) |

# REVIEW

Fill in the blanks with the active or passive voice of the verb given.

In many countries, laws __have been passed__ (1. present perfect: *pass*) that prohibit drivers from using cell phones while driving. In a few countries, such as Japan, both hand-held and hands-free cell phone use _____ (2. present perfect: *ban*). In the United States, the law _____ (3. simple present: *depend*) on the place where you _____ (4. simple present: *live*).

States _____ (5. present perfect: *start*) to become tougher on drivers who use cell phones. In New York, for example, the use of hand-held cell phones while driving _____ (6. simple present: *prohibit*), but the use of hands-free devices _____ (7. simple present: *permit*). A driver who _____ (8. simple present: *not/obey*) this law can be fined $50 for a first offense, $50–$200 for a second offense, and $50–$400 after that. In addition, a driver _____ (9. can/lose) his or her license for two to six months. In Alaska, the fine for using a hand-held device while driving is $10,000. A driver _____ (10. can/even/send) to jail for up to one year. Texting while driving _____ (11. present perfect: *become*) an even greater problem. Drivers _____ (12. simple present: *need*) to look away from the road in order to text. The risk of causing an accident while texting is 23 times higher than it is while driving without this distraction. Each year, nearly 390,000 people _____ (13. simple present: *injure*) in cell phone-related crashes.

But the problem of driver distraction is not only a result of cell phones and texting. According to one study, it _____ (14. simple past: *find*) that 80 percent of accidents _____ (15. simple present: *cause*) by drivers who are not paying attention. This study _____ (16. simple past: *determine*) that drivers _____ (17. simple present: *distract*) by many things: eating, putting on makeup, reading, reaching for things, and changing stations on the radio.

Over 3,000 people _____ (18. simple past: *kill*) in 2018 as a result of driver distraction. It is clear that all drivers _____ (19. simple present: *need*) to give driving their full attention.

# FROM GRAMMAR TO WRITING

## PART 1  Editing Advice

1. Never use *do, does,* or *did* to form the passive voice.

   The criminal ~~didn't find~~ wasn't found.

   Where ~~did~~ were the jurors taken?

2. Don't use the passive voice with *happen, die, become, sleep, work, live, fall, seem,* or other intransitive verbs.

   The accident ~~was~~ happened three weeks ago.

3. Don't confuse the *-ing* form with the past participle.

   The criminal was ~~taking~~ taken to jail.

4. Don't forget the *-ed* ending for a regular past participle.

   My cousin was select**ed** to be on a jury.

5. Don't forget to use *be* with a passive sentence.

   The evidence **was** presented in court.

6. Use the correct word order with adverbs.

   I was ~~selected never~~ never selected to be on a jury.

## PART 2  Editing Practice

Some of the shaded words and phrases have mistakes. Find the mistakes and correct them. If the shaded words are correct, write C.

I ~~wasn't~~ **didn't** come to class last week. My classmates **wanted** to know if I was sick. I explained that I **had**
    1.                                                2.                                                                              3.
jury duty. Only citizens of the United States **can serve** on a jury, so my friends were surprised. But I
                                                                  4.
**was become** a citizen six months ago. Last month, I **was received** a letter in the mail telling me I had to
    5.                                                                                     6.
report for duty. I'm still an ESL student, and my English is far from perfect, but I **was selected**. I **was ask**
                                                                                                                          7.                       8.
a lot of questions, and I **answered** them without a problem. Many people **were rejected**, and I don't know
                                         9.                                                                                  10.
why, but I **chosen**.
              11.

The case was about a traffic accident. Here's what **was happened**: A man **hit** a woman's car and
                                                                              12.                              13.
**was left** the scene of the accident. Her car **was badly damage**. Luckily, the woman **didn't injured**. The
    14.                                                      15.                                                                  16.
woman **saw** the driver's license plate and **wrote** down the number. She also **was taken** a picture of the car
            17.                                                18.                                                              19.
with her cell phone as the driver was leaving. She called the police. The police **caught** him. He **was driven**
                                                                                                                       20.                         21.
without a license. They also determined that the man **was texting** while driving. My friends asked me,
                                                                                        22.

"How **was that determined**? The police checked the phone records and **was found** that at the exact time
          23.                                                                    24.

of the accident, he was texting. The case **lasted** for two days. All the jurors **were agreed** that the man was
                                   25.                                 26.

guilty. The man **was given** a $500 fine. His driver's license **was suspended** for one year.
               27.                              28.

   I think a lot of accidents **are cause** by people talking on the phone or texting while driving. According
                         29.

to the law, **we're not permit** to text and drive. But in some places, you can talk on the phone and drive. I
          30.

hope that the law **will be changed** and talking on a cell phone **will be** against the law, too.
                          31.                               32.

---

### WRITING TIP

When writing, think carefully about whether the active or passive voice is more appropriate. For example, if you choose prompt 1 below, you might use constructions such as:

*I was told/asked/instructed to . . .*

For prompt 2, you might use constructions such as:

*The man was sentenced/convicted/released.*

After you complete a writing assignment, read it through and check for uses of the passive. Confirm that each passive construction is suitable. If you aren't sure, try putting the sentence into active voice and see if this makes the sentence stronger. Sometimes you may need additional information in order to use the active voice.

*The man was sentenced to five years in prison.* (passive) → *Judge Andrews sentenced the man to five years in prison.* (active)

---

## PART 3 Write

Read the prompts. Choose one and write a paragraph about it.

1. Write about an experience you have had with the court system in the United States or your native country.
2. Write about a famous court case that you know of. Do you agree with the decision of the jury?
   (If you research your topic, attach a copy of your sources.)

## PART 4 Edit

Reread the Summary of Unit 13 and the editing advice. Edit your writing from Part 3.

UNIT

# 14

**Articles**
*Other/Another*
**Indefinite Pronouns**

# MONEY

Workers compare blown-up sections of counterfeit, or fake, $100 bills with a real bill enlarged 400 times.

> Making money isn't hard in itself. What's hard is to earn it doing something worth devoting your life to.
> CARLOS RUIZ ZAFÓN

# Millennials AND Money

Read the following article. Pay special attention to the words in bold. 14.1

You've probably been hearing a lot about millennials these days. What, exactly, is **a millennial**? **A millennial** is **a person** born between 1981 and 1996. This is **the** largest **group** of Americans, 78 million. Within the next two years, **millennials** will make up 50 percent of **the workforce**[1]. By 2030, they will be **the majority** of **the workforce** at 75 percent and **the** largest **group** of consumers, so **marketers** are especially interested in this group and their spending habits.

Millennials' attitudes towards **money** and spending are different from those of their parents, **the "Baby Boomers"** (born between 1946 and 1964), or **"Generation Xers,"** (born between 1965 and 1980). First, they often shop online, where they can compare **prices**, **products**, and **vendors**. They are more influenced by **the opinions** of other consumers than by **the recommendations** of family and friends. Second, they prefer to rent **things** rather than own them; they prefer movie and music **subscriptions** rather than **ownership** of DVDs or CDs. They get their music and movies on their smartphones, tablets, or computers. A significant number of them don't even own **a television**. Third, they like to spend their money on life experiences, such as **entertainment**, **restaurants**, and **travel** rather than on **goods**. They often have **the attitude** of "YOLO": You Only Live Once. They want to experience all **life** has to offer. Generally, they are optimistic[2] about **the future**.

What influences these attitudes? At **the end** of 2007, the United States went into a deep economic recession[3]. **The** average **salary** for a person just out of college in 2013 was $34,500. This was **the** lowest starting **salary** for a college graduate since 1998. And recent college graduates have been entering **the** job **market** with huge college **debt**[4]. As a result, millennials have learned to be careful with **money**. They are getting married later than previous **generations**, and many don't believe in spending a lot of **money** on an expensive **wedding**. They often use **public transportation** and **bicycles** for short **trips** or use car-sharing **services**. They prefer to rent **an apartment** rather than buy **a house** because they don't want large financial **commitments**.

American **millennials** spend $600 billion **dollars** a year. **Marketers** need to understand **the mentality** and **habits** of millennnials if they wish to attract their dollars.

---

[1] workforce: all workers employed in a specific area
[2] optimistic: believing that good things will happen
[3] recession: a time when economic activity is not strong
[4] debt: an amount of money owed

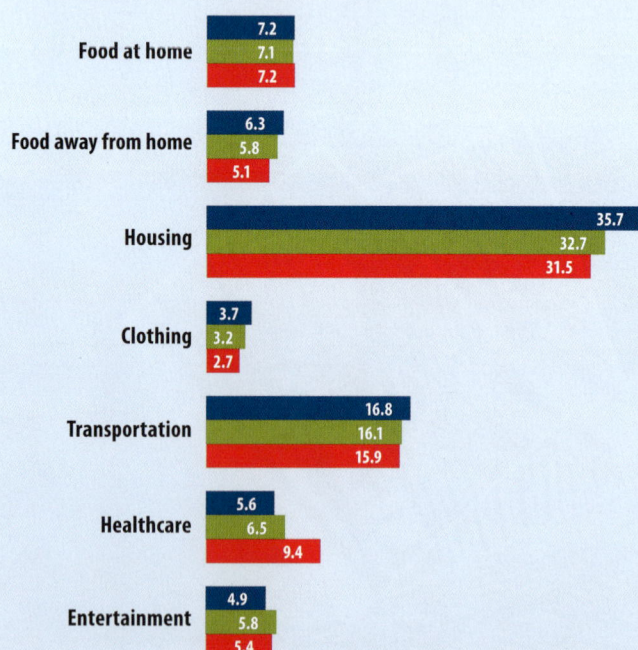

**Percent of Annual Spending on Major Categories**
by Millennials, Gen Xers, & Baby Boomers

| Category | Millennials | Gen Xers | Baby Boomers |
|---|---|---|---|
| Food at home | 7.2 | 7.1 | 7.2 |
| Food away from home | 6.3 | 5.8 | 5.1 |
| Housing | 35.7 | 32.7 | 31.5 |
| Clothing | 3.7 | 3.2 | 2.7 |
| Transportation | 16.8 | 16.1 | 15.9 |
| Healthcare | 5.6 | 6.5 | 9.4 |
| Entertainment | 4.9 | 5.8 | 5.4 |

Data source: Bureau of Labor Statistics

Marketers need to do more research on millennial spending habits. Despite differences in values, these three generations have some similar spending habits.

**COMPREHENSION** Based on the reading, write T for *true* or F for *false*.

1. _____ Millennials make their buying decisions mostly on recommendations from friends.
2. _____ Millenials buy a lot of CDs and DVDs.
3. _____ Millennials make up the largest portion of Americans today.

**THINK ABOUT IT** Discuss the questions with a partner or in a small group.

1. Which generation do you belong to—Millennial? Gen X? Baby boomer? Do you think the article describes these generations correctly?
2. What does "You only live once" (YOLO) mean to you? Do you share the YOLO attitude?

## 14.1 Articles—An Overview

| EXAMPLES | EXPLANATION |
|---|---|
| Do you want **an** expensive wedding?<br>**A** college graduate wants to find **a** good job. | The indefinite articles *a* and *an* are used before a noun to refer to non-specific things and people (singular only). |
| Many people use **the** Internet to shop online.<br>**The** boomers were born between 1946 and 1964. | The definite article *the* is used before a noun to refer to specific things and people (singular or plural). |
| **Marketers** are interested in **millennials**.<br>**Ownership** of DVDs does not interest **millennials**. | A noun can be used without an article to refer to non-specific things and people. |

**EXERCISE 1** Listen to the paragraphs. Then write T for *true* or F for *false*. 14.2

1. _____ Historically, each generation in America has had a better standard of living than their parents.
2. _____ Millennials aren't different from their parents in spending.
3. _____ Getting married isn't a top priority for millennials.

**EXERCISE 2** Listen to the paragraphs again. Fill in the blanks with the article you hear. If you don't hear an article, fill in the blank with Ø. 14.2

___Ø___ Millennials are ___the___ first generation in American history to have
1.                              2.

_____ lower standard of living than their parents. Millennials looking for _____ job
3.                                                                              4.

in 2010 faced _____ unemployment rate of almost 10 percent. _____ average debt for
              5.                                                  6.

_____ millennial college graduate in 2013 was approximately $30,000. In _____
7.                                                                            8.

recent book called _____ *Next America*, _____ author, Paul Taylor, describes
                   9.                          10.

_____ economic changes we will see as boomers retire.
11.

*continued*

Millennials are not only different from their parents' generation in spending. They are _____12._____ first generation to grow up with _____13._____ technology. _____14._____ amount of time it takes _____15._____ product to reach a 50 percent adoption by _____16._____ consumers has become much shorter. It took 31 years for radio to reach 50 percent of consumers; television, 28 years; home computers, 18 years; smartphones, three and a half years. Consumers have adopted _____17._____ smartphones 10 times faster than they adopted _____18._____ computers.

Millennials also have _____19._____ different values from their parents. In 2018, 27 percent of millennials between 18 and 32 were married. In 1980, 48 percent of _____20._____ boomers in this age group were married. Millennials value _____21._____ fun and _____22._____ discovery. Boomers value _____23._____ family and _____24._____ practicality.

## 14.2 Making Generalizations

| EXAMPLES | EXPLANATION |
|---|---|
| **Smartphones** are more popular than **flip phones**.<br>**A smartphones** is more popular than **a flip phone**. | We can make a generalization about a count subject in two ways:<br>no article + plural noun<br>OR<br>*a* or *an* + singular noun |
| **Fun** is important for young people.<br>**Ownership** is not important for millennials. | We don't use an article to make a generalization about a noncount subject. |
| Millennials like **movies**.<br>Millennials value **discovery**. | To make a generalization about an object, count or noncount, we don't use an article. We use the plural form for count nouns. Noncount nouns are always singular. |

**EXERCISE 3** Match the subject on the left with the verb phrase on the right.

1. A shopper
2. TVs
3. Kids
4. Parents
5. Advertising
6. Parents often tell kids that
7. Grandparents
8. A child
9. Life

are expensive.
is short. You only live once (YOLO).
is often directed at millennials.
wants to get a good price.
often buy toys for their children.
like to give gifts to their grandchildren.
money doesn't grow on trees.
needs to learn about money.
want to have toys.

**EXERCISE 4** Complete the sentences to make generalizations about the subjects given. You may work with a partner.

1. Millennials _have different values from their parents._
2. A college graduate _____
3. Consumers _____
4. Life for older Americans _____
5. Good jobs _____
6. A wedding _____
7. Technology _____
8. Marketers _____
9. Boomers _____
10. DVDs _____
11. Money _____

**ABOUT YOU** Put a check (✓) next to the statements that are generally true in your country. Discuss your answers with a partner.

___ 1. A bank is a safe place to keep your money.
___ 2. Doctors make a lot of money.
___ 3. Teenagers have part-time jobs.
___ 4. Children work.
___ 5. Teachers earn a good salary.
___ 6. A government official makes a lot of money.
___ 7. Businesses are closed on Sundays.
___ 8. A college degree is needed to earn a good salary.

## 14.3 Classifying or Defining the Subject

| EXAMPLES | EXPLANATION |
| --- | --- |
| A millennial is **a** person born between 1981 and 1996. "Recession" is **an** economic term. | We classify or define a singular count noun like this: Singular noun + is + a(n) + (adjective) + noun. |
| Boomers are **Americans** born between 1946 and 1964. CDs are compact **discs**. | We classify or define a plural count noun like this: Plural noun + are + (adjective) + noun. |
| **What's** a millennial? **What** are boomers? | We can ask for a definition with *what*. |

**Note:**
We can also use *the* in a definition if the noun is specific.
  The Next America is **the** name of a book.
  A salary is **the** amount of money you get from working at your job.

**EXERCISE 5** In the left column, fill in the blank with the verb and an article if needed. Then match the subject on the left with the definition or classification on the right.

1. YOLO _____is an_____ person born between 1946 and 1964.

2. A boomer _____ owed money.

3. A recession _____ book about the future of the United States.

4. Debt _____ abbreviation.

5. A vendor _____ kids between the ages of 13 and 19.

6. *The Next America* _____ person or company that sells something.

7. Paul Taylor _____ time when the economy isn't strong.

8. Teenagers _____ man who wrote The Next America.

**EXERCISE 6** Define or classify the subject given. You may work with a partner.

1. A CD __is a disk that contains digital music.__

2. A quarter _____

3. A dime _____

4. A credit card _____

5. A debit card _____

6. A diamond _____

7. Silver and gold _____

8. Marketers _____

9. Consumers _____

10. A bank _____

11. A wallet _____

12. Expenses _____

---

**GRAMMAR IN USE**

When defining or classifying a subject, it is important to be aware of the verbs. Use the simple present for things, concrete or abstract, that exist in the current day, and for people who are alive.

*Identity theft **is** the illegal use of another person's private identifying information.*
*Bill Gates **is** an entrepreneur and businessman who founded Microsoft.*

However, to describe something from the past, you would use the simple past.

*Vikings **were** Scandinavian pirates who **attacked** the coasts of Europe from the 8th to 10th centuries.*

Many children have to do chores around the house.

# KIDS and MONEY

Read the following article. Pay special attention to the words in bold. 14.3

Kids like to spend money. With part-time jobs, **an** allowance[1] from their parents, gifts from grandparents and others, and no bills to pay, kids have **the** most disposable income[2] of **any** part of American society. According to **a** 2019 statistic, teens between 15 and 17 have $4,900 **a** year to spend. While **some** teens think about saving their money, about 21 percent say they don't save **any** money at all.

**The** average American child gets **an** allowance of about $800 **a** year. In 90 percent of American homes, kids are expected to do **some** chores[3] in exchange for their allowance. In many cases, this is no more than one hour **a** week. What does **an** allowance teach **a** child about money? Many experts believe **the** answer is nothing!

Parents need to talk to kids about money early. When is **the** best time? **The** earlier **the** better, according to experts. Even preschool children can learn about money. For example, they can learn that you need money to buy things and that you earn money by working. They can learn that there is **a** difference between **the** things you want and **the** things you need. Between six and 10, children can learn to make choices and to compare prices. Between 11 and 13, they can learn that they should save 10 cents of every dollar they receive. Between 14 and 18, they should start to compare **the** cost of different colleges.

Warren Buffet is one of **the** most famous billionaires in **the** world. He says that **the** age at which parents teach their kids good financial habits will determine how successful **the** child will be later in life. Buffet taught his children **the** value of learning from experience. He allowed them to succeed and fail on their own. He did not help them financially if they got in **any** trouble. Interestingly, he is not planning on leaving his grown children **a** large inheritance[4]. He said, "I want to give my kids just enough so that they would feel that they could do anything, but not so much that they would feel like doing nothing."

---

[1] allowance: money children get from their parents for everyday expenses
[2] disposable income: money a person can spend after expenses
[3] chore: a household job, such as washing the dishes
[4] inheritance: money a person receives from someone who died

**COMPREHENSION** Based on the reading, write T for *true* or F for *false*.

1. _____ Many experts believe that giving children an allowance teaches them the value of money.
2. _____ Most kids who get an allowance are expected to do several hours a week of chores.
3. _____ Warren Buffet plans to leave his children the majority of his wealth.

**THINK ABOUT IT** Discuss the questions with a partner or in a small group.

1. What is your opinion about giving a child an allowance? Is this common in your culture?
2. Reread the quote by Warren Buffet at the end of the article. Why might a person who has a lot of money feel like doing nothing? Do you think Warren Buffet is right to have this concern for his kids?

## 14.4 Non-Specific Nouns

| EXAMPLES | EXPLANATION |
| --- | --- |
| She has **a** job.<br>She gets **an** allowance. | We use *a* or *an* to introduce a singular non-specific count noun. |
| He has to do (**some**) chores.<br>He doesn't have (**any**) chores on weekdays.<br>Does he have (**any**) chores on Sunday? | We use *some* or *any* to introduce a plural non-specific count noun. *Some* and *any* can be omitted. |
| He needs (**some**) money.<br>He doesn't have (**any**) cash.<br>Is there (**any**) money in your checking account? | We use *some* and *any* to introduce a non-specific noncount noun. |

Notes:
1. Both *some* and *any* can be used in questions with plural nouns and noncount nouns.
    *Do you have **some** money? Do you have **any** quarters?*
2. *Some* and *any* can be omitted.
    *Do you have money? Do you have quarters?*

**EXERCISE 7** Fill in the blanks with *a, an, some, any,* or Ø (for no article) to complete the conversation between a son (A) and his mother (B). In some cases, more than one answer is possible.

**A:** Mom, I want to get ____*a*____ job.
                              1.

**B:** But you're only 16 years old.

**A:** I'm old enough to work. I need to make _____ money.
                                                2.

**B:** Grandma and Grandpa always give you _____ money for your birthday. And we give you
                                             3.

_____ 15 dollars a week. Isn't that enough money for you?
    4.

**A:** It's not even enough to take _____ girl to _____ movie.
                                       5.                    6.

**B:** What are you going to do about school? You won't have _____ time to study.
                                                                 7.

**A:** You know I'm _____ good student. I'm sure I won't have _____ problems
            8.                                                9.

working part-time. We don't have _____ homework on weekends.
                                    10.

**B:** I'm worried about your grades falling. Maybe we should raise your allowance. Then you won't have to work.

**A:** I want to have my own money. I want to buy _____ new clothes. And I'm going to save
                                                 11.

_____ money each week. Then I can buy _____ car someday.
    12.                                        13.

**B:** Why do you want a car? You have _____ bike.
                                         14.

**A:** Bikes are great for exercise, but if my job is far away, I'll need a car for transportation.

**B:** So, you need _____ job to buy _____ car, and you need _____
                      15.                   16.                          17.

car to get to work.

**A:** Yes. My friends work, and they're good students. I'm not _____ baby anymore. I really want
                                                                 18.

to work.

## 14.5 Specific Nouns

| EXAMPLES | EXPLANATION |
| --- | --- |
| **The reading** on page 365 is about kids and money.<br>**The photos** in this unit are related to money.<br>What did you do with **the money** I gave you? | We use *the* with a specific noun. A noun is specific if it is defined in the phrase or clause after the noun. |
| **The first** reading in this unit is about millennials and money.<br>When is **the right** time to talk to kids about money? | We use *the* when there is only one of something. We usually use *the* with the following words: *first, second, next, last, only, same, back, front,* and *right*. |
| Where's **the teacher**?<br>I have a question about **the reading** on kids and money. | We use *the* when there is a shared experience. Students in the same class talk about *the* teacher, *the* textbook, *the* homework, *the* board. |
| Teenagers should put some of their savings in **the** bank.<br>They want money to go to **the** movies with their friends. | We use *the* with certain familiar places and people:<br>the bank    the beach    the bus<br>the zoo    the post office    the train<br>the park    the doctor    the movies<br>the store    the hospital |
| Warren Buffet is one of **the richest** people in the world.<br>What's **the best** way to teach kids about money? | We use *the* before a superlative form. |
| Millennials often use **the Internet** to shop. | We use *the* before a unique noun. |
| You have **an allowance**. You can use **the allowance** to go out with your friends.<br>There is **some money** on the table. You can use **the money** to go to the movies. | After a non-specific noun is introduced with *a/an/some/any*, we use the definite article to refer to a specific example of this noun. |

*continued*

**Notes:**
1. We don't use *the* to make a generalization. Compare:

    **Life** today is very different from **life** 40 years ago. (Life *is general*.)

    **The life** of my grandparents is different from my life. (The life *is specific*.)

2. When we introduce a noun with *there + be*, we use the indefinite article. We can refer to the noun again with *the*.

    There was **a recession** in 2007. **The recession** affected a lot of people.

---

**EXERCISE 8** Fill in the blanks with *a* or *the*.

**A:** I need to buy _____a_____ new laptop.

**B:** What's wrong with _____ laptop you have now?

**A:** It's too old.

**B:** There's _____ good website that compares computer prices.

**A:** Can you show me _____ website?

**B:** Sure. Let's look at my tablet.

**A:** That's _____ cool tablet you have.

**B:** Thanks. I don't even use _____ computer anymore.

**A:** Was _____ tablet expensive?

**B:** I got _____ good deal online.

**EXERCISE 9** Fill in the blanks with *the, a, some,* or *any*.

**A:** Where are you going after class?

**B:** I'm going to __the__ cafeteria. I want to buy _____ cup of coffee.

**A:** You don't have to go to _____ cafeteria. There's _____ coffee machine on this floor.

**B:** I only have _____ $10 bill. Do you have _____ change?

**A:** I have _____ change, but I need it for the parking meters. There's _____ dollar-bill changer next to _____ coffee machine.

**B:** Uh-oh. _____ coffee machine is out of order. I guess I'll have to go to _____ cafeteria after all. Do you want to go with me?

**A:** Sorry. I don't have _____ time.

**EXERCISE 10** Fill in the blanks with *the, a, an, any, some* or Ø for no article. In some cases, more than one answer is possible.

1. **A:** Mom, I need to buy _____some_____ new jeans.
   a.

   **B:** There are _____ jeans on this rack. Which ones do you like?
   b.

   **A:** I love these. Don't you?

   **B:** But they're torn.

   **A:** That's _____ style these days.
   c.

   **B:** I'll never understand _____ kids. In my day, _____ torn clothes meant you
   d.                                    e.
   were poor.

   **A:** That's silly.

   **B:** I think _____ life was better back then.
   f.

   **A:** You always compare your childhood with today's kids, but _____ times have changed. So,
   g.
   what did you decide about _____ jeans? Can I buy them? I have enough money from
   h.
   _____ job I had last summer.
   i.

   **B:** I suppose so. Go try them on. _____ dressing room is over there.
   j.

2. **A:** Where are you going?

   **B:** To _____ store. I want to deposit _____ check, and I need to get
   a.                                    b.
   _____ cash. There's _____ ATM at _____ supermarket on
   c.                         d.                      e.
   _____ corner.
   f.

   **A:** I'll go with you.

   *(At the ATM)*

   **B:** Oh, no. Look. _____ ATM is out of order.
   g.

   **A:** Don't worry. There's _____ ATM on _____ next corner.
   h.                                   i.

   **B:** That ATM doesn't belong to my bank. If I use it, I'll have to pay _____ fee.
   j.

   **A:** How much is _____ fee?
   k.

   **B:** It's usually $3.00 or $3.50. That's a lot of money to me. _____ more I save,
   l.
   _____ more I have to spend on _____ things I want.
   m.                                       n.

*continued*

3. **A:** I'm going to _____ post office. I need to buy _____ stamps.
   　　　　　　　　　　　a.　　　　　　　　　　　　　　　　b.

   **B:** I'll go with you. I want to mail _____ package to my parents.
   　　　　　　　　　　　　　　　　　　　c.

   **A:** What's in _____ package?
   　　　　　　　　　d.

   **B:** _____ coat for my sister and _____ money for my mother.
   　　　e.　　　　　　　　　　　　　　　　f.

   **A:** You should never send _____ money by mail. You should buy _____ money order at _____ bank.
   　　　　　　　　　　　　　　　g.　　　　　　　　　　　　　　　　　　　　h.
   　　　　　　　　　　i.

   **B:** How much does it cost?

   **A:** Well, if you have _____ account in _____ bank, it's usually free. If not, you'll probably have to pay _____ fee.
   　　　　　　　　　　　　　j.　　　　　　　　　k.
   　　　　　　　　　　　　　　　　　　　　　　　l.

## 14.6 Specific or Non-Specific Nouns with Quantity Words

| EXAMPLES | EXPLANATION |
|---|---|
| **All** children like toys.<br>**Most** American homes have a television.<br>**Few** people are billionaires. | We use *all, most, many, some, (a)/(very) few,* and *(a)/(very) little* before non-specific nouns. |
| **All of the** readings in this unit are about money.<br>**Very few of the** people in my country are rich.<br>**None of the** readings gives information about how to make money. | We use *all of the, most of the, many of the, some of the, (a)/(very) few of the, (a)/(very) little of the,* and *none of the* before specific nouns. |

**Notes:**

1. After *all, of* is often omitted.

    **All the readings** in this unit are about money.

2. After *none of the* + plural noun, a singular verb is correct. However, a plural verb is often used in less formal speech or writing.

    *None of the readings is long.* (correct)

    *None of the readings are long.* (common)

3. Delete *the* when there is a possessive form.

    He spent **all of his money** on a new car.

4. Remember, *few* and *little* without *a* mean "not enough." We often put *very* before these words to emphasize that the quantity is not enough.

**ABOUT YOU** Fill in the blanks with *all, most, some,* or *(a)/(very) few* to make a general statement about your country or another country you know about. Discuss your answers with a partner.

1. ____Some____ people have a car.
2. _____ schools have computers.
3. _____ teachers have a good salary.
4. _____ people use credit cards.
5. _____ kids get an allowance.
6. _____ parents buy a lot of toys for their children.
7. _____ college graduates can find a good job.
8. _____ people have a checking account.
9. _____ grandparents give their grandchildren a lot of gifts.

**ABOUT YOU** Fill in the blanks with a quantity word to make a statement about specific nouns.

1. ____A few of the____ students in this class are boomers.
2. _____ people I know are millennials.
3. _____ my friends shop online.
4. _____ students in this class have a job.
5. _____ people I know have a smartphone.
6. _____ older people in my family use technology.
7. _____ kids in my family use technology.
8. _____ computers at this school are new.

> **FUN WITH GRAMMAR**
>
> Role-play a conversation. Work with a partner. The teacher will write six quantity words on the board. Continue the conversation below for several exchanges, incorporating two of the quantity words correctly. Then role-play your conversation for the class as students listen for the quantity words and correct use of specific or nonspecific nouns.
>
> A: I think **all Americans** are friendly.
> B: Well, . . .

Articles, *Other/Another*, Indefinite Pronouns

Billionaires Jeff Bezos and Mark Zuckerberg

# Billionaires

Read the following article. Pay special attention to the words in bold. 14.4

It's hard to imagine having over a billion dollars. Only about 2,100 people in the world are billionaires. The United States leads the world with the largest number. In 2018, the United States had over 500 billionaires. At the top of the list is Jeff Bezos, the founder of Amazon, with over $130 billion. **Another** area of the world that produces a large number of billionaires is China, with close to 400.

As hard as it is to imagine having over a billion dollars, try to imagine accumulating[1] this wealth before the age of 40! In 2018, Kylie Jenner became the youngest self-made billionaire ever at the age of 21. In 2014, a financial website, Bankrate.com, listed the 10 youngest billionaires in the world at the time. The richest, Mark Zuckerberg, the founder of Facebook, now has a net worth of over $62 billion. But he's not the only one to get rich from Facebook. **Another** person who became a billionaire from Facebook is Dustin Moskovitz. While **other** billionaires prefer to live a life of luxury, Moskovitz rides his bike to work and flies commercial airlines. Both Zuckerberg and Moskovitz have signed the Giving Pledge, which Warren Buffet and **another** famous billionaire, Bill Gates, started. The Giving Pledge has gotten the commitment[2] of Zuckerberg, Moskovitz, and **others** to give the majority of their wealth to philanthropy[3] while they're still alive.

The second richest person on Bankrate's list in 2014 was Yang Huiyan, from China. She made her money in real estate. She also inherited money from her father. She was the only woman on the list of young billionaires in 2014. All **the others** were men. With over $22 billion in 2018, she is on the list of global billionaires along with 241 **other** women.

Some of the billionaires on the list became rich mainly by inheriting family money. One of these is Fahd Hariri of Lebanon. He and his five siblings inherited their father's wealth when their father, the prime minister of Lebanon, was assassinated[4] in 2005. Hariri now owns a furniture company, which supplies furniture to **other** wealthy people, mostly in Saudi Arabia.

If we think about inheriting this large amount of money, we might think of what a nice life we can have. On **the other** hand, we might think, "Would easy money kill our motivation?"

---

[1] to accumulate: to gather together
[2] commitment: a promise
[3] philanthropy: the practice of giving money to people in need
[4] to assassinate: to kill

**COMPREHENSION** Based on the reading, write T for *true* or F for *false*.

1. _____ The wealthiest person in the world is from the United States.
2. _____ The richest person on Bankrate's list is a woman.
3. _____ All of the people on the list inherited money from their family.

**THINK ABOUT IT** Discuss the questions with a partner or in a small group.

1. If you had a billion dollars, would you commit to the Giving Pledge and give the majority of your wealth to philanthropy? Why or why not? If yes, which causes in particular would you contribute to?
2. Do you think easy money could kill your motivation? Do you think motivation is important for a happy life?

## 14.7 *Other* and *Another*

The use of *other* and *another* depends on whether a noun is singular or plural, specific or non-specific.

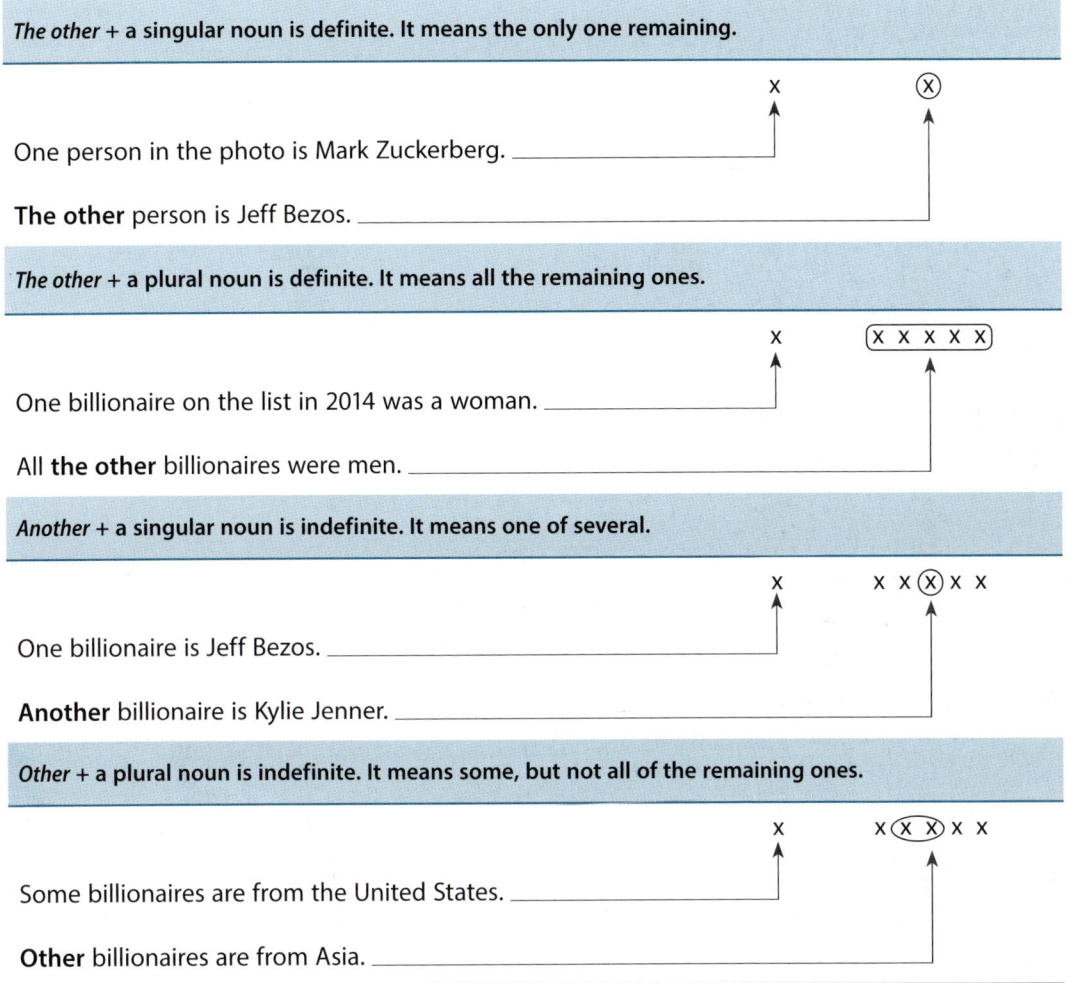

Articles, *Other/Another*, Indefinite Pronouns   373

**EXERCISE 11** Circle the correct words to complete this conversation.

**A:** Last month, I went to the doctor, and she sent me to get an X-ray. I got a bill and paid it, but then I got (**another**/the other) bill. Can you help me figure this out?
　　　　　　　　　　　　　　　1.

**B:** Let's see. Well, one bill is from the doctor. (*The other*/*Another*) bill is from the X-ray lab.
　　　　　　　　　　　　　　　　　　　　　　　　　　　2.

**A:** This is crazy.

**B:** I know, right? Wait for your insurance to pay. After your insurance pays, they'll send you (*another*/*other*) bill that shows the amount you have to pay.
　　　3.

**A:** There are two phone numbers. Which one should I call for information?

**B:** The first number is for telephone service. (*The other*/*Another*) number is a fax number.
　　　　　　　　　　　　　　　　　　　　　　　　4.

**A:** How do I pay?

**B:** There are two methods of payment: One method is by check. (*Other*/*The other*) method is by credit card.
　　　　　　　　　　　　　　　　　　　　　　　　　　　　　5.

**A:** I hate paying bills. Every month, I get a gas bill, a cell phone bill, an electricity bill, a cable bill, and (*other*/*another*) bills. This is so confusing.
　　6.

**B:** Some people send a check, but (*other*/*another*) people set up direct payment. Call the electric company
　　　　　　　　　　　　　　　　　　　　7.
and all (*other*/*the other*) companies to see if you can set up an automatic payment from your checking
　　　　　8.
account. That way, you don't have to think about bills every month.

## 14.8 More about *Other* and *Another*

| EXAMPLES | EXPLANATION |
|---|---|
| One young billionaire is Mark Zuckerberg.<br>**Another billionaire** is Dustin Muskovitz.<br>**Another one** is Dustin Muskovitz.<br>**Another** is Dustin Muskovitz. | After *another* or *the other*, we can substitute a singular noun with *one*. We can also omit *one*. |
| One billionaire is a woman.<br>**The other billionaires** are men.<br>**The other ones** are men.<br>**The others** are men. | After *other* or *the other*, we can substitute a plural noun with *ones*. We can also omit *ones*. If we omit it, we use *others*, not *other*. |
| This $10 bill is torn. Please give me **another** one. | *Another* is sometimes used to mean a different one, or one more. |

**Note:**
We omit *the* when we use a possessive form.
　　*I have two bank accounts. One account is a checking account. **My other** account is a savings account.* (NOT: *My the other*)

**EXERCISE 12** Fill in the blanks with *the other, another, the others,* or *other* to complete the conversation between a grandson (A) and his grandfather (B).

**A:** I want to buy ___another___ pair of sneakers.
                         1.

**B:** You already have about six pairs of sneakers. I bought you a new pair for your last birthday.

**A:** The new pair is fine, but all ___the others___ are too small for me. You know I'm growing very
                                      2.
fast, so I threw them away.

**B:** Why did you throw them away? ___Other___ boys in your neighborhood could use them.
                                     3.

**A:** They wouldn't like them. They're out of style.

**B:** You kids are so wasteful today. What's wrong with the sneakers I bought you last month? If they fit you, why
do you need ___another___ pair?
              4.

**A:** Everybody in my class at school has red sneakers with the laces tied backward.

**B:** Do you always have to have what all ___the other___ kids in school have? Can't you think for
                                             5.
yourself?

**A:** Didn't you ask your parents for stuff when you were in middle school?

**B:** My parents were poor, and my two brothers and I worked to help them. When we outgrew our clothes, we
gave them to ___other___ families nearby. And our neighbors gave us the things that their
               6.
children outgrew. One neighbor had two sons. One son was a year older than me.
___The other___ one was two years younger. So we were constantly passing clothes back and
    7.
forth. We never threw things out. We didn't waste our parents' money. My oldest brother worked in a factory
and gave all his salary to our parents. My ___other___ brother and I helped our father in
                                              8.
his business. My dad didn't give us a salary. It was our duty to help him.

**A:** You don't understand how important it is to look like all ___the other___ kids.
                                                                   9.

**B:** I guess I don't. I'm old-fashioned. Every generation has ___another___ way of looking at
                                                                  10.
things.

# 14.9 Definite and Indefinite Pronouns

| EXAMPLES | EXPLANATION |
|---|---|
| A: Did you read **the article** about **the billionaires**?<br>B: Yes, I read **it** yesterday. Five of **them** are Americans. | We use definite pronouns *him*, *her*, *them*, and *it* to refer to specific count nouns. |
| I'm going to buy a laptop. I need **one** to take notes in class. | We use the indefinite pronoun *one* to refer to a non-specific singular count noun. |
| **NONCOUNT:**<br>My son asked me for money. I didn't give him **any**. Do you think I should give him **some**?<br>**COUNT:**<br>I told him not to buy video games, but he bought **some**.<br>I wanted him to buy books, but he didn't buy **any**. | With noncount nouns and plural count nouns, we refer to a non-specific noun as follows:<br>• *some* for affirmative statements<br>• *any* for negative statements<br>• *some* or *any* for questions. |

Notes:
1. We often use *any* and *some* before *more*.

    Son: *I don't have enough money. I need **some more**.*

    Dad: *I'm not going to give you **any more**.*

2. We can start with a non-specific noun, but when referring to it specifically, we use a definite pronoun.

    *I have **some questions** about one of the billionaires. Can you answer **them** for me?*

---

**EXERCISE 13** Fill in the blanks with *one* or *it* to complete the conversation between a mother (A) and her teenage daughter (B).

A: I have a brochure from the state university. Do you want to look at ___it___ with me?
                                                                                                   1.

B: I don't know, Mom. I don't know if I want to go to college when I graduate.

A: Why not? We've been planning for _____ since the day you were born.
                                                               2.

B: College isn't for everyone. I want to be an artist.

A: Artists don't make any money! You can be _____ and still go to college. Please choose a more
                                                                                  3.

   practical career, like teaching.

B: I'm not really interested in a college degree.

A: But it's good to have _____ anyway.
                                        4.

B: I don't know why. In college, I'll have to study general courses, too, like math and biology. You know I

   hate math. I'm not good at _____.
                                                                             5.

A: Maybe we should look at art schools. There's one downtown. Do you want to visit _____?
                                                                                                                                        6.

B: We can probably find information about _____ online.
                                                                                                7.

**A:** (*Looking at the art school website*) This school sounds great. Let's call and ask for an application.

**B:** I'm sure you can get _____ online.
                                    8.

**A:** Oh, yes. Here it is. Let's print a copy of _____.
                                                    9.

**B:** You can fill _____ out online and submit _____ electronically.
                     10.                              11.

**EXERCISE 14** Fill in the blanks with *one, some, any, it, a, an, the,* or *Ø* (for no article) to complete the conversation between a teenager (A) and her mother (B). In some cases, more than one answer is possible.

**A:** Can I have 15 dollars? I want to buy ____a____ poster of my favorite singer.
                                              1.

**B:** I gave you _____ money last week. What did you do with _____?
                   2.                                                3.

**A:** I spent _____ on a movie.
                4.

**B:** No, you can't have _____ more money until next week. Besides, why do you want a poster? You
                           5.

already have _____ of your favorite singer in your room.
               6.

**A:** I took _____ down. I don't even like her anymore.
              7.

**B:** What happened to all _____ money Grandpa gave you for your birthday?
                              8.

**A:** I don't have _____ money anymore. I spent _____.
                     9.                                  10.

**B:** You have to learn that _____ money doesn't grow on trees. If you want me to give you
                                11.

_____, you'll have to work for it. You can start by cleaning your room.
   12.

**A:** But I cleaned _____ two weeks ago.
                       13.

**B:** That was two weeks ago. It's dirty again.

**A:** I don't have _____ time. I have to meet my friends.
                     14.

**B:** You can't go out. You need to do your homework.

**A:** I don't have _____. Please let me have 15 dollars.
                     15.

**B:** When I was your age, I had _____ job.
                                    16.

**A:** I wanted to get a job last summer, but I couldn't find _____.
                                                              17.

**B:** You didn't try hard enough. When I worked, I gave my parents half of _____ money I earned. You
                                                                             18.

kids today have _____ easy life.
                  19.

**A:** Why do _____ parents always say that to _____ kids?
               20.                                     21.

**B:** Because it's true. It's time you learn that _____ life is hard.
                                                    22.

Articles, *Other/Another*, Indefinite Pronouns

# SUMMARY OF UNIT 14

## Indefinite Articles

|  | COUNT—SINGULAR | COUNT—PLURAL | NONCOUNT |
|---|---|---|---|
| **General** | *A/AN* | *Ø ARTICLE* | *Ø ARTICLE* |
|  | **A child** likes toys. | **Children** like toys.<br>I love **children**. | **Money** can't buy happiness.<br>Everyone needs **money**. |
| **Non-Specific** | *A/AN* | *SOME/ANY* | *SOME/ANY* |
|  | I bought **a toy**. | I bought **some toys**.<br>I didn't buy **any games**.<br>Did you buy **any games**? | I spent **some money**.<br>I didn't buy **any candy**.<br>Do you have **any time**? |
| **Classification/Definition** | *A/AN* | *Ø ARTICLE* |  |
|  | "Recession" is **an economic term**. | Teenagers are **young adults**. |  |

## Definite Articles

|  | COUNT—SINGULAR | COUNT—PLURAL | NONCOUNT |
|---|---|---|---|
| **Specific** | **The reading** on page 365 is about kids and money. | **The photos** in this unit are about money. | **The information** about millennials is interesting. |
| **Unique** | **The Internet** is a great tool. | **The Hawaiian Islands** are beautiful. |  |

## *Other/Another*

|  | SPECIFIC | NON-SPECIFIC |
|---|---|---|
| **Singular** | the other book<br>the other one<br>the other<br>my other book | another book<br>another one<br>another |
| **Plural** | the other books<br>the other ones<br>the others<br>my other books | other books<br>other ones<br>others |

## Indefinite Pronouns

We use *one/some/any* to substitute for non-specific nouns.

| Singular Count | I need a quarter. Do you have **one**? |
|---|---|
| Plural Count | I need some pennies. You have **some**. |
| Noncount | I don't have any change. Do you have **any**? |

# REVIEW

Circle the correct words to complete the conversation. (Ø means no article is needed.)

**A:** I bought my daughter (**a**/the/some) new doll for her birthday. Now she's asking me to buy her
1.

(the other/another/other) one. There's nothing wrong with (a/the/Ø) doll I bought her last month. She just got
2.                                                                                        3.

bored with it.

**B:** That's how (Ø/the/a) kids are. They don't understand (a/the/Ø) value of money.
4.                                                            5.

**A:** You're right. They think that (a/the/Ø) money grows on trees.
6.

**B:** I suppose it's our fault. We have to set (Ø/a/the) good example. On the one hand, we tell them to be careful
7.

about money. On (the other/other/another) hand, we buy a lot of things we don't really need. We use (a/the/Ø)
8.                                                                                                   9.

credit cards instead of (a/the/Ø) cash and worry about paying (a/the/Ø) bill later.
10.                                                            11.

**A:** I suppose you're right. Last month, we bought (the/a/Ø) new TV.
12.

**B:** I thought you bought (it/one) last year.
13.

**A:** We did. But we were at the appliance store last month looking for (the/a/Ø) new dishwasher when we saw a
14.

much bigger, better TV. We decided to get (it/one).
15.

**B:** What did you do with (the other/another/other) TV?
16.

**A:** We put (it/one) in (the/a/Ø) basement. I suppose we didn't really need (other/any other/another) one.
17.          18.                                                              19.

**B:** Last weekend, my husband bought (a/some/the) new phone. He said (a/the/Ø) new one has better apps than
20.                                                21.

(another/other/the other) one. And it has better games. He got tired of (another/the others/the other) games.
22.                                                                      23.

**A:** Our kids are imitating us. We need to make (some/any/the) changes in our own behavior. I'm going to start
24.

(a/the/Ø) budget tonight. I'm going to start saving (a/any/some) money each month.
25.                                                  26.

**B:** Do you need (a/any/the) help with it? There's (a/the/Ø) course at the community college on how to manage
27.                                       28.

your money. Do you want to take it with me?

**A:** That's (a/Ø/the) good idea. How much does it cost?
29.

**B:** I'm not sure. Some courses are $50 a course. (Others/Other/Another) courses are $100 a credit hour. We should
30.

take it no matter what it costs.

# FROM GRAMMAR TO WRITING

## PART 1  Editing Advice

1. Choose the correct article or Ø for no article.

   Warren Buffet is ^a^ famous billionaire.

   What is ^the^ first job you had?

   You should save ~~a~~ money for college.

2. Use *the* after a quantity word when the noun is specific.

   I spent most of ^the^ money my grandparents gave me.

3. Use a plural count noun after a quantity expression.

   A few of my friend^s^ have a part-time job.

4. *Another* is always singular.

   Some teenagers save their money. ~~Another~~ ^Other^ teenagers spend it without thinking about their future.

5. *A* and *an* are always singular.

   Mark Zuckerberg and Warren Buffet are ~~a~~ billionaires.

6. Use *a* or *an* for a definition or a classification of a singular count noun.

   A millennial is ^a^ person born between 1981 and 1996.

7. Don't use the definite article with a possessive form.

   I use two cards for my purchases. One is my credit card. My ~~the~~ other card is a debit card.

8. Don't use *the* to make a general statement about a noun.

   ~~The~~ ^M^money doesn't buy happiness.

   ~~The~~ ^C^children like toys.

9. Use an indefinite pronoun to substitute for a non-specific noun.

   I have a checking account. Do you have ~~it~~ ^one^?

10. Before a plural noun or pronoun, use *other*, not *others*.

    Some billionaires are from the United States. Other~~s~~ billionaires are from Asia.

## PART 2 Editing Practice

Some of the shaded words and phrases have mistakes. Find the mistakes and correct them. If the shaded words are correct, write C.

I'm a teenager and I know this: the teenagers think a lot about the money. We want money to
    1. C                        2.                        3.                  4.

buy a new jeans or sneakers. Or we want money to go out with our friends. We sometimes want
     5.

to go to the restaurant or to a movie. Most of the my friends try to get a job in the summer to
     6.                7.                8.

make some money. At the beginning of every summer, my friends always say, "I need a job. Do
      9.                                                            10.

you know where I can find it?"
                     11.

One of my friend found a summer job at Bender's. Bender's is small bookstore. Another
          12.                                              13.      14.

friend found a job at a summer camp. But I have the other way to make money. I prefer to
                                                  15.

work in my neighborhood. Most of people in my neighborhood are working or elderly. I ask
                            16.

my neighbors for work. Some neighbors pay me to take care of the lawn in front of their house.
                                                                     17.

Another neighbors pay me to clean their garage. In the winter, I shovel a sidewalks in front of
 18.                                                                                   19.

their houses. I like these jobs. I love a music, and I listen to my favorite music while I work.
                                       20.

What do I do with the money I get from my jobs? I buy songs on Internet. I used to buy
                         21.                                       22.

CDs, but I only liked a few songs. Some of songs on the CDs were great, but I never listened to
                                      23.

anothers. Now I can download the songs I like and not pay for all the others songs on a CD. This
 24.                         25.                                     26.

helps me save money. With the money I save, I can buy the other things I want.
                                                             27.

---

### WRITING TIP

When writing an introduction, grab the readers' attention with an interesting piece of information. If you choose prompt 1, you can start with some statistics. For example, *Did you know that kids in the U.S. earn an average of $67.80 per month?* For prompt 2, one possible way to pull in the reader is with a series of questions directed at a teen. For example, *Do you need money to upgrade your phone or to get a new pair of sneakers?* Engaging openers captivate readers and make them want to read more.

---

## PART 3 Write

Read the prompts. Choose one and write about it.

1. Do you think children should get an allowance from their parents? How much? Does it depend on the child's age? Should the child have to do chores for the money? Write a few paragraphs explaining your point of view.
2. Write a short essay giving advice to teenagers on how to earn and save money.

## PART 4 Edit

Reread the Summary of Unit 14 and the editing advice. Edit your writing from Part 3.

# APPENDIX A

## SUMMARY OF VERB TENSES

| VERB TENSE | FORM | MEANING AND USE |
|---|---|---|
| SIMPLE PRESENT | I **have** class Mondays.<br>He **doesn't have** class today.<br>**Do** you **have** class today?<br>**What do** you **do** every day? | • facts, general truths, habits, and customs<br>• used with frequency adverbs, e.g., *always, usually, sometimes, never*<br>• regular activities and repeated actions |
| PRESENT CONTINUOUS | I **am studying** biology this semester.<br>He **isn't studying** now.<br>**Are** you **studying** this weekend?<br>**What is** she **studying** at college? | • actions that are currently in progress<br>• future actions if a future time expression is used or understood |
| PRESENT PERFECT | I **have seen** the movie *Titanic*.<br>He **has seen** *Titanic* five times.<br>**Have** you **seen** *Titanic*?<br>**Why have** you never **seen** *Titanic*? | • action that started in the past and continues to the present<br>• action that repeats during a period of time from the past to the present<br>• action that occurred at an indefinite time in the past |
| PRESENT PERFECT CONTINUOUS | She **has been working** there for years.<br>I **haven't been working** regularly in a while.<br>**Have** you **been working** here long?<br>**Where have** you **been working** lately? | • an action that started in the past and continues to the present |
| SIMPLE PAST | The students **liked** the class discussion.<br>They **didn't like** the homework.<br>**Did** you **like** the discussion?<br>**What did** you **like** about the discussion? | • a single, short, past action<br>• a longer past action<br>• a repeated past action |
| PAST CONTINUOUS | She **was watching** TV when I called.<br>I **wasn't watching** TV when you called.<br>**Were** you **watching** TV around 10?<br>**What were** you **watching**? | • an action in progress at a specific past time<br>• often with the simple past in another clause to show the relationship of a longer past action to a shorter past action |
| PAST PERFECT | I **had** just **left** when she arrived.<br>We **hadn't left** yet when she arrived.<br>**Had** you already **left** the party when she arrived?<br>**How long had** you **known** each other before you got married? | • used to indicate the first of two past events |
| PAST PERFECT CONTINUOUS | The movie **had been playing** for 10 minutes when they arrived.<br>The movie **hadn't been playing** for too long when they arrived.<br>**How long had** the movie **been playing**? | • a continuous past action that was completed before another past action<br>• used with action verbs, e.g., *arrive, ask, eat, enter* |
| FUTURE WITH *WILL* | I **will go** to the store<br>He **won't go** to the store.<br>**Will** you **go** to the store?<br>**When will** you **go** to the store? | • future plans/decisions made in the moment<br>• strong predictions<br>• promises and offers to help |

| | | |
|---|---|---|
| **FUTURE WITH *BE GOING TO*** | He**'s going to study** all weekend.<br>He **isn't going to study** Saturday.<br>**Are** you **going to study** Saturday?<br>**What are** you **going to study** Saturday? | • future plans that are already made<br>• predictions |
| **FUTURE CONTINUOUS** | I **will be sleeping** at midnight.<br>They**'re going to be attending** a concert at that time. | • actions that will occur in the future and continue for an expected period of time |
| **FUTURE PERFECT** | She **will have finished** by 10 o'clock. | • actions that will be completed before another point in the future |
| **FUTURE PERFECT CONTINUOUS** | I **will have been standing** here for an hour when the train finally arrives. | • actions that will continue up until a point in the future |

# APPENDIX B

# NONACTION VERBS

| DESCRIPTION | FEELINGS | DESIRES | MEASUREMENTS | MENTAL STATES | SENSES |
|---|---|---|---|---|---|
| appear*<br>be*<br>consist of<br>look*<br>look like<br>resemble<br>seem | appreciate<br>care<br>dislike<br>forgive<br>hate<br>like<br>love<br>mind<br>miss | hope<br>need<br>prefer<br>want<br>wish | cost<br>measure*<br>weigh* | agree<br>believe<br>concern<br>disagree<br>doubt<br>forget<br>guess<br>know<br>imagine<br>mean<br>recognize<br>remember*<br>suppose<br>surprise<br>think*<br>understand | belong<br>contain<br>feel*<br>have*<br>hear*<br>hurt<br>notice<br>own<br>possess<br>see*<br>smell*<br>sound* |

*Words that also have an active meaning

# APPENDIX C

## IRREGULAR VERB FORMS

| BASE FORM | PAST FORM | PAST PARTICIPLE | BASE FORM | PAST FORM | PAST PARTICIPLE |
|---|---|---|---|---|---|
| be | was/were | been | fight | fought | fought |
| bear | bore | born/borne | find | found | found |
| beat | beat | beaten | fit | fit | fit |
| become | became | become | flee | fled | fled |
| begin | began | begun | fly | flew | flown |
| bend | bent | bent | forbid | forbade | forbidden |
| bet | bet | bet | forget | forgot | forgotten |
| bid | bid | bid | forgive | forgave | forgiven |
| bind | bound | bound | freeze | froze | frozen |
| bite | bit | bitten | get | got | gotten |
| bleed | bled | bled | give | gave | given |
| blow | blew | blown | go | went | gone |
| break | broke | broken | grind | ground | ground |
| breed | bred | bred | grow | grew | grown |
| bring | brought | brought | hang | hung | hung |
| broadcast | broadcast | broadcast | have | had | had |
| build | built | built | hear | heard | heard |
| burst | burst | burst | hide | hid | hidden |
| buy | bought | bought | hit | hit | hit |
| cast | cast | cast | hold | held | held |
| catch | caught | caught | hurt | hurt | hurt |
| choose | chose | chosen | keep | kept | kept |
| cling | clung | clung | know | knew | known |
| come | came | come | lay | laid | laid |
| cost | cost | cost | lead | led | led |
| creep | crept | crept | leave | left | left |
| cut | cut | cut | lend | lent | lent |
| deal | dealt | dealt | let | let | let |
| dig | dug | dug | lie | lay | lain |
| dive | dove/dived | dove/dived | light | lit/lighted | lit/lighted |
| do | did | done | lose | lost | lost |
| draw | drew | drawn | make | made | made |
| drink | drank | drunk | mean | meant | meant |
| drive | drove | driven | meet | met | met |
| eat | ate | eaten | mistake | mistook | mistaken |
| fall | fell | fallen | overcome | overcame | overcome |
| feed | fed | fed | overdo | overdid | overdone |
| feel | felt | felt | overtake | overtook | overtaken |

| BASE FORM | PAST FORM | PAST PARTICIPLE | BASE FORM | PAST FORM | PAST PARTICIPLE |
| --- | --- | --- | --- | --- | --- |
| overthrow | overthrew | overthrown | stick | stuck | stuck |
| pay | paid | paid | sting | stung | stung |
| plead | pled/pleaded | pled/pleaded | stink | stank | stunk |
| prove | proved | proven/proved | strike | struck | struck/stricken |
| put | put | put | strive | strove | striven |
| quit | quit | quit | swear | swore | sworn |
| read | read | read | sweep | swept | swept |
| ride | rode | ridden | swell | swelled | swelled/swollen |
| ring | rang | rung | swim | swam | swum |
| rise | rose | risen | swing | swung | swung |
| run | ran | run | take | took | taken |
| say | said | said | teach | taught | taught |
| see | saw | seen | tear | tore | torn |
| seek | sought | sought | tell | told | told |
| sell | sold | sold | think | thought | thought |
| send | sent | sent | throw | threw | thrown |
| set | set | set | understand | understood | understood |
| sew | sewed | sewn/sewed | uphold | upheld | upheld |
| shake | shook | shaken | upset | upset | upset |
| shed | shed | shed | wake | woke | woken |
| shine | shone/shined | shone/shined | wear | wore | worn |
| shoot | shot | shot | weave | wove | woven |
| show | showed | shown/showed | wed | wedded/wed | wedded/wed |
| shrink | shrank/shrunk | shrunk/shrunken | weep | wept | wept |
| shut | shut | shut | win | won | won |
| sing | sang | sung | wind | wound | wound |
| sink | sank | sunk | withdraw | withdrew | withdrawn |
| sit | sat | sat | withhold | withheld | withheld |
| sleep | slept | slept | withstand | withstood | withstood |
| slide | slid | slid | wring | wrung | wrung |
| slit | slit | slit | write | wrote | written |
| speak | spoke | spoken | | | |
| speed | sped | sped | | | |
| spend | spent | spent | | | |
| spin | spun | spun | | | |
| spit | spit/spat | spit/spat | | | |
| split | split | split | | | |
| spread | spread | spread | | | |
| spring | sprang | sprung | | | |
| stand | stood | stood | | | |
| steal | stole | stolen | | | |

**Note:**
The past and past participle of some verbs can end in *-ed* or *-t*.

burn — burned or burnt
dream — dreamed or dreamt
kneel — kneeled or knelt
learn — learned or learnt
leap — leaped or leapt
spill — spilled or spilt
spoil — spoiled or spoilt

# APPENDIX D

## GERUNDS AND INFINITIVES

### Verbs Followed by Gerunds

| | | | |
|---|---|---|---|
| admit | detest | miss | resent |
| advise | discuss | permit | resist |
| anticipate | dislike | postpone | risk |
| appreciate | enjoy | practice | stop |
| avoid | finish | put off | suggest |
| can't help | forbid | quit | tolerate |
| complete | imagine | recall | understand |
| consider | keep | recommend | |
| delay | mention | regret | |
| deny | mind | remember | |

### Verbs Followed by Infinitives

| | | | |
|---|---|---|---|
| agree | claim | know how | seem |
| appear | consent | learn | swear |
| ask | decide | manage | tend |
| attempt | demand | need | threaten |
| arrange | deserve | offer | try |
| be able | expect | plan | volunteer |
| beg | fail | prepare | want |
| can afford | forget | pretend | wish |
| care | hope | promise | would like |
| choose | intend | refuse | |

### Verbs Followed by Either Gerunds or Infinitives

| | | |
|---|---|---|
| begin | love | start |
| continue | prefer | stop* |
| hate | remember* | try (in past form *tried*)* |
| like | can (not) stand | |

*Difference in meaning between use of gerund and infinitive

### Adjectives Followed by Infinitives

| | | | |
|---|---|---|---|
| afraid | easy | lucky | sad |
| ashamed | embarrassed | necessary | shocked |
| careful | excited | pleased | sorry |
| certain | glad | prepared | stupid |
| challenging | good | proud | surprised |
| delighted | happy | ready | upset |
| determined | hard | relieved | useful |
| difficult | important | reluctant | willing |
| disappointed | impossible | rewarding | wrong |
| eager | likely | right | |

# APPENDIX E

## VERBS AND ADJECTIVES FOLLOWED BY A PREPOSITION

**MANY VERBS AND ADJECTIVES ARE FOLLOWED BY A PREPOSITION.**

| | | |
|---|---|---|
| accuse someone of | (be) familiar with | (be) prepared for/to |
| (be) accustomed to | (be) famous for | prevent (someone/something) from |
| adjust to | (be) fond of | prohibit (someone/something) from |
| (be) afraid of | forget about | protect (someone/something) from |
| agree with | forgive (someone) for | (be) proud of |
| (be) amazed at/by | (be) glad about | recover from |
| (be) angry about | (be) good at | (be) related to |
| (be) angry at/with | (be) grateful (to someone) for | rely on/upon |
| apologize for | (be) guilty of | (be) responsible for |
| approve of | (be) happy about | (be) sad about |
| argue about | hear about | (be) satisfied with |
| argue with | hear of | (be) scared of |
| (be) ashamed of | hope for | (be) sick of |
| (be) aware of | (be) incapable of | (be) sorry about |
| believe in | insist on/upon | (be) sorry for |
| blame someone for | (be) interested in | speak about |
| (be) bored with/by | (be) involved in | speak to/with |
| (be) capable of | (be) jealous of | succeed in |
| care about | (be) known for | (be) sure of/about |
| care for | (be) lazy about | (be) surprised at |
| compare to/with | listen to | take care of |
| complain about | look at | talk about |
| concentrate on | look for | talk to/with |
| (be) concerned about | look forward to | thank (someone) for |
| consist of | (be) mad about | (be) thankful (to someone) for |
| count on | (be) mad at | think about |
| deal with | (be) made from/of | think of |
| decide on | (be) married to | (be) tired of |
| depend on/upon | object to | (be) upset about |
| (be) different from | (be) opposed to | (be) upset with |
| disapprove of | participate in | (be) used to |
| (be) divorced from | plan on | wait for |
| dream about/of | pray to | warn (someone) about |
| (be) engaged to | pray for | (be) worried about |
| (be) excited about | | worry about |

# APPENDIX F

## NONCOUNT NOUNS

| GROUP A | **Nouns that have no distinct, separate parts** | | | |
|---|---|---|---|---|
| | milk | juice | paper | cholesterol |
| | oil | yogurt | rain | blood |
| | water | poultry | air | electricity |
| | coffee | bread | soup | lightning |
| | tea | meat | butter | thunder |
| GROUP B | **Nouns with parts too small or insignificant to count** | | | |
| | rice | hair | sand | |
| | sugar | popcorn | corn | |
| | salt | snow | grass | |
| GROUP C | **Nouns that are classes or categories** | | | |
| | money or cash (nickels, dimes, dollars) | | mail (letters, packages, postcards, flyers) | |
| | furniture (chairs, tables, beds) | | homework (compositions, exercises, readings) | |
| | clothing (sweaters, pants, dresses) | | jewelry (necklaces, bracelets, rings) | |
| GROUP D | **Abstract nouns** | | | | | |
| | love | happiness | nutrition | patience | work | nature |
| | truth | education | intelligence | poverty | health | help |
| | beauty | advice | unemployment | music | fun | energy |
| | luck/fortune | knowledge | pollution | art | information | friendship |
| GROUP E | **Subjects of study** | | | |
| | history | grammar | biology | |
| | chemistry | geometry | math (mathematics*) | |

*__Note:__ Even though *mathematics* ends with *s*, it is not plural.

## Quantity Words with Count and Noncount Nouns

| SINGULAR COUNT | PLURAL COUNT | NONCOUNT |
|---|---|---|
| **a** tomato | tomatoes | coffee |
| **one** tomato | **two** tomatoes | **two cups of** coffee |
| | **some** tomatoes | **some** coffee |
| **no** tomato | **no** tomatoes | **no** coffee |
| | **any** tomatoes (with questions and negatives) | **any** coffee (with questions and negatives) |
| | **a lot of** tomatoes | **a lot of** coffee |
| | **many** tomatoes | **much** coffee (with questions and negatives) |
| | **a few** tomatoes | **a little** coffee |
| | **several** tomatoes | **several cups of** coffee |
| | **How many** tomatoes? | **How much** coffee? |

# Count or Noncount Nouns with Changes in Meaning

| COUNT | NONCOUNT |
|---|---|
| Avocados and nuts are **foods** with healthy fats. | We have a lot of **food** at home. |
| He wrote a **paper** about hypnosis. | I need some **paper** to write my composition. |
| He committed three **crimes** last year. | There is a lot of **crime** in a big city. |
| I have 200 **chickens** on my farm. | We ate some **chicken** for dinner. |
| I don't want to bore you with my **troubles**. | I have some **trouble** with my car. |
| She went to Puerto Rico three **times**. | She spent a lot of **time** on her project. |
| She drank three **glasses** of water. | The window is made of bulletproof **glass**. |
| I had a bad **experience** on my trip to Paris. | She has **experience** with computers. |
| I've learned about the **lives** of my grandparents. | **Life** is sometimes happy, sometimes sad. |
| I heard a **noise** outside my window. | Those children are making a lot of **noise**. |
| Some **fruits** have a lot of sugar. | I bought some **fruit** at the fruit store. |

# APPENDIX G

## USES OF ARTICLES

### The Indefinite Article

#### A. To classify a subject

| EXAMPLES | EXPLANATION |
|---|---|
| Chicago is **a** city.<br>Illinois is **a** state.<br>Abraham Lincoln was **an** American president. | • We use *a* before a consonant sound.<br>• We use *an* before a vowel sound.<br>• We can put an adjective before the noun. |
| Chicago and Los Angeles are cities.<br>Lincoln and Washington were American presidents. | We do not use an article before a plural noun. |

#### B. To make a generalization about a noun

| EXAMPLES | EXPLANATION |
|---|---|
| **A dog** has sharp teeth.<br>**Dogs** have sharp teeth.<br>**An elephant** has big ears.<br>**Elephants** have big ears. | We use an indefinite article *(a/an)* + a singular count noun or no article with a plural noun.<br>Both the singular and plural forms have the same meaning. |
| **Coffee** contains caffeine.<br>**Love** makes people happy. | We do not use an article to make a generalization about a noncount noun. |

#### C. To introduce a new noun into the conversation

| EXAMPLES | EXPLANATION |
|---|---|
| I have **a cell phone**.<br>I have **an umbrella**.t | We use the indefinite article *a/an* with singular count nouns. |
| I have **(some) dishes**.<br>Do you have **(any) cups**?<br>I don't have **(any) forks**.<br>I have **(some) money** with me.<br>Do you have **(any) cash** with you?<br>I don't have **(any) time**. | We use *some* or *any* with plural nouns and noncount nouns.<br>We use *any* in questions and negatives.<br>*Some* and *any* can be omitted. |
| There's **an elevator** in the building.<br>There isn't **any money** in my wallet. | *There* + a form of *be* can introduce an indefinite noun into a conversation. |

# The Definite Article

## A. To refer to a previously mentioned noun

| EXAMPLES | EXPLANATION |
| --- | --- |
| There's **a dog** in the next apartment. **The dog** barks all the time. | We start by saying *a dog*. We continue by saying *the dog*. |
| We bought **some grapes**. We ate **the grapes** this morning. | We start by saying *some grapes*. We continue by saying *the grapes*. |
| I need **some sugar**. I'm going to use **the sugar** to bake a cake. | We start by saying *some sugar*. We continue by saying *the sugar*. |
| Did you buy **any coffee**? Yes. **The coffee** is in the cabinet. | We start by saying *any coffee*. We continue by saying *the coffee*. |

## B. When the speaker and the listener have the same reference

| EXAMPLES | EXPLANATION |
| --- | --- |
| **The number** on this page is 391. | The object is present, so the speaker and listener have the same object in mind. |
| **The president** is talking about **the** economy. | People who live in the same country have things in common. |
| Please turn off **the lights** and shut **the door** before you leave **the house**. | People who live in the same house have things in common. |
| **The house on the corner** is beautiful. I spent **the money you gave me**. | The listener knows exactly which one because the speaker defines or specifies which one. |

## C. When there is only one in our experience

| EXAMPLES | EXPLANATION |
| --- | --- |
| **The sun** is bigger than **the moon**. There are many problems in **the world**. | The *sun*, the *moon*, and the *world* are unique objects. |
| Write your name on **the top** of the page. | The page has only one top. |
| Alaska is **the biggest** state in the U.S. | A superlative indicates that there is only one. |

## D. With familiar places

| EXAMPLES | EXPLANATION |
| --- | --- |
| I'm going to **the store** after work. Do you need anything? **The bank** is closed now. I'll go tomorrow. | We use *the* with certain familiar places and people—*the bank, the zoo, the park, the store, the movies, the beach, the post office, the bus, the train, the doctor, the dentist*—when we refer to the one that we habitually visit or use. |

**Notes:**

1. Omit *the* after a preposition with the words *church, school, work,* and *bed*.
   - He's **in church**.
   - They're **at work**.
   - I'm going **to school**.
   - I'm going **to bed**.

2. Omit *to* and *the* with *home* and *downtown*.
   - I'm going **home**.
   - Are you going **downtown** after class?

*continued*

### E. To make a formal generalization

| EXAMPLES | EXPLANATION |
|---|---|
| **The shark** is the oldest and most primitive fish. | To say that something is true of all members of a group, use *the* with singular count nouns. |
| **The computer** has changed the way people deal with information. | To talk about a class of inventions, use *the*. |
| **The ear** has three parts: outer, middle, and inner. | To talk about an organ of the body in a general sense, use *the*. |

**Note:**

For informal generalizations, use *a* + a singular noun or no article with a plural noun.
  **The computer** has changed the way we deal with information. (Formal)
  **A computer** is expensive. (Informal)
  **Computers** are expensive. (Informal)

## Special Uses of Articles

| NO ARTICLE | ARTICLE |
|---|---|
| Personal names:<br>　John Kennedy | The whole family:<br>　the Kennedys |
| Title and name:<br>　Queen Elizabeth | Title without name:<br>　the Queen |
| Cities, states, countries, continents:<br>　Cleveland<br>　Ohio<br>　Mexico<br>　South America | Places that are considered a union:<br>　the United States<br>Place names: the _____ of _____<br>　the District of Columbia |
| Mountains:<br>　Mount Everest | Mountain ranges:<br>　the Rocky Mountains |
| Islands:<br>　Staten Island | Collectives of islands:<br>　the Hawaiian Islands |
| Lakes:<br>　Lake Superior | Collectives of lakes:<br>　the Great Lakes |
| Beaches:<br>　Palm Beach<br>　Pebble Beach | Rivers, oceans, seas:<br>　the Mississippi River<br>　the Atlantic Ocean<br>　the Dead Sea |
| Streets and avenues:<br>　Madison Avenue<br>　Wall Street | Well-known buildings:<br>　the Willis Tower<br>　the Empire State Building |
| Parks:<br>　Central Park | Zoos:<br>　the San Diego Zoo |

| NO ARTICLE | ARTICLE |
|---|---|
| Seasons:<br>    summer    fall    spring    winter<br>    Summer is my favorite season.<br>**Note:** After a preposition, *the* may be used.<br>    In (the) winter, my car runs badly. | Deserts:<br>    the Mojave Desert<br>    the Sahara Desert |
| Directions:<br>    north    south    east    west | Sections of a piece of land:<br>    the West Side (of New York) |
| School subjects:<br>    history    math | Unique geographical points:<br>    the North Pole    the Vatican |
| Name + *College* or *University*:<br>    Northwestern University | The University/College of _____<br>    the University of Michigan |
| Magazines:<br>    *Time*    *Sports Illustrated* | Newspapers:<br>    the *Tribune*    the *Los Angeles Times* |
| Months and days:<br>    September    Monday | Ships:<br>    the *Titanic*    the *Queen Elizabeth II* |
| Holidays and dates:<br>    Mother's Day<br>    July 4 (month + day) | The day of month:<br>    the fifth of May<br>    the Fourth of July |
| Diseases:<br>    cancer    AIDS<br>    polio    malaria | Ailments:<br>    a cold    a toothache<br>    a headache    the flu |
| Games and sports:<br>    poker<br>    soccer | Musical instruments, after *play*:<br>    the drums    the piano<br>**Note:** Sometimes *the* is omitted.<br>    She plays (the) drums. |
| Languages:<br>    English | The _____ language:<br>    the English language |
| Last month, year, week, etc. = the one<br>before this one:<br>    I forgot to pay my rent last month.<br>    The teacher gave us a test last week. | The last month, the last year, the last<br>week, etc. = the last in a series:<br>    December is the last month of the year.<br>    Vacation begins the last week in May. |
| In office = in an elected position:<br>    The president is in office for four years. | In the office = in a specific room:<br>    The teacher is in the office. |

# APPENDIX H

# CONNECTORS

## Sentences Types

There are three basic sentences types: simple, compound, and complex.
**Simple sentences** usually have one subject and one verb.

    S    V
    Students love textbooks.

Simple sentences can have more than one subject and/or verb.

    S        S    V
    Children and adults like pizza.

**Compound sentences** are usually made up of two simple sentences (independent clauses) with a **connector** (a coordination conjunction such as *and*, *but*, *or*, *yet*, *so*, and *for*):

                            coord
    S   V                conj  S      V
    They worked hard all semester, **but** they did not finish the project.

**Complex sentences** have one independent clause and at least one dependent clause. The dependent clause is often an adverb clause, which begins with a **connector** (a subordinating conjunction such as *while*, *although*, *because*, and *if*):

    sub
    conj  dependent clause               independent clause
    **Although** the test was very difficult, all the students received a passing grade.

## Coordinating Conjunctions

Coordinating conjunctions join two independent clauses to form a compound sentence. Use a comma before a coordinating conjunction in a compound sentence.

                        coord
    independent clause   conj    independent clause
    The test was very difficult, **but** all the students received a passing grade.

## Subordinating Conjunctions

Subordinating conjunctions introduce a dependent clause in a complex sentence. When a dependent clause begins a sentence, use a comma to separate it from the independent clause.

       dependent clause              independent clause
    **Although** the test was very difficult, all the students received a passing grade.

When a dependent clause comes after an independent clause, no comma is used.

       independent clause             dependent clause
    All the students received a passing grade **although** the test was very difficult.

# Transition Words

Transition words **show the relationship between ideas in sentences**. A transition followed by a comma can begin a sentence.

<u>The test was very difficult.</u> **However**, <u>all the students received a passing grade.</u>
(independent clause) (transition) (independent clause)

# Connector Summary Chart

| PURPOSE | COORDINATING CONJUNCTIONS | SUBORDINATING CONJUNCTIONS | TRANSITION WORDS |
|---|---|---|---|
| To give an example | | | For example, To illustrate, Specifically, In particular, |
| To add information | and | | In addition, Moreover, Furthermore, |
| To signal a comparison | | | Similarly, Likewise, In the same way, |
| To signal a contrast | but yet | while, although | In contrast, However, On the other hand, Conversely, Instead, |
| To signal a concession | yet | although, though, even though | Nevertheless, Even so, Admittedly, Despite this, |
| To emphasize | | | In fact, Actually, |
| To clarify | | | In other words, In simpler words, More simply, |
| To give a reason/cause | for | because, since | |
| To show a result | so | so | As a result, As a consequence, Consequently, Therefore, Thus, |
| To show time relationships | | after, as soon as, before, when, while, until, since, whenever, as | Afterward, First, Second, Next, Then, Finally, Subsequently, Meanwhile, In the meantime, |
| To signal a condition | | if, even if, unless, provided that, when | |
| To signal a purpose | | so that, in order that | |
| To signal a choice | or | | |
| To signal a conclusion | | | In conclusion, To summarize, As we have seen, In brief, In closing, To sum up, Finally, |

# APPENDIX I

## CAPITALIZATION AND PUNCTUATION

### Capitalization Rules

| RULE | EXAMPLES |
|---|---|
| The first word in a sentence | **M**y friends are helpful. |
| The word *I* | My sister and **I** took a trip together. |
| Names of people | **A**braham **L**incoln; **G**eorge **W**ashington |
| Titles preceding names of people | **D**octor (**D**r.) **S**mith; **P**resident **L**incoln; **Q**ueen **E**lizabeth; **M**r. **R**ogers; **M**rs. **C**arter |
| Geographic names | the **U**nited **S**tates; **L**ake **S**uperior; **C**alifornia; the **R**ocky **M**ountains; the **M**ississippi **R**iver<br>**Note:** The word *the* in a geographic name is not capitalized. |
| Street names | **P**ennsylvania **A**venue (**A**ve.); **W**all **S**treet (**S**t.); **A**bbey **R**oad (**R**d.) |
| Names of organizations, companies, colleges, buildings, stores, hotels | the **R**epublican **P**arty; **C**engage **L**earning; **D**artmouth **C**ollege; the **U**niversity of **W**isconsin; the **W**hite **H**ouse; **B**loomingdale's; the **H**ilton **H**otel |
| Nationalities and ethnic groups | **M**exicans; **C**anadians; **S**paniards; **A**mericans; **J**ews; **K**urds; **I**nuit |
| Languages | **E**nglish; **S**panish; **P**olish; **V**ietnamese; **R**ussian |
| Months | **J**anuary; **F**ebruary |
| Days | **S**unday; **M**onday |
| Holidays | **I**ndependence **D**ay; **T**hanksgiving |
| Important words in a title | *Grammar in Context; The Old Man and the Sea; Romeo and Juliet; The Sound of Music*<br>**Note:** Capitalize *the* as the first word of a title. |

# Punctuation Rules

| PUNCTUATION | EXAMPLES |
|---|---|
| A period (.) is used at the end of a declarative sentence. | This is a complete sentence. |
| A question mark (?) is used at the end of a question. | When does the movie start? |
| An exclamation mark (!) is used at the end of an exclamation. It expresses a strong emotion. It can also be called an exclamation point. | This book is so interesting! |
| A comma (,) is used: | |
| • before the connectors *and*, *but*, *so*, and *or* in a compound sentence. | • She gave Tomas a pen, but he wanted a pencil. |
| • between three or more items in a list. | • He needs a notebook, a pen, and a calculator. |
| • after a dependent clause at the beginning of a complex sentence. Dependent clauses include time clauses, *if* clauses, and reason clauses. | • If it's cold outside, you should wear a coat. |
| • between the day and the date and between the date and the year. | • The test will be on Friday, May 20.<br><br>The school opened on September 3, 2010. |
| • between and after (if in the middle of a sentence) city, state, and country names that appear together. | • She lived and taught in Shanghai, China, for five years. |
| • after time words and phrases, prepositional phrases of time, and sequence words (except *then*) at the start of a sentence. | • Finally, the test was over, and the student could leave.<br><br>After the movie, they decided to go out for coffee. |
| An apostrophe (') is used to indicate either a contraction or a possession: | |
| • Use an apostrophe in a contraction in place of the letter or letters that have been deleted. | • I'm happy to see you.<br><br>You've read a lot of books this year. |
| • Add an apostrophe and the letter *-s* after the word. If a plural word already ends in *-s*, just add an apostrophe. | • That is Yusef's book.<br><br>The teachers' books include the answers. |
| Quotation marks (" ") are used to indicate: | |
| • the exact words that were spoken by someone. Notice that the punctuation at the end of a quote is inside the quotation marks. | • Albert Einstein said, "I have no special talent. I am only passionately curious." |
| • language that a writer has borrowed from another source. | • The dictionary defines punctuation as "the use of specific marks to make ideas within writing clear." |
| • when a word or phrase is being used in a special way. | • The paper was written by a "professional" writer. |

# GLOSSARY

- **Adjective** An adjective gives a description of a noun.

    It's a *tall* tree.      He's an *old* man.      My neighbors are *nice*.

- **Adverb** An adverb describes the action of a sentence or an adjective or another adverb.

    She speaks English *fluently*.      I drive *carefully*.

    She speaks English *extremely* well.      She is *very* intelligent.

- **Adverb of Frequency** An adverb of frequency tells how often an action happens.

    I *never* drink coffee.      They *usually* take the bus.

- **Affirmative** Affirmative means "yes."

    They *live* in Miami.

- **Apostrophe '** We use the apostrophe for possession and contractions.

    My *sister's* friend is beautiful. (possession)

    Today *isn't* Sunday. (contraction)

- **Article** An article comes before a noun. It tells if the noun is definite or indefinite. The indefinite articles are *a* and *an*. The definite article is *the*.

    I have *a* cat.      I ate *an* apple.      *The* teacher came late.

- **Auxiliary Verb** An auxiliary verb is used in forming tense, mood, or aspect of the verb that follows it. Some verbs have two parts: an auxiliary verb and a main verb.

    You *didn't* eat lunch.      He *can't* study.      We *will* return.

- **Base Form** The base form of the verb has no tense. It has no ending (*-s*, *-ed*, or *-ing*): *be, go, eat, take, write*.

    I didn't *go*.      We don't *know* you.      He can't *drive*.

- **Capital Letter** A B C D E F G . . .

- **Clause** A clause is a group of words that has a subject and a verb. Some sentences have only one clause.

    *She speaks Spanish.*

Some sentences have a **main clause** and a **dependent clause**.

| MAIN CLAUSE | DEPENDENT CLAUSE (reason clause) |
|---|---|
| *She found a good job* | *because she has computer skills.* |
| MAIN CLAUSE | DEPENDENT CLAUSE (time clause) |
| *She'll turn off the light* | *before she goes to bed.* |
| MAIN CLAUSE | DEPENDENT CLAUSE (*if* clause) |
| *I'll take you to the doctor* | *if you don't have your car on Saturday.* |

- **Colon** :
- **Comma** ,
- **Comparative** The comparative form of an adjective or adverb is used to compare two things.

    My house is *bigger* than your house.

    Her husband drives *faster* than she does.

    My children speak English *more fluently* than I do.

- **Consonant** The following letters are consonants: *b, c, d, f, g, h, j, k, l, m, n, p, q, r, s, t, v, w, x, y, z*.

    NOTE: *Y* is sometimes considered a vowel, as in the world *syllable*.

- **Contraction** A contraction is two words joined with an apostrophe.

    *He's* my brother.                *You're* late.                    They *won't* talk to me.

    (*He's = He is*)                  (*You're = You are*)              (*won't = will not*)

- **Count Noun** Count nouns are nouns that we can count. They have a singular and a plural form.

    1 *pen*–3 *pens*                  1 *table*–4 *tables*

- **Dependent Clause** See **Clause**.
- **Exclamation Mark** !
- **Frequency Word** Frequency words (*always, usually, generally, often, sometimes, rarely, seldom, hardly ever, never*) tell how often an action happens.

    I *never* drink coffee.           We *always* do our homework.

- **Hyphen** -
- **Imperative** An imperative sentence gives a command or instruction. An imperative sentence omits the subject pronoun *you*.

    *Come* here.                      *Don't be* late.                  Please *help* me.

- **Infinitive** An infinitive is *to* + the base form.

    I want *to leave*.                You need *to be* here on time.

- **Linking Verb** A linking verb is a verb that links the subject to the noun, adjective, or adverb after it. Linking verbs include *be, seem, feel, smell, sound, look, appear,* and *taste*.

    She *is* a doctor.                She *looks* tired.                You *are* late.

- **Main Clause** See **Clause**.
- **Modal** The modal verbs are *can, could, shall, should, will, would, may, might,* and *must*.

    They *should* leave.              I *must* go.

- **Negative** *Negative* means "no."

    She *doesn't speak* Spanish.

- **Nonaction Verb** A nonaction verb has no action. We do not use a continuous tense (*be* + verb *-ing*) with a nonaction verb. Nonaction verbs include: *believe, cost, care, have, hear, know, like, love, matter, mean, need, own, prefer, remember, see, seem, think, understand, want,* and sense-perception verbs.

    She *has* a laptop.               We *love* our mother.             You *look* great.

- **Noncount Noun** A noncount noun is a noun that we don't count. It has no plural form.

    She drank some *water*.           He prepared some *rice*.

    Do you need any *money*?          We had a lot of *homework*.

- **Noun** A noun is a person, a place, or a thing. Nouns can be either count or noncount.

    My *brother* lives in California. My *sisters* live in New York.

    I get *advice* from them.         I drink *coffee* every day.

- **Noun Modifier** A noun modifier makes a noun more specific.

    *fire* department                 *Independence* Day                *can* opener

- **Noun Phrase** A noun phrase is a group of words that form the subject or object of a sentence.

    *A very nice woman* helped me.    I bought *a big box of cereal*.

- **Object** The object of a sentence follows the verb. It receives the action of the verb.

    He bought *a car*.    I saw *a movie*.    I met *your brother*.

- **Object Pronoun** We use object pronouns (*me, you, him, her, it, us, them*) after a verb or preposition.

    He likes *her*.    I saw the movie. Let's talk about *it*.

- **Paragraph** A paragraph is a group of sentences about one topic.

- **Parentheses** ( )

- **Period** .

- **Phrasal Modal** Phrasal modals, such as *have to* and *be able to,* are made up of two or more words.

    You *have got to* see the movie.    We *have to* take a test.

- **Phrase** A group of words that go together.

    *Last month* my sister came to visit.    There is a strange car *in front of my house*.

- **Plural** *Plural* means "more than one." A plural noun usually ends with *-s*.

    She has beautiful *eyes*.    My *feet* are big.

- **Possessive Form** Possessive forms show ownership or relationship.

    *Mary's* coat is in the closet.    *My* brother lives in Miami.

- **Preposition** A preposition is a short connecting word. Some common prepositions are: *about, above, across, after, around, as, at, away, back, before, behind, below, by, down, for, from, in, into, like, of, off, on, out, over, to, under, up,* and *with*.

    The book is *on* the table.    She studies *with* her friends.

- **Present Participle** The present participle of a verb is the base form + *-ing*.

    She is *sleeping*.    They were *laughing*.

- **Pronoun** A pronoun takes the place of a noun.

    John likes Mary, but *she* doesn't like *him*.

- **Punctuation** The use of specific marks, such as commas and periods, to make ideas within writing clear.

- **Question Mark** ?

- **Quotation Marks** " "

- **Regular Verb** A regular verb forms the simple past with *-ed*.

    He *worked* yesterday.    I *laughed* at the joke.

- **-s Form** A simple present verb that ends in *-s* or *-es*.

    He *lives* in New York.             She *watches* TV a lot.

- **Sense-Perception Verb** A sense-perception verb has no action. It describes a sense. Some common sense-perception verbs are: *look, feel, taste, sound,* and *smell*.

    She *feels* fine.         The coffee *smells* fresh.         The milk *tastes* sour.

- **Sentence** A sentence is a group of words that contains a subject and a verb and gives a complete thought.

    SENTENCE: She came home.

    NOT A SENTENCE: When she came home

- **Singular** *Singular* means "one."

    She ate a *sandwich*.         I have one *television*.

- **Subject** The subject of the sentence tells who or what the sentence is about.

    *My sister* got married last April. *The wedding* was beautiful.

- **Subject Pronoun** We use a subject pronoun (*I, you, he, she, it, we, you, they*) before a verb.

    *They* speak Japanese.         *We* speak Spanish.

- **Superlative** The superlative form of an adjective or adverb shows the number one item in a group of three or more.

    January is the *coldest* month of the year.

    My brother speaks English the *best* in my family.

- **Syllable** A syllable is a part of a word. Each syllable has only one vowel sound. (Some words have only one syllable.)

    change (one syllable)              after (af·ter = two syllables)

    look (one syllable)                responsible (re·spon·si·ble = four syllables)

- **Tag Question** A tag question is a short question at the end of a sentence. It is used in conversation.

    You speak Spanish, *don't you*?         He's not happy, *is he*?

- **Tense** Tense shows when the action of the sentence happened. Verbs have different tenses.

    SIMPLE PRESENT: She usually *works* hard.

    PRESENT CONTINUOUS: She *is working* now.

    SIMPLE PAST: She *worked* yesterday.

    FUTURE: She *will work* tomorrow.

- **Verb** A verb is the action of the sentence.

    He *runs* fast.         I *speak* English.

    Some verbs have no action. They are linking verbs. They connect the subject to the rest of the sentence.

    He *is* tall.         She *looks* beautiful.         You *seem* tired.

- **Vowel** The following letters are vowels: *a, e, i, o, u*.

    NOTE: *Y* is sometimes considered a vowel, as in the world *syllable*.

# INDEX

Note: All page references in blue are in Split Edition B

## A

*A few, several, a little*, 143–144, 146
Ability/permission, modals, 202–203
Action verbs, present continuous, 53–54
Active voice, 341–342, 354
    summary, 354
Adjectives, 168
    adverbs versus, 162–163
    clauses, 284–307
    comparatives, 317–319
    gerunds, with, 267
    infinitives after, 273–274
    modifiers, 154–156
    possessive, 98–99
    superlatives, 311–313
    *too, too much, too many, enough,* 165–166, 168
    *too, very,* 166–168
Adjective clauses, 284–307
    relative pronouns, objects, 291–294, 304
    relative pronouns, objects of prepositions, 295–297, 304
    relative pronouns, place, 301–304
    relative pronouns, possessive, 298–299, 304
    relative pronouns, subjects, 288–290, 304
    relative pronouns, time, 301–304
    summary, 304
    *where* and *when,* 301–304
    *who/that,* 290
    *whose* + noun, 298–299, 304
Adverbs, modifiers, 153–154, 160–162, 168
    adjectives versus, 162–163
    comparatives, 317–319
    nouns, modifying, 153–154
    present perfect, 233
    summary, 168
    superlatives, 311–313
Advice, modals, 205–207
Affirmative statements
    simple present, 16–17
*Another* and *other,* 373–375, 378
Articles, 361–381
    *another* and *other,* 373–375, 378
    definite pronouns, 376–378
    generalizations, 362–363
    indefinite pronouns, 376–378
    nonspecific nouns, 366–367, 370–371
    quantity words, 370–371
    specific nouns, 367–371
    subjects, classifying, 363–364
    subjects, defining, 363–364
    summary, 378
*As . . . as,* comparatives, 324–325, 334
*As many/much . . . as,* comparatives, 326–327

## B

*Be*
    contractions, 5, 10–11
    forms, simple present, 5–10, 36
    *going to,* 60–64
    negative statements, 8
    present continuous, 43–44
    simple past, 76–77, 88
    *there + be,* 138–140
    uses, 7
    *wh-* questions, 12–14
*Be + not,* 8
*Be going to,* 60–64
*Be supposed to,* 201–202

## C

*Can, could,* modals, 202–203
Clauses, adjectives, 284–307
Comparatives, 316–337
    adjectives, 317–319
    adverbs, 317–319
    *as . . . as,* 324–325, 334
    *as many/much . . . as,* 326–327
    *like* and *alike,* 331–334
    long words, 334
    *same . . . as,* 327–329, 334
    short words, 334
    similarity, 331–333
    summary, 334
    use, 319–322
Comparison nouns, 141
Complements, questions about, 114–116, 118
Comprehension exercises
    *a few, several, a little,* 142–143
    adjective clauses, 286–287, 300–301
    adverbs, modifiers, 152–153
    articles, 360–361, 365–366, 372–373
    *as . . . as,* 323–324
    *be* forms, 4–5
    comparatives, 316–317
    count and noncount nouns, 130–131
    frequency words, 28–29
    future, 57–58

gerunds, 260–261
habitual past, 85–86
infinitives, 270–271
*like* and *alike*, 330–331
modals, 196–197, 204–205, 211–212, 216–217
nouns, plural, 124–125
object pronouns, 102–103
past continuous, 179–180, 185–186
possessive forms, 94–95
present continuous, 42–43
present perfect, 226–227, 234–235, 240–241
present perfect continuous, 248–249
relative pronouns, objects of prepositions, 295–296
simple past, 72–73, 75–76
simple past negatives, 81–82
simple present affirmative, 15–16
simple present questions, 20–21
simple present vs. present continuous, 50–51
superlatives, 310–311
time words, 174–175
transitive and intransitive verbs, 349–350
voice, 340–341
Conclusions, deductions, modals, 212–213
Contractions
   *be*, 5, 10–11
Count and noncount, 131–136, 141, 146

# D

Definite pronouns, 376–378
Direct and indirect objects, 109–111, 118
   complements, questions about, 114–116, 118
   questions, 112–117
   *say* and *tell*, 110–111
   subjects, questions about, 113–116, 118
   *wh-* questions, 117
Discussion questions
   *a few, several, a little,* 143
   adjective clauses, 287, 301
   adverbs, modifiers, 153
   articles, 361, 366, 373
   *as . . . as,* 323–324
   *be* forms, 5
   comparatives, 317
   count and noncount nouns, 131
   frequency words, 29
   future, 58
   gerunds, 261
   habitual past, 86
   infinitives, 271
   *like* and *alike,* 331
   modals, 197, 205, 212, 217

nouns, plural, 125
object pronouns, 103
objects, direct and indirect, 108
past continuous, 180, 186
possessive forms, 95
present continuous, 43
present perfect, 227, 235, 241
present perfect continuous, 249
relative pronouns, objects of prepositions, 296
simple past, 73, 76
simple past negatives, 82
simple present affirmative, 16
simple present questions, 21
simple present vs. present continuous, 51
subject, 113
superlatives, 311
time words, 175
transitive and intransitive verbs, 350
voice, 341

# E

*Ever,* simple present questions with, 32–33
Expectation, modals, 201–202

# F

Frequency words/expressions, 29–31, 36
Future, 57–66
   *be going to*, 60–64
   *if* clause, 64–65
   present continuous, 62–64
   summary, 66
   time +, 64–65
   *will,* with, 58–60, 62–64

# G

Generalizations, 128, 362–363
Gerunds, 258–269, 278–280
   adjective +, 267
   after verb, 278–279
   form, 262
   *go* + gerund, 265
   infinitives versus, 280
   objects, 265–266
   phrase, 261, 265
   preposition +, 267–269
   subjects, 262–264
   summary, 280
*Go* + gerund, 265

# H

Habitual past, 85–88
*How often,* simple present questions with, 33–35

# I

*If* clause, future, 64–65
Indefinite pronouns, 376–378
Indefinite time, present perfect, 243–245
Infinitives, 271–280
    after adjectives, 273–274
    after *it*, 272–273
    after verbs, 274–276, 278–279
    gerunds versus, 280
    objects before, 276
    phrase, 274–275
    show purpose, 277
    summary, 280
    *to* +, 277–278
Intransitive verbs, 350–353
Irregular verbs, simple past, 78–80, 88
*It*, infinitives after, 272–273

# L

*Like* and *alike*, comparatives, 331–334
Long words, comparatives, 334

# M

*May*, modals, 200–201
*May/might*, modals, 214–215
Modals, 194–223
    ability/permission, 202–203
    advice, 205–207
    *be supposed to*, 201–202
    *can, could,* and, 202–203
    conclusions, deductions, 212–213
    expectation, 201–202
    *may* and, 200–201
    *may/might*, 214–215
    *must* and, 199–200, 212–213
    negatives, 207–210
    obligation/necessity, 199–200
    permission/prohibition, 200–201
    phrasal, 197–200, 220
    politeness, 217–219
    possibility, 214–215
    *should, ought to, had better*, 205–207
    summary, 220
Modifiers; *see also* Adjectives, Adverbs, Nouns
    adjectives as, 154–156
    adverbs as, 153–154, 160–162, 168
    nouns, 153–154, 157–158, 168
*Must*, modals, 199–200, 212–213

# N

Negative statements
    *be*, 8
    modals, 207–210
    passive voice, 347–348, 354
    simple past, 82–84
    simple present, 18–19, 36
Nonaction verbs, present continuous, 53–54
Non-specific nouns, 366–367, 370–371
Nouns
    *a few, several, a little,* 143–144, 146
    comparison, 141
    count and noncount, 131–136, 141, 146
    generalizations, 128
    modifiers, 153–154, 157–158, 168
    non-specific, 366–367, 370–371
    plural, 125–129
    possessive, 96–97, 118
    quantity, 135–136
    singular, 129
    specific, 367–371
    summary, 146
    *there + be*, 138–140, 146
    *too much/too many, a lot of*, 145–146

# O

Object pronouns, 103–105, 118
Objects
    gerunds, 265–266
    infinitives after, 276
    relative pronouns, 291–294, 304
Objects of prepositions, relative pronouns, 295–297, 304
Obligation/necessity, modals, 199–200
*Other* and *another*, 373–375, 378

# P

Passive voice, 341–348, 354
    form, 342–343
    negatives, 347–348
    questions, 347–348
    summary, 354
    use, 345–347
Past continuous, 180–184, 190
    present participle, 180
    simple past versus, 188
    specific time, 182–183
    summary, 190
    verb + *ing*, 189
    *wh-* questions, 180
    *when* clause, 184, 188
    *while* clause, 186–187
    *yes/no* questions, 180
Past participle, present perfect, 228–232
Past to present continuation, present perfect, 236–237
Past to present repetition, present perfect, 241–243
Permission/ability, modals, 202–203
Permission/prohibition, modals, 200–201

Phrasal modals, 197–200, 220
Phrases
   gerunds, 261, 265
   infinitives, 274–275
Place, relative pronouns, 301–304
Plural nouns, 125–129
Politeness, modals, 217–219
Possessive forms, 95–101, 118
   adjectives, 98–99
   nouns, 96–97, 118
   pronouns, 95–96, 99–100, 118
   summary, 118
   *whose*, questions with, 101
Possessive nouns, 96–97, 118
Possessive relative pronouns, 298–299, 304
Possibility, modals, 214–215
Preposition + gerund, 267–269
Present continuous, 41–56, 62–64, 66
   action verbs, 53–54
   *be* verb form, 43–44
   future with, 62–64
   nonaction verbs, 53–54
   use, 45–46
   questions, 46–48
   summary, 66
   versus simple present, 51–53, 55–56
   *wh-* questions, 46
   *yes/no* questions, 47
Present participle, past continuous, 180
Present perfect, 227–247
   adverb with, 233
   forms, 227–228
   indefinite time, past, 243–245
   past participle, 228–232
   past to present continuation, 236–237
   past to present repetition, 241–243
   simple past, 238–239, 246–247, 254
   simple present, 238–239
   summary, 254
   uses, 235
Present perfect continuous, 249–254
   forms, 249–251
   summary, 254
   use, 251–253
   *wh-* questions, 249
   *yes/no* questions, 249
Pronouns, 95–96, 99–107, 118
   object pronouns, 103–105, 118
   possessive forms, 95–96, 99–100, 118
   reflexive, 106–107
Purpose, show, 277

## Q
Quantity nouns, 135–136, 146
Quantity words, articles, 370–371
Questions
   complement, 114–118
   passive voice, 347–348

## R
Reflexive pronouns, 106–107, 118
Regular verbs, simple past, 77–78, 88
Relative pronouns
   objects, 291–294, 304
   objects of prepositions, 295–297, 304
   place, 301–304
   possessive, 298–299, 304
   subjects, 288–290, 304
   time, 301–304

## S
*Same . . . as*, comparatives, 327–329, 334
*Say* and *tell*, 110–111
Short words, comparatives, 334
*Should, ought to, had better*, modals, 205–207
Similarity, comparatives, 331–333
Simple past, 72–84
   *be*, 76–77, 88
   habitual past, *used to*, 86–88
   irregular verbs, 78–80, 88
   negatives, 82–84
   past continuous versus, 188
   present perfect, 238–239, 246–247, 254
   regular verbs, 77–78, 88
   summary, 88, 254
   use, 74
   *wh-* questions, 82–84
   *yes/no* questions, 82–84
Simple present, 3–39, 66
   affirmative statements, 16–17, 36
   *be*, 5–10, 36
   *ever*, questions with, 32–33
   frequency words/expressions, 29–31, 36
   *how often*, questions with, 33–35
   negative statements, 18–19, 36
   present perfect, 238–239
   questions, 21–27
   summary, 36
   use, 17–18
   versus present continuous, 51–53, 55–56
   *wh-* questions, 21, 25–27, 36
   *yes/no* questions, 21, 32, 36
Singular nouns, 129
Specific nouns, 367–371

Specific time, past continuous, 182–183
Subjects
    classifying, articles, 363–364
    defining, articles, 363–364
    gerunds, 262–264
    questions about, 113–116, 118
    relative pronouns, 288–290, 304
Superlatives, 308–315
    adjectives, 311–313
    adverbs, 311–313
    summary, 334
    use, 313–315

# T

*There + be*, 138–140, 146
Time + future, 64–65
Time words, 175–178, 189–190
    relative pronouns, 301–304
    summary, 190
*To* + infinitives, 277–278
*Too, too much, too many, enough*, 165–166, 168
*Too, very*, 166–168
*Too much/too many, a lot of*, 145–146
Transitive verbs, 350–353

# U

Units of measure, 133–134
*Used to*, habitual past, 86–88

# V

Verb + *ing*, past continuous, 189
Verbs
    gerunds after, 278–279
    infinitives after, 274–276, 278–279
    intransitive verbs, 350–353
    transitive verbs, 350–353

Voice
    active voice, 341–342, 354
    negatives, 347–348
    passive voice, 341–348, 354
    questions, 347–348
    summary, 354

# W

*Wh-* questions
    *be*, 12–14
    direct and indirect objects, 117
    past continuous, 180
    present continuous, 46
    present perfect continuous, 249
    simple past, 82–84
    simple present, 21, 25–27, 36
*When, whenever*, 178
*When* clause, past continuous, 184, 188
*Where* and *when*, 301–304
*While* clause, past continuous, 186–187
*Who/that*, 290
*Whose*, questions with, 101
*Whose* + noun, 298–299, 304
*Will*, future with, 58–60, 62–64

# Y

*Yes/no* questions
    past continuous, 180
    present continuous, 47
    present perfect continuous, 249
    simple past, 82–84
    simple present, 21, 32, 36

# CREDITS

**ILLUSTRATIONS**

© Cengage Learning

**PHOTOS**

**194–195 (c)** ©martin–dm/E+/Getty Images; **196** (bc) ©Maskot/Getty Images; **204** (t) ©Syed Mahabubul Kader/EyeEm/Getty Images; **208** (bc) ©Hinterhaus Productions/DigitalVision/Getty Images; **211** (t) ©Hero Images/Getty Images; **216** (t) ©Alex Potemkin/E+/Getty Images; **219** (b) ©Alexander Spatari/Moment/Getty Images; **224–225** (c) ©Eduardo Munoz/National Geographic Image Collection; **226** (t) ©Jb Reed/Bloomberg/Getty Images; **231** (b) ©Ashley Gilbertson/VII /Redux; **234** (b) ©TPG/Getty Images Entertainment/Getty Images; **240** (t) ©Robyn Twomey/Redux; **248** (b) ©Rick Friedman/Corbis Historical/Getty Images; **258–259** (c) © Zay Yar Lin; **260** (t) ©Frances Roberts/Alamy Stock Photo; **270** (t) ©Gary Friedman/Los Angeles Times/Getty Images; **279** (b) ©SolStock/E+/Getty Images; **284–285** (c) ©Photograph by Tyler Metcalfe; **286** (t) ©ZUMA Press Inc/Alamy Stock Photo; **295** (t) ©Hero Images/Getty Images; **300** (b) ©kate_sept2004/E+/Getty Images; **308–309** (c) ©Handout/Getty Images Sport/Getty Images; **310** (b) ©GREGG TREINISH/National Geographic Image Collection; **315** (b) ©Alexander Hassenstein/Getty Images Sport/Getty Images; **316** (t) ©Meg Oliphant/Getty Images Sport/Getty Images; **321** (c) ©Al Bello/Getty Images Sport/Getty Images; **323** (bl) ©Abramorama/Courtesy Everett Collection; **329** (b) ©Adam Pretty/Getty Images Sport/Getty Images; **330** (t) ©Tom Szczerbowski/Getty Images Sport/Getty Images; **338–339** (c) ©CSP_teshimine/AGE Fotostock; **340** (t) ©Photo by Mike Kline (notkalvin)/Moment/Getty Images; **344** (t) ©Hero Images/Getty Images; **349** left ©DAVID SLATER; **353** (b) ©Bill Perry/Shutterstock.com; **358–359** (c) ©KAZUHIRO NOGI/AFP/Getty Images; **365** (t) ©kate_sept2004/E+/Getty Images; **372** (t) ©Photo Courtesy of Kleiner Perkins

# NOTES

# NOTES

# NOTES

# NOTES

# NOTES